ATLAS
OF WORLD
INTERIOR DESIGN

IMPRINT

The Deutsche Bibliothek lists this publication in the Deutsche Nationalbibliographie; detailed
bibliographical information can be found on the Internet at http://dnb.ddb.de

ISBN 978-3-03768-061-2

© 2011 by Braun Publishing AG
www.braun-publishing.ch

1st edition 2011

Project coordination: Jennifer Kozak, Manuela Roth
English text editing: Judith Vonberg
Layout: Michelle Galindo
Graphic concept: Michaela Prinz

ATLAS
OF WORLD
INTERIOR DESIGN

Markus Sebastian Braun | Michelle Galindo (ed.)

BRAUN

Preface → page 009

North, Central & South America

CONTENT

REGIONS

Every piece of architecture has two faces: An exterior, which creates an initial impression as a kind of business card in the context of its surroundings, and the interior, which plays a much more important role in terms of functional considerations as well as the more lasting impression of the designed surroundings. However the bulk of literature about architecture deals with the building structure and the interior construction and seldom with the "finishing", the art of interior design that ranges from the interior construction down the smallest detail work. With its complete catalogue of building types and the many contemporary styles represented by 500 projects from around the world, this volume does exactly that.

During times when economic circumstances are not exactly conducive to new construction, increasing attention is being paid to the conversion of existing architecture. In addition, conversion and renovation contribute to the consciousness of factors of ecology (soil sealing, recycling) and history (monument preservation, cityscape). In comparison with new construction, an updated interior design can create a completely new space relatively economically.

But also in the case of new construction it is the interior design which creates the areas for living, work or other purposes out of empty volumes of built space. But interior design as the high art of dealing with the interior is much more than furnishings: individually or serially produced furniture, but also hung ceilings, floor coverings, drywall construction and lighting are the raw materials of the design goal, which first emerges out of combination and arrangement, through contrast and emphasis, or restraint, as the case may be. The role of precise lighting plays an especially important role here. This pertains not only to artificial light but also to the deployment of daylight (and also shade!), both of which lend the space depth as well substance in equal measure. Just as Leonardo da Vinci's use of light distinguishes his paintings from those of his predecessors, and light in Caravaggio's paintings has another, completely different spatial effect, reflexes which are dependent on materials, clear light, diffuse shadows or the "sfumato" emitted by cloth also exert a decisive influence on interiors. In that sense the Atlas of World Interior Design is not simply a catalogue of 500 spatial works of art. It is a wellspring of countless ideas for transforming empty volumes of built space with color combinations, use of materials or the staging and arrangement of the experience of space.

PREFACE

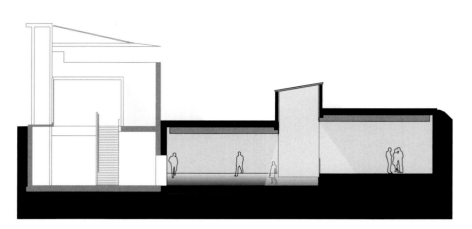

Archeological Museum Eggenberg

The purpose of the new building for this museum was the underground extension of the existing lapidarium along with the new presentation of the Joanneum's archeological exhibition. The zones of the two-part exhibition hall with a skylight extending through its center are defined by different floor levels. Exposed concrete walls and flooring create an understated background for the small-scale exhibits that seem to float in highly transparent, fully glazed showcases. Architecture and showcases are combined into a contemporary and elegant room structure that is very light and bright.

MUMUTH

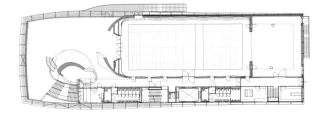

The architecture of this building clearly communicates that this is a place where music lives. Two main themes dominate the construction: The first one is the so-called "spring structure" which bears a direct relationship to music. As the organizing element, the spiral offers structure to the volumes that make up the theater, auditorium, rehearsal and utility spaces. The spiral splits into many smaller interconnected spirals that take on a vertical and a diagonal direction. This is the second theme which creates a free and fluent internal spatial arrangement, and is an important design model, named by the architects as "blob-to-box".

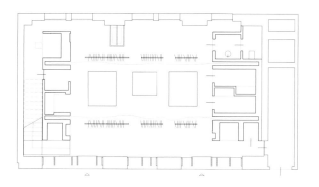

2006Feb01

BEHF Architekten are famous for professional concept of design. Two worlds — the busy streets outside and the stillness of the garden — are the framework for the store's "living area". The historical stone façade of the former bank building was playfully re-interpreted for its new purpose. The hardware (such as floors) bear the typical BEHF signature: untreated, smooth cement surfaces in a pure gray. Niches, shelves, drawers and changing rooms are decorated using different luxurious materials, for example polished stainless steel or magnificent tapestry fabric. These can be varied and changed like in a puppet theater or stage.

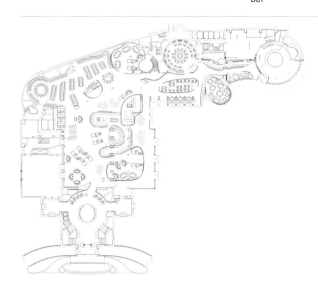

Do&Co Baden

Strong connections and intensive blending of the gaming and gastronomy functions wherever possible merge the different contents and differently designed, separate areas to one exciting, eventful whole, a dialogue between the past and the future. By systematically covering the existing substance in shades of deep black, the space acquires new elegance while at the same time providing a neutral backdrop for all new interventions. The color red runs like a thread from the lobby to the dining room, where it multiplies in the many different materials, surfaces and patterns and dominates the room. An organically-shaped, 70-meter-long bar redefines the structure of the gaming room, creates new space within the space and connects all the Casino's different content areas like a clip.

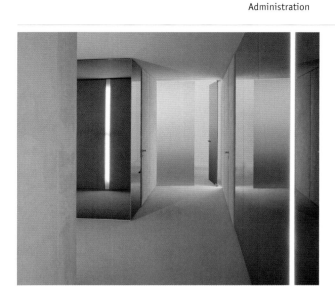

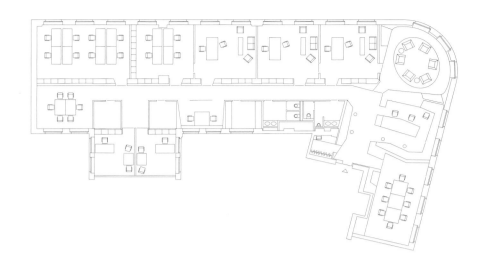

Harisch Rutter offices

The concept for the branch office of a law firm and project development company was made subordinate to the needs of later utilization. Consistent use of select, high-quality materials creates a dense atmosphere, presenting itself malleable to the needs of other users according to their discretion and image. The rooms' textural and acoustic qualities answer to the needs of sensitive and confidential interactions with customers. All rooms maintain a discreet simplicity, while all presentation and multimedia technology is integrated in a way that effectively hides it. Large mirrored surfaces continuously offer new vistas both inside and out, breaking the perspective and even giving the corridor area spatial breadth and openness.

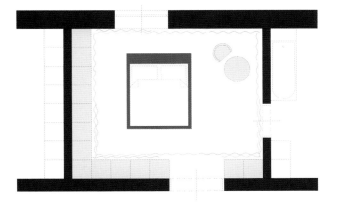

Bedroom Apartment W

It was the goal to create a sensual room from an existing bedroom inside a generous older apartment. This was achieved by using textiles and haptic materials. By being "dressed" in curtains, the room received a flowing drape which smoothes over all sharp contours. At the same time, the curtains hide all functional elements such as closets, doors and windows. The curtain rails sport various earthy tones. A special effect is created using a double-layered drape arrangement, resulting in a color play with a three-dimensional property. The bed is clad in hand-waxed buffalo leather, and harmonizes with the drape.

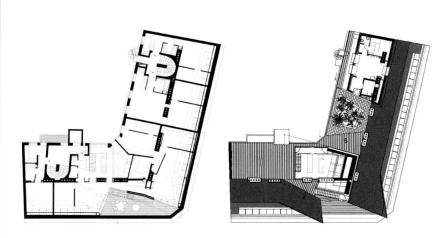

KLG19

The Wilhelminian corner building was overhauled and its roof was raised, creating four new roof apartments. The roof consists of two intersecting structures. The room design of the corner apartment is based on an open layout with the individual living areas simply created by the spatial division. The upper level uses the entire roof area of the corner building and is divided into two large outdoor areas. This level features the transparent kitchen cube and the sauna clad in wood panels. The turret is a pure steel construction, with a mostly invisible frame.

Beaudevin

This is a contemporary interpretation of the traditional wine cellar. In this concept wine as a product for pleasure produced through a sophisticated craftsmanship was translated by using well-known materials with an honest character like oak in contrast to glass which is transparent and light. The atmosphere of this concept gets the inspiration from the encounter between wine grower and wine lover in the grower's wine castle or cellar, combined with modern comfort. Wood is the base material and is used for the furniture, the bar, ceiling and the floor. The honest materials radiate warmly in the space. Women find the space open and inviting because of the simple and clearly defined areas.

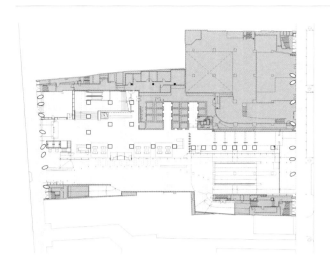

Dominican Hotel

The Art-Deco building La Mondiale (designed around 1930): was named for the former insurance company that had the corner building on the Schildknaapstraat and the Leopodstraat in 1937. The project involved the renovation and restoration of one of the most centrally located city eyesores in the heart of Brussels. The seriously neglected building is located just next to shopping areas, just behind the Theâtre Royale de la Monnaie, and within walking distance of the Grand Place and many other tourist attractions. Residential properties are planned for the top floors of the old buildings while the ground floor is reserved for business propertie.

Be Manos

The luxurious boutique hotel Be Manos is located in the center of Brussels only a few minutes from the railway station. The former townhouse dating back to the 1920s was renovated and restructured into a hotel with 60 rooms. Its elegant interior combines designer elements, simple furniture and materials such as leather, plexiglas, slate and stainless steel. The dominant shades of black and cream are loosened up by contemporary photographs and color accents. The Be Lella restaurant and breakfast room, for example, features apple-green elements that complement the furnishings. The Bar Noir and Black Lounge located on the third floor invite guests to relax on a beautiful terrace.

Woonburo Custers

Designers laid gray parquet interiorly and chose to go for a linear concept: with four long lines, as three long black boxes and one wall cabinet. When entering the office, you are led to the reception desk, made from the same material as the floor: gray oak. This desk was given the shape of the roof of a house for obvious representative reasons; being two V forms, in which, currently, the presentation books are stored for renting and for selling. At the back, a complete work space was installed in black MDF; this also being the area where the fax machine and the coffee machine are located.

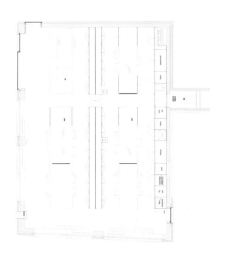

Falkensteiner Punta Scala Residence & Vacation Club

Ten kilometers from Zadar, on a 29.6-hectare seaside plot on the Dalmatian coast of Croatia; a distinguished resort is taking shape. Besides hotels, apartments and villas, the complex includes shopping centers, restaurants, sporting facilities, parks and swimming areas. The structural plan places a lot of weight on environmental protection and conservation of natural living spaces. Punta Scala's colors – white beach, emerald green forests, clear turquoise water and sun-bleached gray rocks – are incorporated in the project's details. The sea horizon provides a continuous orientation for all structures of the complex.

National Technical Library in Prague

This project is the architects' answer to the role of the library in today's society. The building should be urban developmentally important and environmentally friendly. The ground floor houses public spaces like the cafe, exhibition hall, bookshop, cloak room and night study room. The entry to the library is right in the middle of the atrium. The actual library occupies the upper four floors. Part of the concept is the surrounding area – social spaces on the west and a green park on the east. Finally, the building was designed including the interior. Art and the graphic design follow the concept "the technological schoolbook", so that illustrations are deliberately shown to better understand the building's design and functions.

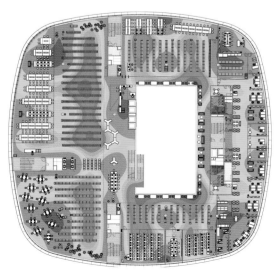

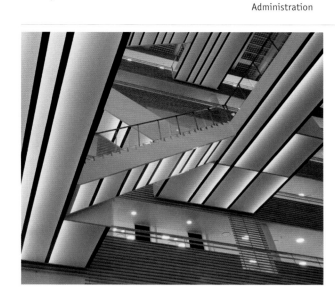

Deloitte Headquarters

The three solitary buildings are located at the edge of land and water. Their openings, which prolong the outer perimeter, position all offices along the façades with panoramic views and fresh air access. The façades consist of double glass elements. The office areas and the central atrium form a single room with a large light installation at the bottom of the stairs. This supports an open and transparent business structure and informal knowledge sharing. The office areas are mostly designed as landscapes, with a number of back-up rooms such as study cells and meeting rooms also present at all levels.

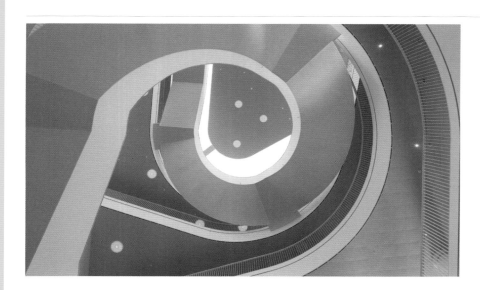
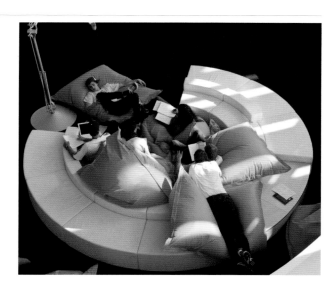

Ørestad College

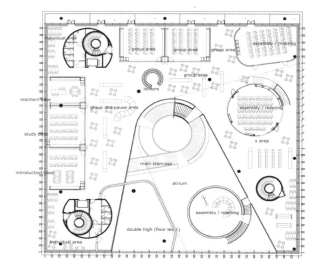

Ørestad College is the first college in Denmark based on the new visions of content, subject matter, organisation and learning systems in the reform of the educational system of the Danish "high-school" (gymnasium) for students of the age of 16–19. Communication, interaction and synergy has been key issues. The project displays a visionary interpretation of openness and flexibility regarding team sizes, varying from the individual over groups to classes and assemblies, and reflects international tendencies aiming at achieving a more dynamic and life-like studying environment and introducing IT as a main tool. The intention is also to enforce the students' abilities to care for own learning, both through team-work and individual assignments.

FRONT

With its combination of discrete Scandinavian forms and international brightly colored and voluminous elements throughout, FRONT, located by Copenhagen's prime harbour promenade, is a hotel for guests who appreciate design. In the FRONT's lobby, a 24-meter long counter, which functions as a reception desk, a bar and a restaurant, combines the hotel's most central service functions in a long succession of pleasant and discrete impressions. The interior is decorated with a mix of old paintings and candlesticks in addition to new furniture, contemporary art and lighting design from Italy and Denmark. The color scheme is dominated by dark brown and black nuances, complemented by strong accents such as the pink sofa modules and the vibrant paintings.

Cubion Office

Located in the heart of Copenhagen the consultant company Cubion A/S now occupies the lower floor in a protected house dating from 1793. The main office supports and stimulates the exchange of knowledge. The office space is suited for eight employees divided into two groups of vibrant green tables. The office is lit up by two (1500 x 100 x 1000 millimeters) suspended lamps also designed for the room by Jackie-B. The office walls are inhabited with synthetic grass islands that help to secure a dreamy and calm atmosphere and with which the employees can interact. The kitchen is designed as a social meeting room with a bright yellow table that centers the room.

Clubhouse for the Royal Danish Yachting Club

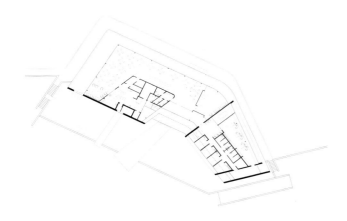

The clubhouse by Vilhelm Lauritzen Architects with its mellow form is a reference to the curves of a boat and the soft character of water. It addresses the waterfront, with fully exposed façades in glass from floor to ceiling. Materials are limited to a selection of hardwood, steel, glass and concrete. To ensure and support the desire for a homogeneous form, the building is clad in black roofing felt without indicating seam joints – framed by a white painted steel profile as a reference to a large ship's white hull. The form is internally implemented with wood as a direct reference to a ship's wooden decks and internal fittings.

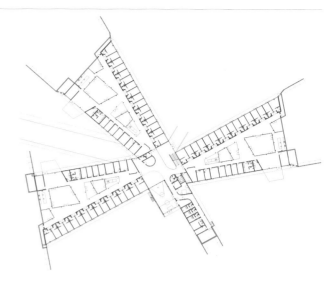

Helsingor Psychiatric Hospital

As the base of design the architects interviewed patients, personnel and relatives related to the psychiatric hospital. No truth emerged, but a series of paradoxes became evident. The PSY needs to combine the efficiency of a central organization with the freedom and autonomy of a decentralized complex. It needs to allow control and protection while maintaining a free and open atmosphere. In terms of function the PSY is a logistically optimized hospital and in terms of experience it is all but a hospital.

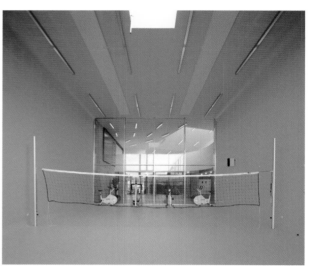

House Kekkapää - Wood In Rock

The house was built in a historically significant agricultural landscape in North Espoo. The simple form topped with a pitched roof integrates the building into the wider context. The western slope of the woodland site is divided into two areas of differing character; the back part with pines and the rocky ground covered with moss. The main building comprises three zones: living and working, and a glass-roofed conservatory linking the two. During the day the living area is used for in-home child-care, while the conservatory acts as a shared dining space and as the meeting room of the office. The office can later be transformed into a separate apartment.

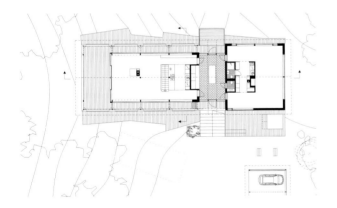

Humlegård House

The building is in the village of Fiskars, a few kilometers away from the center of the old ironworks. It stands on a small knoll at the edge of an overgrown glade and is orientated in a north-south direction. The garden is bounded on the west by a shed and a carport, by a field on the south with an old village winding road, and is sheltered by a high cliff on the north. A log sauna has been built to the east of the house where Fiskars Lake can be seen through the forest. The house consists of three parts: two kitchen/living rooms linked by a balcony, a bathroom and a walk-in wardrobe below. The high window openings catch the first rays of the sun, which are reflected into the interior by the ceiling.

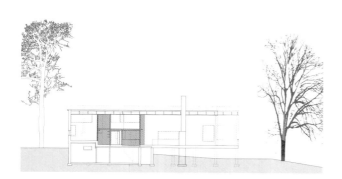

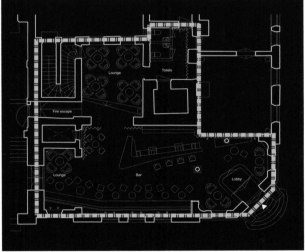

Bar Grotesk

The interior of Bar Grotesk is finished in white, black and gold. A custom designed white leather sofa stretches luxuriously for 14 meters under the windows, sharing the space with black designer plastic chairs, black leather chairs, and black glass tables. The bar is the heart of nightclub. The designers wanted it to be a freeform, bone-like element, as if a spaceship had landed in the middle of the room. They chose a material with a satiny feel and look. The solid surfacing was ideal for creating the complex, yet stable shapes.

Klaus K

Klaus K is a personal contemporary hotel inspired by the emotional contrasts of Finland's national epic, the Kalevala, its nature and drama. The Klaus Kurki hotel, located in the late-19th century Rake building and a landmark for many years, has been transformed into the Klaus K with the help of renowned Finnish architects SARC Group and international interior design by Stylt Trampoli. The lead architects of the Klaus K, Antti-Matti Siikala and Sarlotta Narjus of SARC Architects, have created some of Finland's foremost modern architectural projects: an ultra-designed lifestyle experience where contrast abound, an upmarket experience of tradition and cutting-edge Nordic modernity.

Chalet Le Marti

This boutique hotel-styled chalet was once the village school in the old village of Argentière at the foot of Mont Blanc. It later became a hostel for walkers and climbers and it was also for a while a restaurant. Today Le Marti is a modernized chalet designed by HIP Chalets, blending contemporary design with rustic features. The 340 square meter of living area holds a sauna and outdoor hot tub, eight bedrooms with ensuite bathrooms, an open plan lounge and dining area separated by a modern fireplace. Le Marti is the perfect modern getaway for ski lovers as its location is right below the world famous ski area Les Grands Montets in the heart of the Mont Blanc valley.

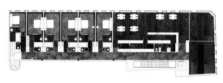

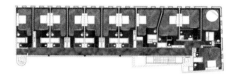

Seeko'o Hotel

A regular pattern of evenly proportioned openings covers the two façades of the hotel. These windows and French windows ensure a remarkable visual continuity in the extension of the 18th century's façade of the waterfront. The project emphasizes the lack of decoration and the pure, clean lines of its design. The choice of a smooth, abstract outer skin made up of large, immaculately white plates of Corian® creates the strong identity of the project. The final level of the hotel, an attic, is set recessed from the façades. The rooms there benefit from an unspoiled view of the surroundings.

Chalet des Drus

Le Chalet des Drus has bespoke furnishings designed exclusively for the chalet and original works of art from the owner's personal collection. The chalets' façade and interiors combine burned and sand blasted rustic wood, beautiful stonework and stucco plaster work on some interior walls. The use of these traditional materials contrasts beautifully with the modern design features such as the glass stairway and slate dining table using iron legs from the workshop of Mr. Eiffel, (architect of the Eiffel Tower). This creates a stunning harmony respecting traditional building materials, and techniques with modern design features and technology.

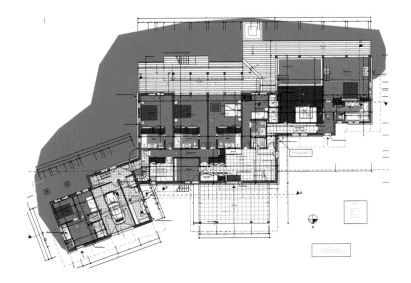

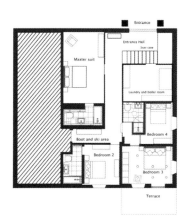

Ferme du Bois

Ferme du Bois was built by Jean Couttet in 1740. It is one of the oldest buildings in the Chamonix valley. Some time before Second World War the house underwent some changes where the hayloft was turned into living quarters and the fireplace was cut to its current position. It was used as a family home for many years and there are stunning authentic antique furniture throughout the house. The rustic structure and history of the chalet have been lovingly maintained, integrating modern features where necessary. Ferme du Bois gives a homely and comfortable atmosphere with an unequalled sense of social space and a perfect location at the foot of Mont Blanc with views of the entire mountain range.

Hotel Les Airelles

In these interiors, furniture, woodwork and friezes harmonize with antique furnishings, pictures and art objects. The interior designer completed the last phase of the renovation, following spa and restaurant. The goal was to create a different world filled with marvels and perfect dreams. The use of wood, warm colors, unusual furniture and accessories was inspired by centuries-old traditions of mountain decor. In addition to the lobby, spa, restaurant, bedrooms and suites, an area dedicated entirely to children has also been created.

Lycée Louis Armand

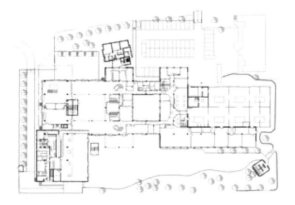

Behind the perforated aluminum-clad façade a 1000 square meter atrium with a height of three storeys can be found. All three floors have their own colors dedicated to. The colors meet again in the atrium and form a work of art in the style of Mondrian. The architects have managed to establish a connection between old and new building to enable a stable educational work.

Epinay Nursery School

The nursery is located on the edge of a 1970s estate characterized by tall, massive and rectangular features. With its bright colors and modern look, this nursery is at odds with the surrounding built context, but entirely in tune with the imaginative world of childhood. The project consists of five entities, all linked to childhood, but each one distinct and requiring its own configuration and access. These small units lie at right angles to the main access road and alternate with strips of vegetation. Each unit has a panelled roof whose slope differs according to the activities underneath. The height to ridge beam and the resulting available internal space are linked to the room's importance.

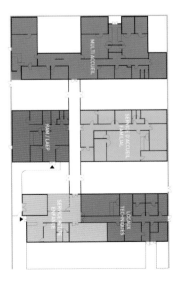

Boutique Lancel

This boutique resembles a gallery in which a great number of bags and other leather goods are displayed on rows of chromed shelves and may be viewed through arches crisscrossing the space. The arches combine the concept of the existing building with the elegant atmosphere created by stylish white leather armchairs and delicate transparent lamps suspended in midair. Featured products are showcased in glass cases and illuminated by LED lamps, whose light is reflected in mirrors distributed around the space, giving the boutique a scintillating ambiance.

Hotel B Design

The luxury hotel offers 14 open suites each measuring 44 to 86 square meters. To reach each suite, a dark, narrow corridor must be crossed. This architectural feature ensures the element of surprise experienced when entering the luminous suites lit using big glass panes facing a private terrace of about 30 square meters each. The main quarters may be separated by mirrored sliding doors, which prevents their contracting the space's intended depth. The modest and accurately selected appointments as well as the interior's light color create a calm and homelike atmosphere.

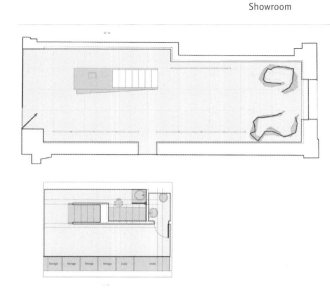

Me Boutique, Issey Miyake

AEDS has worked with Issey Miyake for more than five years to create the Pleats Please spaces and Me line boutique. The Me line boutique is a practice in minimalism. Existing in an all white color palette, the featured element of the boutique is a lacquered, reflective floor and ceiling with recessed light fixtures. This unique lighting method prevents direct spot light, creating an even, ambient light environment. The forthcoming fitting rooms, digitally designed and using 3D print technology, will be an ornamental installation within the esthetically pure Me boutique space. AEDS has matched this sentiment by using cutting edge digital technology and new materials.

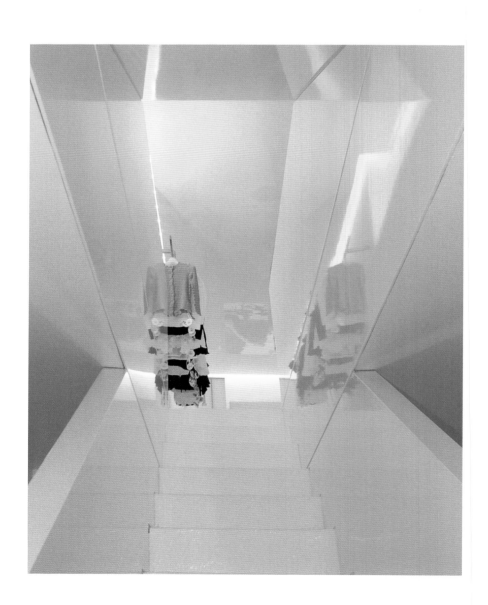

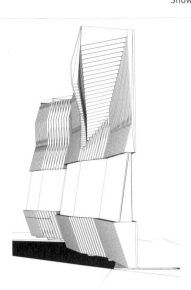

Silvera Wagram Shop

The ground floor measuring 5 x 20 meters leads to the 400 square meter basement with no direct street access. A wooden panel "canyon" draws visitors inside, creating an impression of walking through a Parisian passage with small objects located to either side. The far wall has a shiny red surface, from which chairs are suspended. These elements are continued down the staircase, where a window showcases a range of iconic armchairs. The path continues with a ceiling with a dark wood treatment and rough concrete walls. A few lights create vignettes around selected objects and furniture.

Stella McCartney Store Paris

The gilded ceiling in the main room was carefully restored using gold leaf; the custom furniture was made carefully and with great attention to detail, and handmade ceramics were combined with detailed metal pieces created using modern laser cutting techniques. The result is a meticulously balanced space with simple forms and lines, which juxtaposes the luxury and fullness of Parisian mentality against moderation of lines, forms and mass of the modern city. Stable but warm, feminine materials create an individual character.

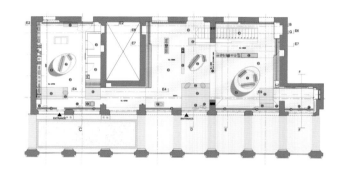

Maxalto Store

The Maxalto store expands a 145 square meter addition to its existing space. A leading name in the world of high-quality furniture, Maxalto uses traditional furniture-making techniques, modern technologies and prestigious materials, predominantly wood, to create furnishing collections with timeless and precious lines. The dark wood floors and the soft atmosphere are in perfect harmony with the space. The latest Maxalto collections are displayed in the boudoir atmosphere of this extraordinary space.

Fauchon Flagship Store

The creation of this gourmet and specialty company was based on the idea of varying atmospheres. The concept of luxury is expressed through the rigor of design and the quality of materials, as well as a generous display of a delicious profusion of foods. The golden ambience of the bakery, pastry and coffee bar fills the space with light. The luminous and crystalline silver atmosphere of the restaurant melts into a pale pink evoking subtle Parisian elegance. The black, white and gray air of the grocery, catering and wine cellar brings light and structure to Fauchon's diverse universe.

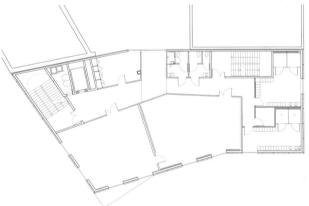

Lilas Animation Center

Lilas Animation Center is a new building in Paris. The architects designed it to accommodate cultural, sporting and social events. The façade is pulled into a skin made of black rectangles, white and silver. The skin folds on the roof to provide residents in the towers with views of the building. The basement hosts a theater of 150 seats. There is an exhibition hall, multipurpose room and a kitchen on the ground floor. First floor studios are for dance and sports activities and the second level workshops are for visual arts. The whole space is full of energy and youthful spirit with colorful decoration.

Espace PAYOT

In the spirit of classic bathing parlours, the only elements present are water, stone and light. The purity of the lines and materials here contribute to restfulness, the decorative qualities residing uniquely in the rhythm of the volumes and the monolithic spirit. This ubiquitous mineral presence lends a timeless character to the whole setting. Set out in the infrastructure of a building dating from the beginning of the last century, the ensemble is situated on two levels: the ground floor combines the reception area, dressing rooms and services, and the underground level features a swimming pool, Jacuzzi, hammams, saunas, a gymnasium and cubicles for health and beauty treatments.

Hotel Lumen

The hotel is set in the center of Paris, between Place Vendôme and the Tuileries gardens. In perfect harmony with the location's name, light was placed at the core of the concept using subtle interplay of light and different contrasting materials. The bedrooms reflect a morphing of contexts by mixing baroque and modern styles. In the hotel's restaurant, the Bistrot Parisien, classic space has been revisited. The hotel has 33 rooms and suites, two meeting rooms equipped with the latest communication technologies and a restaurant with an occupancy of 60.

My Berry Restaurant

Punctuated by white and featuring curved, elegant shapes, the space physically illustrates the "0% fat yogurt" restoration concept. The outer façade clearly presents the idea and invites the passersby for a tasting. The bar counter is nothing more than the logical continuity of the dominant white, elegant and dynamic surface. It features a variation of refreshing colors, reminiscent of toppings which complement the yogurt. Colors and materials appear from behind the white surfaces, as if the color has been ingeniously removed to create space with features like bright niches.

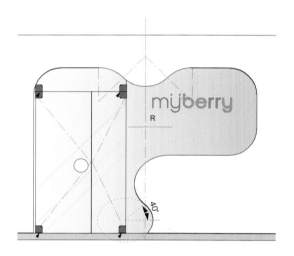

Cardboard Office

The challenge in converting an industrial space into a twenty-desk office was to provide it with a flexible space which would accommodate various activities such as advertising and Internet departments for a duration ranging from a few months to several years, instead of a more permanent design. The concept was executed using a water-resistant honeycomb cardboard which may be folded, glued and taped to be transformed into needed furniture elements. This unusual interior design offers a functional and flexible space, which can be executed in a very short time and for a competitive price. The office's special ambience conveys the client's creative image.

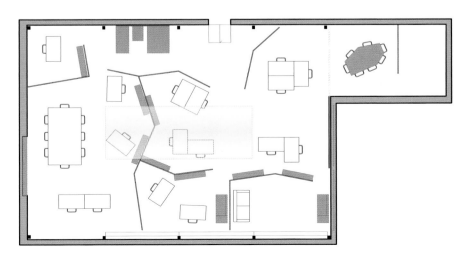

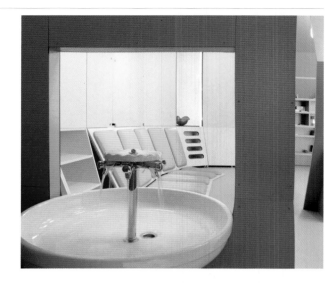

Cent-Quatre Day Care Center

This place welcomes local children aged from zero to five years accompanied by their parents for meeting, mediation, discovery, encounters and listening. It is made up of various areas put to use according to children's ages and their relative autonomy. The space is very luminous and airy thanks to a sky-blue shell and radiates dynamism with shades of bright colors. An artificial garden placed inside a shell offsets the industrial character of the place. In the garden, mushrooms of various sizes organize it into child-sized sub-sections and act as supports for activities.

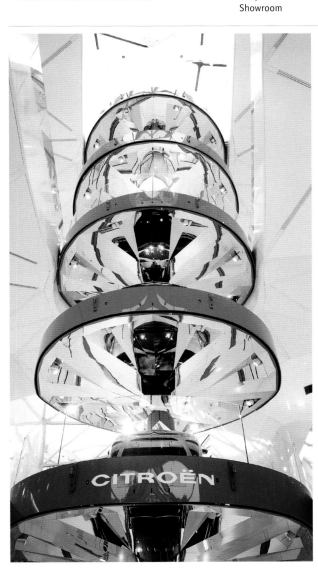

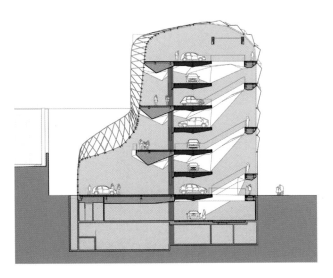

C42 Citroën Flagship Showroom

The tall, cavernous space of the Citroën exhibition building has an unusual form and a spiraling ramp along the outer walls. The white space without any separations into stories stands in contrast to a highly noticeable, shiny red shelf unit with seven "shelves". Four of the shelf levels with presented cars may be viewed at close range, while the last three offer staged scenes not accessible from the floor. For pedestrians striding past the façade facing Champs-Élysées, the shop window offers a unique, dizzying view through the glazed bay on the illustrious Parisian shopping promenade.

LaboBrain

LaboBrain is the office of the founder of Le Laboratoire, a Think Tank that links art and science. The room resembles a living room with distinguished designer furniture (Cork Chair by Jasper Morrison, Bentwood chair by Frank Gehry) and a geodetic cathedral transformed into an easy chair conceived by the interior designer, rather than a conventional work place. Lehanneur's "Delicious" boxes and plant-based room filter "Andrea" complete this section of the room that is enclosed in a large rounded delineable wall disc. In contrast to the emotional "frontal lobe" section of the room, the back section represents the rational memory with white drawers and a large work desk.

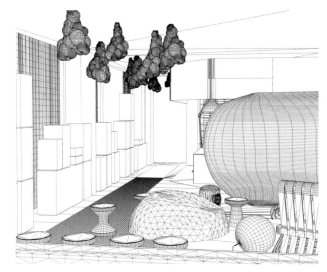

Hotel Jules

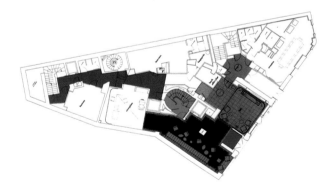

Hotel Jules, which was designed by the Touch of Grace team (G.L.A. Hotels), is located in a very busy section of Paris. The hotel's casual chic atmosphere, incorporating style elements from the 1950s, 1960s and 1970s, is an instant eye catcher. A black-and-white diamond motif on a carpet and round ceiling lights in the lobby, combined with simple room design in chocolate or blue tones in 94 guestrooms, invite guests to stay a while and relax. The six junior suites maintained in warm colors feature heavy curtains and black lamps of bottle glass.

Germain

This exceptional bar and restaurant was placed in the former Brasserie Arbuci and provided with an entirely new interior design. The most striking element is the yellow sculpture in the form of a woman, originating on the ground floor in the middle of the restaurant and continuing to the second story, where it enters the VIP room with the upper part of the body. The rest of the furnishings are just as extraordinary and inventive, combining various patterns and bright colors on floors, walls and furniture elements to create a highly varied interior.

Maison des 3 thés

Turning an old laundrette into master Tseng's nest was the challenge to be faced here. But the space was strangely working for the designers, as the shape was not that different from the Chinese dwellings studied by the designer in Guangzhou. The space had been organized around a huge tea counter and a back wall displaying the tea collection. Following the soul of this 1930s bricks and concrete building, the designers formulated a mix of Chinese and European spirit. The furniture was made in China and the raw material was kept on the walls. Large sheets of paper with Chinese poems cover the plaster walls.

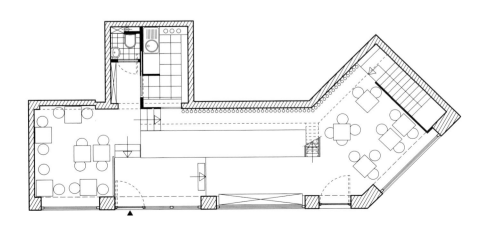

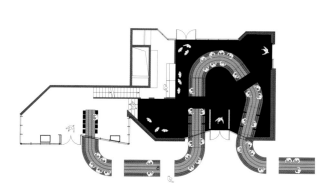

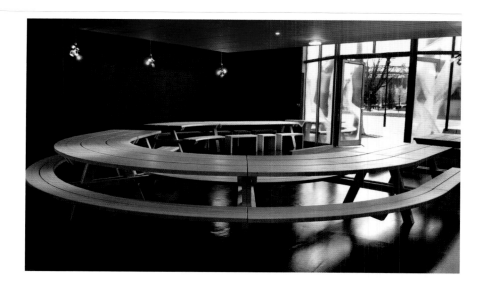

Restaurant le 51

Connecting the restaurant's interior to the park was an important element of the overall concept. A 40 meter long curved picnic table of Swiss pinewood continues with almost no transition into and out of the building. The atmosphere of festive communal meals invites people from the park and the neighboring area inside. Scrap furniture remained in the épicerie after the construction work. Instead of conventional legs, seven pairs of rubber fishermen's boots serve as rests for the counter which supports the restaurant's register and electronics.

Mama Shelter Hotel

In this hotel, standard rooms are as big as 20 square meters and offer a modern and cozy atmosphere thanks to materials such as cotton and satin as well as comprehensive multimedia technology. Luxury suites reach 35 square meters in size and additionally feature large terraces with Paris views. Common rooms invite gatherings at simple family tables or comfortable armchairs illuminated by candlelight. Mama Shelter was designed not only as a place of habitation but also as a retreat which offers a homely feeling.

Restaurant Le Meurice

Here, stone, gold and warm colors render the noble character of each space and are amplified by the dreamlike atmosphere created using unusual lighting, secret alcoves, ochre, wood and leather. The grand foyer is characterized by the harmony of beige accented with red and black, and the association of wood, glass and metal with scattered touches of velvet, satin and leather. A historic yet completely timeless space is created. The atmosphere of the bar is subtly warmed by the crackling glow of tobacco shades and accented by the sparkle of rare crystal decanters, to be filled at leisure.

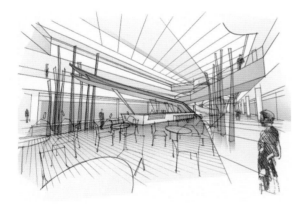

Domus Furniture Mall

The challenge was to develop the design of the interior space of the 62,000 square meter mall using a contemporary architectural language, which would frame and complement the furniture retail offers within. The mall stretches 200 meters and consists of three floors of dedicated retail space. The commission also included the lighting scheme for both the external and internal spaces. Daylight was an important element with an 8,400 square meter glass roof to the main atrium adding natural light throughout the day. At Domus the landscape is not just about commerce. Some of the atrium spaces are devoted to non-commercial uses — spaces to rest, refresh, and refuel or simply to contemplate.

Musée de la Bretagne

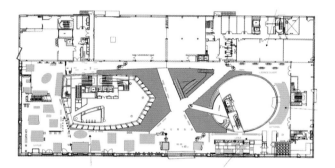

Unlike conventional museum buildings based on enclosed spaces, Elizabeth de Portzamparc has designed a museography inspired on an open city-walk type itinerary. The museum's scenography unfolds over the various historical epochs, while the visitor passes streets and crosses places. Large boxes of differing dimensions and empty spaces represent the earliest periods one after the next, recalling buildings and places. A street ambiance embodies subsequent periods, while two dark, dramatic, tunnel-like enclosed spaces stand for the two wars. Designed with modern technical fixtures, the Museum of Breton civilization includes periods up to and including contemporary 21st century history.

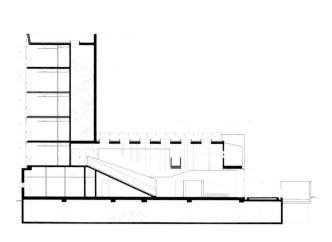

Saint-Denis Police Station

Given the reduced size and the location of the land parcel, the idea was to insert most of the program elements into a high vertical volume which will stand as an emblematic tower. The "special" elements of the program will have their own volumes. The composition is constrained on both ends with glass walls. These spaces enclose the ground floor and the first level, creating a pedestal for the rest of the masses to stand on. The plinth unfolds along the elevation, forming setbacks and notches where various volumes nestle or detach themselves. This volume interaction creates a tension link between them.

Bar du Port

Created in 2001, the Bar du Port has been entirely remodeled in 2008, giving center stage to the interplay of mirrors, shadows and light as an element of decor. Glass, smoked mirrors, white stone and furnishings create a dazzling ambiance which subtly changes as the hours pass and LED screens diffuse various colored light effects. Open seven days a week, the sparkling atmosphere attracts and enchants a diverse international and local clientele over the course of the day. A top-notch brasserie-style menu and an appetizing selection of complimentary tapas are offered for lunch and dinner.

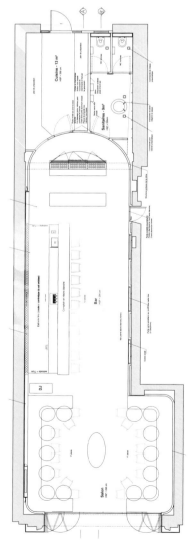

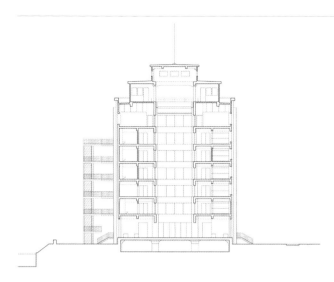

André Malraux Library

The river landscape demands to be understood horizontally. Everything in the setting complies with the logic of the river – the linearity of the quays, the stretch of the jetty, the alignment of the trees. Even the buildings themselves are lined up from one end of the jetty to the other, perfectly regular in their continuity parallel to the quays, vertically punctuated at their ends, like prows, by their silos. On this long tongue of land surrounded by water, it is less the buildings that define the space than the relation between them; the succession of masses and voids, the play of horizontals and verticals, the axes, as well as their strict alignment with the quays.

Hotel Le Grand Balcon

The building, where the pioneers of air mail service had been living, was remodelled. Instead of converting the space into a museum to display engravings and photos retracing the history of the Aéropostale, a modern hotel radiating the same spirit of adventure and enterprise exemplified by those young pioneers has been designed. The space communicates the dreams, carefree attitude and poetry that inspired these men. Aviation, travel and wide open spaces are at the heart of this new universe, whose overall decoration concept was to give guests a feeling of space, freedom and well-being.

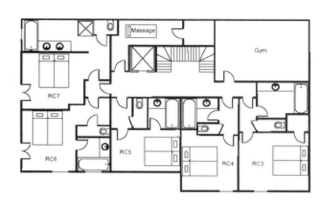

Le Rocher

The chalet is beautifully finished, mixing a rustic Alpine style with reclaimed wood from Mongolia, intricately carved furnishings and designer pieces, to create the perfect blend of new and old. Le Rocher, which literally translates as "the rock", has been constructed into the mountainside with the natural rock face exposed in the massage room and one of the bathrooms - a spectacular feature! The spacious interior also boasts an indoor swimming pool with jet stream, a Hammam, massage room, a home gym and solarium. A beautiful red cedar hot tub is situated on the balcony.

Trianon Palace Hotel

Opened in 1910, the Trianon Palace Hotel in Versailles is 500 meters from Louis XIV's royal residence with a splendid view of the Palace. It is not just a hotel, but a historic location... the Treaty of Versailles was actually signed in one of its rooms, the Clémenceau. Andromeda has created the hotel's decorative lighting, which combines with the setting of each room to enhance the architectural and functional context. The result is a mix of Murano handmade glass structures characterized by different styles and moods. The entrance and galleries feature for the first time the Knit element, designed by Karim Rashid, in a structural and decorative concept developed by Michela Vianello, Art Director of Andromeda. In the la Veranda brasserie five Le Roi c'est moi, the classical style is reinterpreted with a touch of contemporary.

Concrete Apartment

The main material utilized by this interior design of this unusual apartment is compact concrete. The walls consist of untreated rough concrete and, together with dark floors and high ceilings, give the space a loft feel. Almost all furniture pieces are cast from concrete and left in the original color. Even armchairs and sofas consist of this hard material and are rendered comfortable by seat cushions in a warm brown color. The simple, unornamented shapes and surfaces contribute to the apartment's modern and stylish atmosphere. Inventive lighting provides the uniformly gray space with necessary warmth.

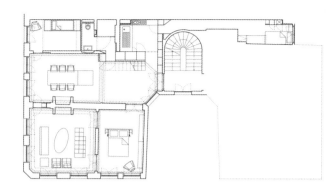

Apartment Hanovre

The 95 square meter apartment has an original ceiling height of approximately 4.2 meters. Dating from 1790, the apartment occupies the piano nobile, or the first level above an intermediate story. Previously, the space was used as an office, and neither kitchen nor sanitary amenities existed. The task involved connecting two units, one classical-bourgeois, the other functional-contemporary, executed completely in teak. A section of the apartment was split into two levels to create two new rooms to house the kitchen and bathroom.

Yacht Riela

The challenge of this interior was to make it a reflection of the owner's personality. The interior is pure and sophisticated, light and calm with some subtle dark ebony lines to add contrast while keeping in harmony with the atmosphere. The sensuality of the interior is a combination between natural materials and high-tech complexity. Particular attention was given to lighting design creating a unique effect which obscures its source while providing adequate illumination. All these elements create a pure and natural, but still warm and comfortable interior ambiance.

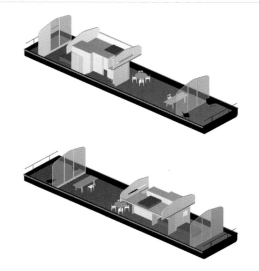

Floating House

This house boat was created to serve as a place for artists and authors to find refuge and be inspired. The house floats on a river, which can be viewed from the two main rooms through two completely glazed fronts, and therefore the calming effect of the water played a big role in the concept. The interior design is dominated by wooden walls and floors, and together with simple furnishings, creates a rustic atmosphere on an area of about 110 square meters. Climbing plants will grow on the terrace to integrate the building into the surrounding nature.

VitaSol Thermal Baths

The pleasure of bathing meets the experience of wellness in the newly designed bathing hall of the VitaSol thermal baths in Bad Salzuflen. The conversion of Hall 1 has not only extended the choice of bathing opportunities offered by the thermal baths but has also created an atmosphere that encourages well-being and relaxation. The architects set certain essential design criteria for this "metamorphosis": transparent, smooth transitions coupled with warm materials, powerful shades of color and special light effects define the appearance of the bathing hall and give the space its distinctive character. The dynamic lighting gives the bathing hall a lively and friendly atmosphere. The name VitaSol is after all derived from "life" and "sun", so visitors should experience the baths accordingly as a sunny oasis in which to discover the joy of life.

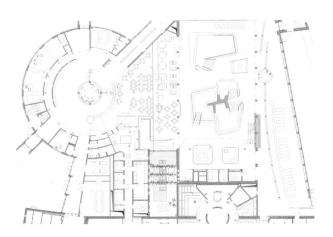

Alexa

East Berlin's largest shopping center is located on one of the last city hubs still undergoing development – Alexanderplatz. The architecture plays with the motifs from the roaring twenties with its art deco elements, recalling a mythical period for the metropolis on the Spree. The forms are not simply copied, but varied and amplified. The structure of the façade with an enlarged rounded arch frieze acts on the art deco principle of motif repetition and variation of architectonic vocabulary, simultaneously creating a counterpart to the neighboring arches of the elevated train viaduct. The volume is externally separated into individual building volumes, while inside a comprehensive circulation concept unites the entire space.

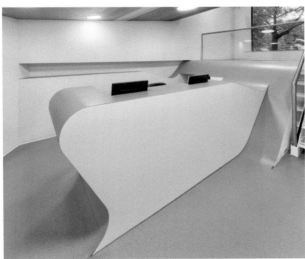

Children's Dental Practice

To eliminate children's fear of visiting the dentist, a new type of practice was developed. Upon entering, each patient is pulled into an underwater world created by full wall murals that result in a breathtaking atmosphere. Right at the entrance to the clinic a wave rises and flows throughout the entire building assuming the functions of a ceiling, wall, reception and lounge, while interweaving the rooms with each other. The aquatic theme is present in all areas of the practice and implemented by the specific application of light and materials. The color scheme with shades of ocean blue also extends throughout the premises. Diving into this underground world can easily help patients forget everything around them.

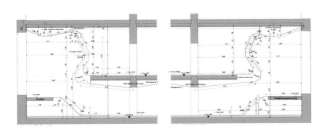

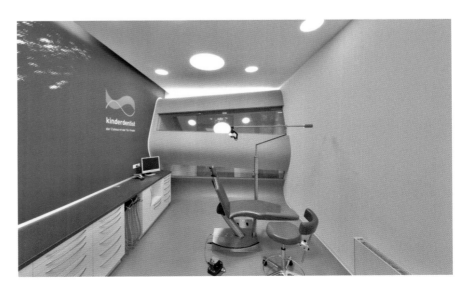

Dentist's practice KU64

The very thought of a dentist's practice evokes an image of hygiene and sterility, the everlasting mono-
logue of white, not to mention the unmistakable odour. But everything is different here. The image
evoked is that of a landscape of dunes in which the beach visitor seeks a spot in the sand, lays out his
towel and gazes off into the distance. It is a room in which the floor warps upward and the ceiling forms
waves. The arrangement of dune summits and valleys preserves privacy and fosters intimacy while allowing a generously open view through the entire practice. The floor, which folds to form waves and merges
with walls, has a striking orange surface consisting of four layers: colorless spray elastomers, a coloured
seal, anamorphic motifs as white rasters, and a final transparent seal.

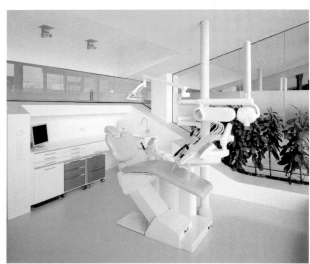

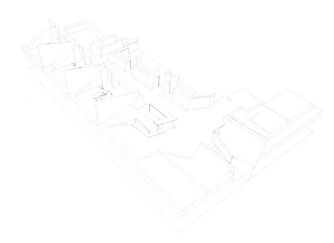

flip*flop Store

Initially, with their all-in-white combination of wood, ceramic tiles with an embossed relief pattern and various fabrics, flip*flop stores resemble art galleries. Yet this material mix also conveys a friendly attitude and openness. The neutrally colored ambience, the straight lines and cubic forms, coupled with a multifunctional wall panel create an ideal setting for presenting the flip*flop collection. The flip*flop lettering and logo are unobtrusively integrated into the design of the wall panel. The sound of birds chirruping in the background conveys the spirit of spring, while fresh flowers in a variety of colors usher in the summer – but in fact flip*flop stores are worth discovering in any season of the year.

Galeria Kaufhof Alexanderplatz

The Galeria Kaufhof on Alexanderplatz has a history that is as colorful as its surroundings. The store's origins lie with the Hermann Tietz Department Store, which was built on this area at the beginning of the 20th Century. The Centrum Emporium occupied the space as a fine example of 1970s zeitgeist. The current reconstruction and expansion of the Kaufhof building took place between 2004 and 2006. The building's character is defined by its new façade, which is a modern interpretation of classic department store architecture that includes large entrances, a two-story plinth and sculpturally structured natural stone surfaces. The domed, light-filled atrium with escalators is at the center of the building.

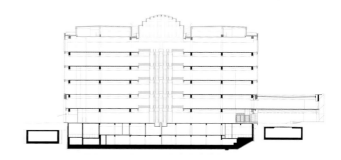

Geometry

Plajer & franz studio created an entirely new ambience in this space. True to the motto "how weird can you get", Geometry seems to be the apartment of someone eccentric but with good taste. It takes you by surprise like the first visit to your professor's home. The professor is not only obscure but also has a cultivated taste for proportions and moods. He collects all kinds of strange items photos of skeletons and lamps including that look like jackstraws. Everything refers to symmetry (skeleton) and asymmetry (overlapping reflections of the angled bronze mirrors). Everything is also very stylish — the mud-colored wall, the dark wooden floor and the brushed white oak furniture.

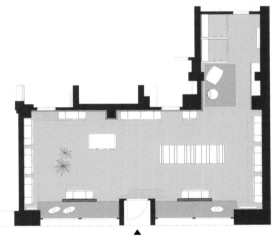

Yi Spa

The Yi presents a holistic spiritually balanced lifestyle concept – understated elegance, natural elements like slate stone, mother-of-pearl and dark wood are contrasted with colored glass, exotic plants and delicate fragrances. The idea was to allow all these elements to interact distinctively, while certain design features, like the tone-in-tone gravel between big stone slabs that imposes a path through a riverbed in Chiang Mai, exemplify the correlation between interior design and tradition. The Yi Spa integrates Asian culture into a modern realistic ambiance.

Rocco Forte Hotel de Rome

With its combination of stylish design and exceptional comfort, Hotel de Rome is one of the few luxury hotels of Berlin located in a historical building. Constructed in 1889, the building formerly housed the head office of the Dresdner Bank until 1945 and, more recently, the Central Bank of the German Democratic Republic. Hotel de Rome retained many of the building's original features while the architectural style has been maintained throughout, even with the addition of two new floors. All of the Hotel de Rome's 101 spacious bedrooms and 45 suites offer a contemporary fusion of "Berlin Style" incorporating glass and steel, inspired by the well-known classicist Prussian architect Schinkel.

O₂ World Berlin

The modern multifunctional arena provides a cultural experience scenario of the O_2 Germany brand. The telecommunications provider presents itself in two suites and a lounge, the so-called "Blue Room". The entrance hall conveys the world of O_2 with an individual wall and ceiling design including light and media with spatial dimensions. The design quality and corporate design are consistently applied and made palpable. The suites and the lounge create a landscape that is accentuated by dynamic blue incisions and the precise application of blue light. At the same time, these elements define various functional areas such as seating, bar and catering.

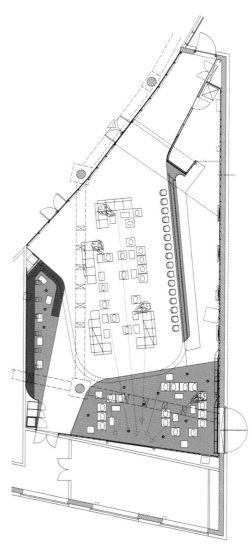

Roof Apartment near the Spree

The attic floor was designed as the private retreat of an internationally active businesswoman. Modern design in combination with collector's items and design classics create individual accents. The light colored sideboards that extend throughout the area feature integrated lighting that provides the room with a pleasant atmosphere and lightness. The fitted furniture and objects in various shades of white are in contrast to the warm natural hue of the parquet floor. Deliberate dabs of color highlight the originality and individuality of the inhabitant. The generously proportioned living area with a fireplace extends into the roof terrace with olive trees, herb garden, outdoor shower and an integrated bench with a view across the roofs to the Spree River.

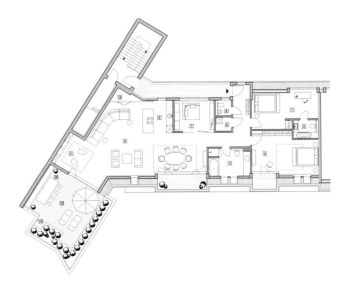

Townhouse am Friedrichswerder

The interior design provides the residents with the opportunity to apply their own concepts and display their individuality, since all fittings have understated colors and materials. Their extension gives them a presence that predefines a specific utilization concept. The ground floor and first floor levels are connected via a six-meter high open space and the vertically meandering furniture. On the lower floor it consists of a sequence of reception, bar, fire place and salon, while upstairs contains a cooking and dining piece of furniture measuring 15 meters. The rooms are denser and more private in the upper floors, with more contrasting materials and colors. The lateral illumination of the stairs underscores the linearity of the rooms. The existing structural design was adopted and reinterpreted as an immaterial white room sculpture.

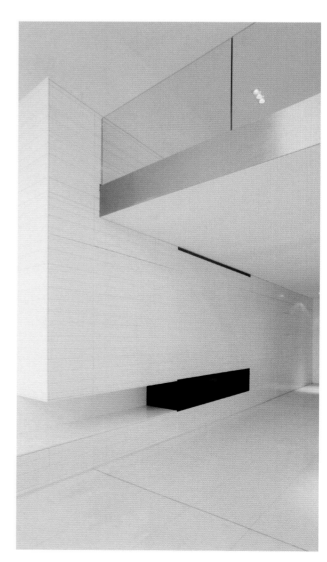

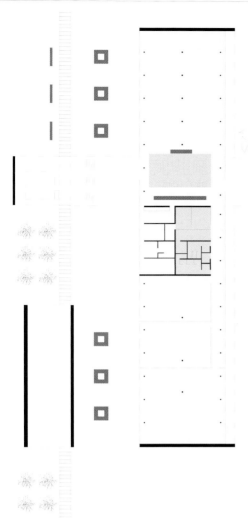

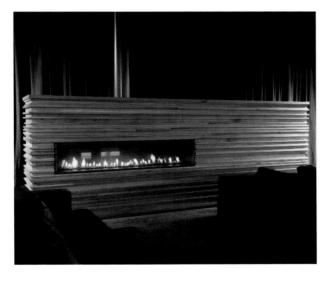

Roma Forum

In line with the corporate design of the globally leading rolling shutter manufacturer, the strictly arranged ensemble of buildings and outdoor areas was exclusively implemented in black-dyed exposed concrete. It serves as a multi-functional platform for the sophisticated interaction between customers, architects and manufacturer. An extensive lounge with an espresso bar and fireplace welcomes guest to the extended concrete bar-like building. Along both of its sides there are generous exhibition areas and offices, as well as a lecture hall and training rooms. In summer and winter the core-activated building is exclusively heated and air-conditioned via energy-intensive ground water feed- in and heat pumps.

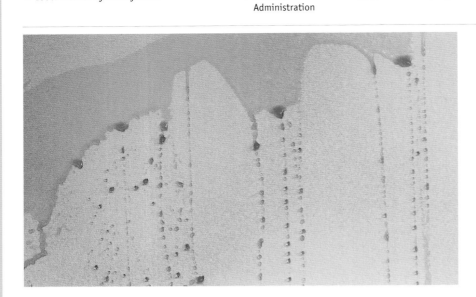

stardust

Following a move to new premises, the meeting room of the company was redesigned in white coupled with organic and crystalline shapes. Designed in cooperation with Evonik, the unique wall covering ccflex Stardust is not a regular wallpaper pattern, but an award-winning design product with its very own character. Due to its surface structure, the pattern of macro-sized diffused foam structures generates different optical impression such as shadows or projections, depending on the viewing angle and movement. The name "stardust" is derived from the NASA spacecraft, which rang in a new era of space research and brought stardust back to earth. These components constitute the very individual, yet subtle and understated setting that distinguishes the conference room.

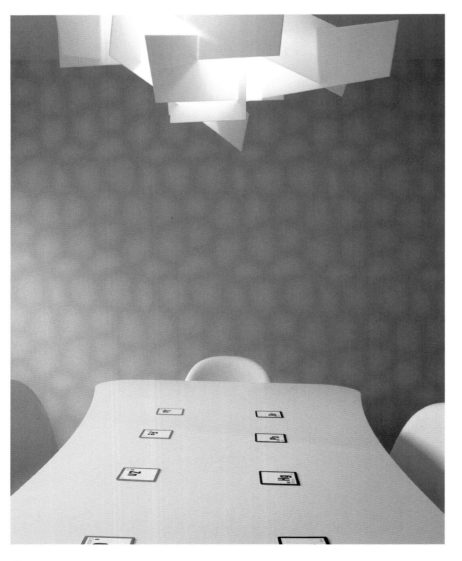

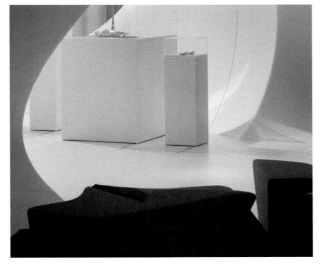

ideal house

The eye-catching red cubes are a trademark feature of Cologne's international furniture fair. Innovative designers can use them to realize their visions of future living space. In Hadid's ideal house rooms lose all orthogonality, and come together not as cubes, but stretch out inside the cube as asymmetrical space bubbles, erasing it along the edges and in corners. As in a group of soap bubbles, the closed volume of space, not the skin, determines the material's staying in the shape of surfaces and bridges. All the same, the stretching of space is not determined by physical laws, but guided by the designer's will, function and abstraction. For modeling of the rounded edges on the metal frame, 400 cubic meters of polystyrene were used. The continuous surface received a coating of 1.8 tons polyurethane.

Archititonic Lounge

The whole lounge can be completely reused and modified for any purpose. The umbrella frame is crafted by 100% recyclable aluminum, and the lightweight stretchable membrane minimizes the material usage. The lounge seats are carved from off cuts from industrial products and can be reused for a diverse range of products, including packaging and fill material. Each lounge seat weighs 6 kilograms, much less tahn the weight of a standard office chair and the lounge is therefore easily and environmentally friendly to transport. Umbrellas were designed to be projected with media that contribute to the atmosphere as they present information for the visitors.

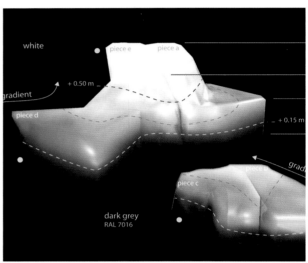

The Deutsche Bank Lounge

Karim Rashid's digipop sensuous world serves as a communication forum for the Deutsche Bank's many clients and discussion events. The exterior custom print wallpaper becomes a large artwork, blurring the borders of design, art and architecture. The influence of these fields on each other is strongly visible, creating one strong memorable experience. Visitors enter the main area of the lounge through reflections and refractions of color, light and pattern, while the backlit floor provides an intimate atmosphere. All rooms are separated by a glowing border of fluorescent color to create a visual distinction between the individual spaces. In harmony with Rashid's lounge concept in Cologne, Deutsche Bank is presenting the series of Winter garden prints by Marc Quinn.

Pediatric Clinic "Princess Margaret"

The 80-bed children's hospital was constructed in the park of the Alice hospital near Mathildenhöhe in Darmstadt. Its petal-shaped design is particularly suited to this setting. The patients' rooms are located on the two upper floors, while the treatment and auxiliary rooms are on the ground floor, which simultaneously serves as an entrance and reception area. The hospital stay is not intended to shut the children off from the outside world in a sterile hospital environment, but to stimulate them with new impressions, thus contributing to their healing.

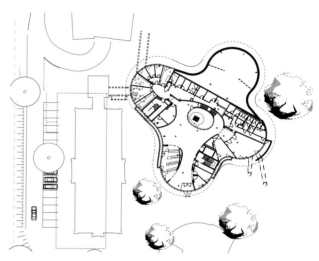

Hotel Ritter

The 2008 design for the hotel building created a bridge between modernity and its 500-year tradition as well as additions and renovations from all eras. Created in the tradition of wine and culinary delights, the modern hotel reflects all these historic themes, occasionally commenting on them tongue in cheek. The original suit of armor plays as big a role as the custom-made wallpaper with large bunches of grapes with shimmering morning dew made of silver leaf. Wine bottles were artistically turned into lamps, clothing hooks and toothbrush tumblers. The old wine cellar is dominated by red (Pinot Noir) and green (Riesling) fully glazed refrigeration rooms, located next to an archaic table made from a tree trunk.

THING Euroshop

The D'ART DESIGN GRUPPE presented its own meeting place at Euroshop 2008 in Düsseldorf. In terms of content, the stand was dedicated to the THING, turning Kant's philosophic concept of the "thing in it-self" upside down. Initially it is not clear what the THING is, since to the interdisciplinary designers the THING is synonymous with the offer of an open-ended exploratory voyage of their image presentation. To them, design consists of a shared and playful process and not of a ready-made solution. Of course, this means an according reflection in their own fair presence. The result is an enchanting all-round communication process as an entire network of possible interpretations and connections unfolds around the concept of the THING.

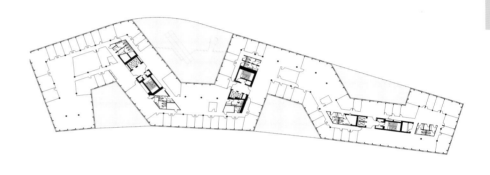

Capricornhaus

The unique new building with its red glass paneling is distinguished by its i-module façade. The location of the building, which is subject to a large degree of noise pollution, led to the design of a multifunctional façade module containing the entire individual room climate control technology. The façade features a ventilation system for cooling, heating and heat recovery, in addition to lighting, noise absorption, and room acoustics elements. The elimination of conventional building technology areas by the decentralized concept provided the interior planning with a great degree of freedom.

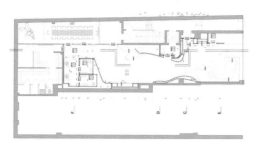

Dental Lounge

The main source of inspiration was the Aesculapius Staff; the image of a snake winding around a staff is the common symbol for the medical profession and proved to be an enticing concept. The narrow confinement of the floor plan helps accentuate this experience, as one is beckoned to delve further into the room, and gradually comprehend the full scope of the interior. The commonly associated cold and sterile environment yields to the lounge atmosphere; warm colors of brown, orange, and red along with a successful space sculpture are all important elements within the effect of the practice, signifying the patients' comfort and well-being.

Julia Stoschek Collection

The building used to be a factory in the last century. The task was to maintain the exterior of the original layout and to reorganize the interior to suit the new purpose. The interior spaces are stacked up vertically, starting with a cinema space in the basement and culminating in a panoramic terrace at the top of a glass box placed on the factory roof. The collection's focus is on works of video art that are presented to the public with yearly changing themed exhibitions. The exhibition spaces can therefore be changed easily. Areas for watching videos are enclosed by soundproof walls. The spaces dividing each video installation create a break between one piece and another.

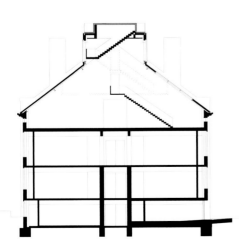

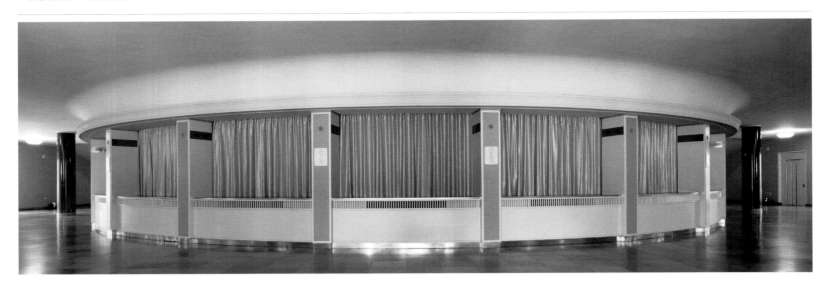

Deutsche Oper am Rhein

Constructed in neo-Renaissance style, the theater was renovated in the 1950s, and experienced a re-furbishment and addition of a light-filled orchestra and a ballet rehearsal space in 2007. During the latest modernization of the complete foyer, new lounge furnishings, information/exhibition stands and catering areas were created. The tiers with VIP lounges and dining facilities are individually designed using not only layout, but also through varied furnishings, thereby creating various spatial effects with the help of carefully chosen materials. The elegant lines found in the architecture are continued in the building's appointments.

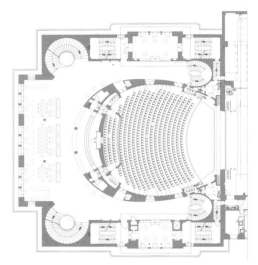

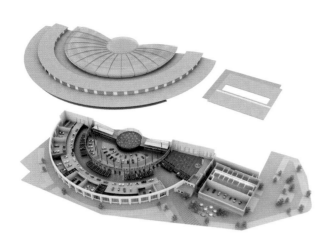

Meilenwerk

A listed former locomotive warehouse with 30 doors has been transformed into a specialty mall for vintage car enthusiasts. The structure from 1930 has been preserved where possible, with additions in the ring hall planned as nested houses. Along the workshops and showrooms located in the outer ring, a gallery offers views inside the hall and onto pedestals that present specialty cars. The central restaurant is built to replicate the former swivel platform. The central space is roofed over with a foil cushion construction, which appears to float above the eaves of the inner ring. Existing structure and addition communicate only through this 130 meter long transparent material.

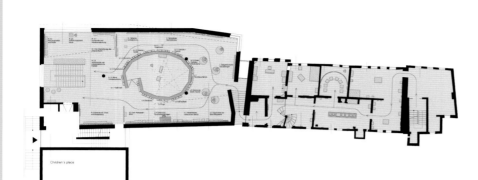

Bachhaus Eisenach

The highlight of the exhibition is, in the center of the space, the so-called "Accessible Piece of Music" (APM). At the exterior walls of the oval, the fugue is explained as a musical form. Inside the body the visitor can view a large format media interpretation of three contemporary performances of Bach's work. They refer to three exhibits first edition "Kunst der Fuge", a text notebook "Tönet ihr Pauken" and a manual organ from the year of 1702, on which Bach personally played. The illusionistic medial space performance fascinates its viewers and allows them to immerse themselves in the inspiring music of Johann Sebastian Bach.

z-room

The opening of z-room, an atmospheric info lounge on the fifth floor of the Zeilgalerie was the first step of the planned restructuring of the entire shopping center, which will incorporate the new design of the façade as well as the public areas of the interior. The z-room showcases the future style, which will be distinguished by a light-colored primarily white interior, atmospheric light installations, flowing room transitions, as well as attractive leisure areas consisting of comfortable lounges. In the showroom, a meeting lounge with a coffee bar, an event and exhibition area, and the so-called private room, an exemplary shopping area, are seamlessly integrated with each other.

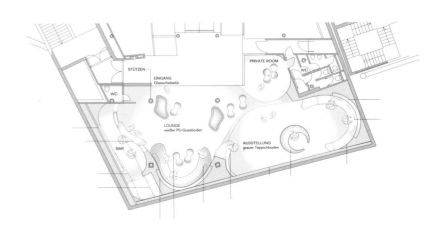

German Stock Exchange

An important feature of the design is the LED band displaying information regarding international trade. The band is integrated into a stylized world map above the gallery, where news and guiding- indices from all continents are shown. The new design allows a view of the commercial hall from the entrance space of the stock market building. This is archieved by incorporating a glass lobby in between the two spaces, which maintains physical distance but is visually open. Here, the glass can be switched from transparent to opaque in order to accommodate conferences or IPO festivities. The main trading hall radiates a new light.

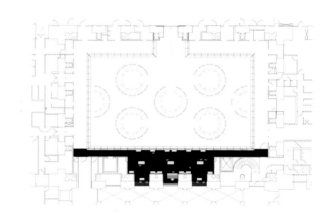

smart IAA

Smart is the young brand of Mercedes Car Group that is uniquely positioned as an urban and environmentally conscious automobile lifestyle brand. The architectural concept of the smart fair presence uses the shop window as a metaphor. Meandering glass facades generate different spaces allowing a diversified perception of smart's core competences. The cars are displayed on innovative glass truss, while materials and colors are presented fashion-like as a collection. The different stand areas are connected by a back wall passe-partout that is used for multi-media applications. Typography with high affinity for the architecture transports the core brand values and creates a dynamic interaction with the shop windows.

25hours Hotel by Levi's

The 25hours Hotel Frankfurt by Levi's is a lifestyle cooperation between the young urban 25hours Hotel Company and the iconic jeans label Levi's. Featuring different shades of blue, the new design hotel in Frankfurt's city center is timeless and familiar like an old pair of blue jeans and has already been awarded European Hotel Property of the Year 2008. The furniture, lamps, carpeting, wallpaper and fabrics used on each floor were carefully selected by the local designers to evoke a different decade of the 20th century. The atmosphere ranges from a classic, crisp and clean to a casual cool stonewashed look. Apart from the 76 themed guestrooms, the hotel features a laid-back slow food restaurant, a roof deck terrace in the midst of the Frankfurt skyline, and a Gibson Music Session Room for hotel guests and local bands.

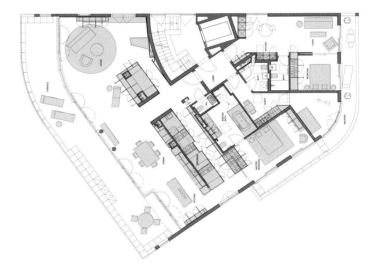

Penthouse Sachsenhausen

Hollin + Radoske designed this apartment all in white with a few contrasts in graphite gray and gray oak. Nearly everything is hidden behind built-in doors. Four dressing rooms provide specially designed space for the clothes collection of the owner, a lady with a special interest in haute couture. The layout of the apartment is open and fluent; the whole glass façade is visible in the huge living and dining area. The designers formed the sculpture of the dining table as a concept together with the cooking block in the centre of the kitchen zone. The kitchen comes as a hanging frame integrated in the white core of the apartment.

Garment Garden

Each city fabric needs space for nature and retreat. Garment Garden by Nya Nordiska offers a place for relaxation within the busy urban context of the first Design Annual in Frankfurt. Vertical elliptical columns are covered with folded fabric. They can simultaneously be perceived as mini highrises and tree like struktures, and their surfaces oscillate between curtain wall façades and bark. Mirrored walls reflect the pocket park into an endless display forest for the numerous products of Nya Nordiska — the experience is one of strolling in a park, only to get lost in a city jungle.

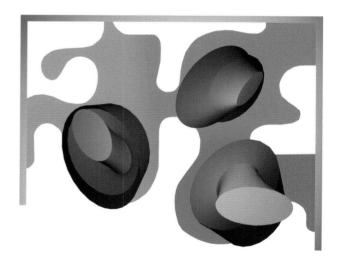

Dornbracht Elemental Spa

Ritual architecture is the result of the interaction of space and acts of cleansing, in which human beings are at the center of the architectural design. The bath becomes the interface between the user and his/her rituals. Emphasizing the archaic, the products of the Elemental Spa concept were deliberately designed for this ritual architecture purpose and constitute a contemporary interpretation of elementary water springs. These water springs have a clear, cubical shape distinguished by the mouthpiece with the crystalline-like inner shape. The soft water discharge accentuates the feeling of standing near a natural spring.

AUDI trade fair stand IAA

The architecture of the fair stand designed by Schmidhuber + Partner for Audi plays with the concept of a marketplace. It steers visitors in a way that immediately submerges them in the world of Audi. The skywalk, a shiny white floor and ceiling track, takes them through interactive stations via a show stair-case to the Showdrive, a media display area made of glass, which stages the A4 and culminates in the highlight grandstand including seating stairs for observation and relaxation. The dynamism of the car becomes very palpable in the A4 lounge – where it seems to glide through space as if through a wind tunnel. By focusing on high-tech materials and the intelligent use of media, the stand highlights the design competency and innovative power of the Audi brand.

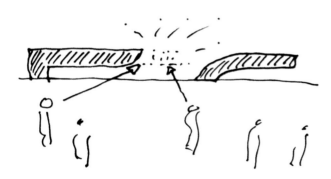

Berkhan House

This building is best understood as a three-dimensional body, a kind of habitable sculpture. A simple, elongated form was chosen in order to make optimal use of the plot. Two elements were deployed to divide the space: the staircase and two sanitation and technology units, which were designed as built-in wardrobes that are colored on the inside to set them apart. The overhanging roof above the entrance area and veranda, and expansive glazing facing the garden, allow the interior and exterior spaces to interconnect. A huge curtain suspended from the front edge of the roof acts as a privacy and sun screen, while also creating an interim zone; an intimate exterior area and veranda.

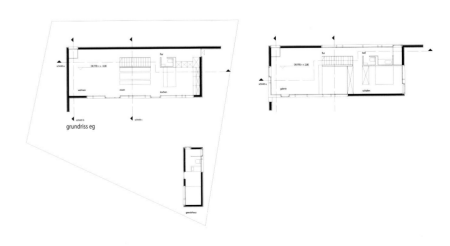

Grünwälder Papeterie und Accessoires

The floor covers, installations and furniture of the store consist of vertically and horizontally enmeshed timber floor planks that create an interesting pattern and an unusual relationship between the floor and the furnishings. Three variably sized vending tables can be arranged by themes and equipped with the relevant seasonal products. They divide the sales floor allowing customers to move freely around the furniture. In addition to the natural timber colors, the presentation furniture contains inserted drawers made of chip board laminated in white. To optimally highlight the colored accents of the objects on sale and to create a neutral backdrop, natural colors were deliberately used for the interior.

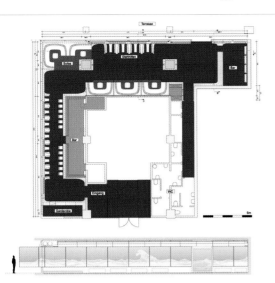

La Nuit

With their elegant lines and daring combination of corian and teak, the furnishings work in concert with the white surroundings and ceiling to suggest the atmosphere of a yacht by the water. The space integrates all elements and directs the attention across the room to the water. The abstract velvety and 3D graphic contours of a wave flow along the wall to the dance floor. The ceiling features three dimensional elements with computer programmed back lighting design. In order to allow the club to generate ever new atmospheres in the greatest possible range the creative team paid special attention to the medial aspect of the project. A projection spanning sixteen meters along the windows between the club and the restaurant interacts with the graphics of the space. The interactions between the installation, the striped patterns of the furniture and the windows constantly create new perspectives with the exterior.

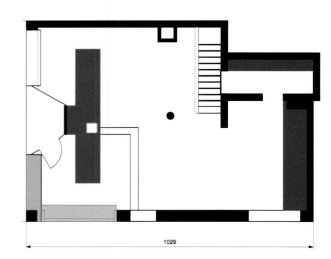

1029

Mutter

The move of the design office in the vibrant St. Georg district was part of a concentration process that allowed the office owner to once again work as a designer instead of managing a design company. In an interactive process, the customer together with the architect conceived a design that combines a modern working atmosphere with the listed building structure. The previous spatial structure was highlighted, for example through a five-meter-long table that balances out different levels, existing structures were maintained and even complemented, and the old structures were incorporated into a functional office concept. An eat-in kitchen was established into a small basement thanks to custom-made furniture.

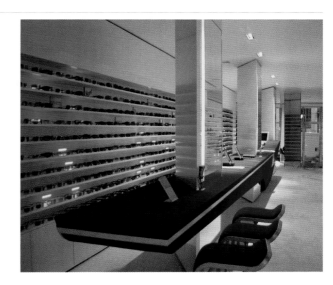

OPTICON Hamburg

The construction of a store in a historic building in Hamburg created a unique and very personalized sales venue, whose design incorporated the large number of offered products. The goods are always visible, freely accessible, but never obtrusive. The presentation areas and room borders are interwoven, with walls turning into shelves, closets, or even display cases. Rounded wall segments expand and constrict the space in between, create different store areas, and accentuate transitions. With its bright colors and velvety surfaces, the furniture dominates the room areas. Dynamic lighting behind the presented eyeglasses underscores the flow of the architecture and captures the attention of buyers.

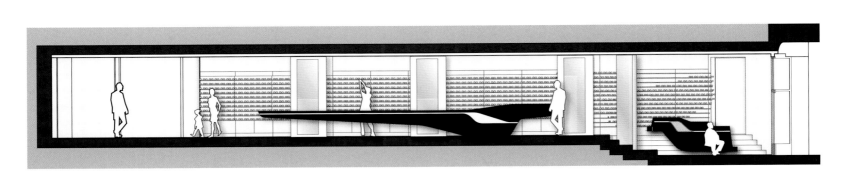

Astra Turm

The physical differentiation of the venue is achieved via the division into "office with carpet" and "hall-way with timber boards" as well as a lighting strip extending along the ceiling. The fixed central lighting is juxtaposed to flexible illumination with floor lamps in the office areas. Thanks to motion detectors and the almost exclusive use of energy saving lamps, energy consumption could be significantly reduced. All interior areas were designed with the greatest possible clarity and a continuous style of shapes that is also found in the white cladding of the inner core, the hallways, elevators and sanitary installations. The highest floor was fitted with tables, carpets and shelf systems specifically designed for the DWI Group.

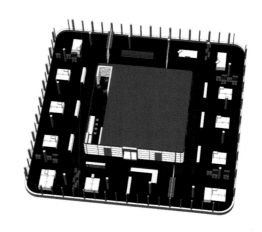

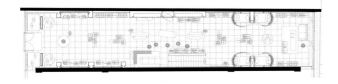

Laurèl Flagship Store

The Munich-based design studio, which is in charge of the international shop and showroom concept as well as the global roll-out of the brand, implemented a comprehensive project for the special location at Neuer Wall street. The world of the Laurèl brand is presented on two completely core-renovated floors. Clearing the skylight created a light-flooded sequence of rooms reaching to the lounge area next to the town canal in the rear. The feminine nature of the brand is highlighted by elegant arched shapes, organic fitted furniture, and room-high curtains. A formally understated, intelligent illumination concept underlines the generous layout, stages the collection, and accentuates individual areas. An exclusive VIP section and bar/lounge area was integrated into the mezzanine level.

climate and man - life in eXtremes

The concept of the exhibition seeks to awaken in the public an admiration for the adaptability and sur-vivability of our ancestors who were facing extreme climate changes. By walking along a climate curve, the exhibition is arranged like an expedition, as a travel through time and space. Themes and objects such as the development of flora and fauna, climate changes and the evolution of man become a walk-through experience. The concept is structured via clear information levels, designed as a multilayered il-lusion of a landscape. This landscape is created by overlapping imagery, graphics, texts and background painting and visualizes the development of landscape and life over the millennia.

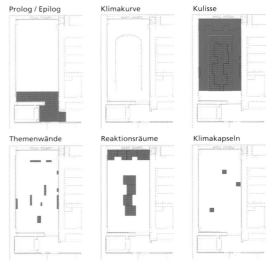

Prolog / Epilog   Klimakurve   Kulisse

Themenwände   Reaktionsräume   Klimakapseln

Budersand Hotel-Golf & Spa-Sylt

Materials from the indigenous nature were applied by the designer sparingly by the interior designer, who defines himself as Italian, as the key elements of the design, resulting in a sporty-elegant, understated composition. Furnished with linen, cotton, oak and pine, the rooms are not overloaded with furniture, but offer the luxury of extensive open spaces. Light natural colors ensure a friendly atmosphere. The clearly discernible careful attention to details and the selection of a few special decoration items results in high quality. The wonderful light of the island enters the building to allow guests to experience the different seasons inside as well. The rooms have different layouts, but all are equipped with large bathrooms, terraces and balconies.

TechniKomm

In close cooperation with Bayers advertising and events department, GOLDEN PLANET developed the idea to create a space which would link the laboratories where the materials are developed and optimized to the finished products and applications showing the possibilities of hi-tech engineered polymers. The entire ceiling and parts of the walls are clad with the most well-known polycarbonate material Bayer produces: translucent Makrolon® sheets. With light shining through these diffusing panels, and a special light choreography, the space has an almost floating, clean atmosphere.

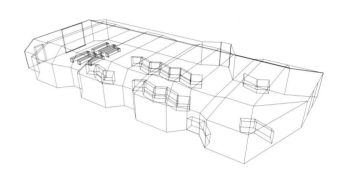

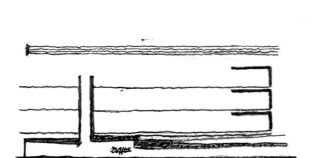

Peek & Cloppenburg Department Store

The Peek & Cloppenburg Department Store is a clear cube resting on beams with a steel-and-glass façade that lets plentiful light into the sales spaces. True to its "Light is life" motto, Richard Meier has created a transparent cuboid that radiates openness and allows an unrestricted view of the surrounding urban life. Glass, white aluminium panels, light natural stone and oak parquet define the elegant structure, whose geometry reflects the right-angled geometry of Mannheim's center. Thus, Roman travertine creates a strong contrast to the glass surfaces of the façade stretching the height of four floors.

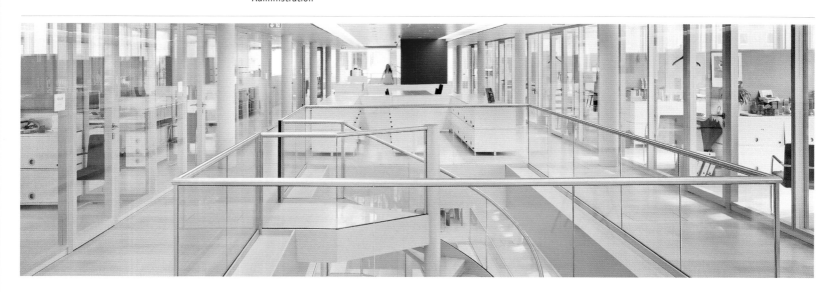

E.ON Headquarters

With its ground floor canteen and several meeting rooms in the penthouse, the newly built corporate headquarters of E.ON Energie AG offers 120 combination offices on four floors. They are connected via three air spaces with spiral staircases. On the ground floor, the cafeteria is in part located on a deck extending across six meeting rooms. The staff lounge on the ground floor connects the glass-covered piazza with the new inner courtyard. Designed in cooperation with Dietmar Tanterl, building A's roof floor hallway connects the executive level with the supervisory board meeting room.

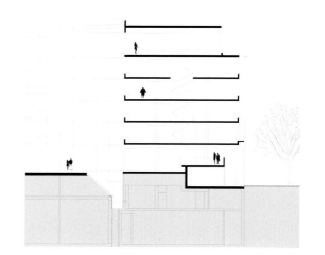

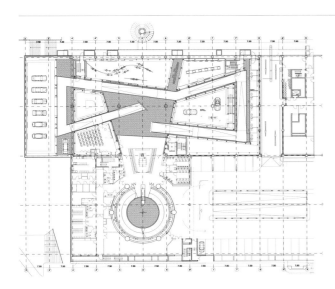

BMW Museum

Part of the corporate headquarters, the BMW Museum can be experienced within the scope of the land-marked building substance. The leading idea of the museum is the "continuation of the street in enclosed space" (Karl Schwanzer, 1973), which is perceived as a principle of a dynamic architecture in the new permanent exhibition. The west wing was gutted and developed into an exhibition area. The "Museum Bowl" was architecturally connected to it and now forms an epilogue with the "Visual Symphony". On an asphalted street the visitor is immersed into an urban ambience whose luminescent white thematic houses constitute a media display around the BMW Platz. More than 1.7 million LEDs are employed behind satin finish glass panes.

dress code

The managing director of the fashion label Irma Mahnel who designs fashion not only for small sizes desired a new presentation venue. She innovatively approached the spirit of the times and a new sense of being. The new store design was intended to increase the wellbeing of the customers. The focus of the design is on an all-round mirror consisting of 5,000 attached mirror panes, which creates playful illusionary interactions. Similar to the way clothing wraps the body, this establishes a relationship with the customer. Round shapes that are a main design feature are also replicated in the changing rooms as well as the waiting bench of gold-colored leather. The rounded shape reflects the sensuality and femininity of the customers. The core essence of the concept is the desire to evoke self-love.

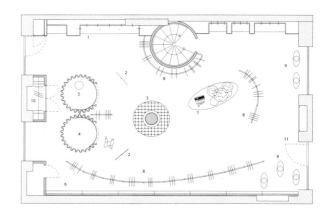

Ege Trade Fair Stand

For Ege, the wall-to-wall carpet was intended to be the central design element in planning the trade fair stand for BAU 2007. The concept included covering the entire floor and wall areas of the stand with fitted carpeting. Similar to the copies of a sketchbook or the blueprint of a plan at a scale of 1:1, floor plans, sections, views and perspectives stretched across the surfaces clearly visible from a distance. The technical implementation of this concept was made possible with the help of the latest technology. CAD-driven production systems and programming expertise ensured the precise production of the textiles. The carpet as a construction material thus exited the two-dimensional pettiness and exchangeability expressed in small patterns to become a bearer of identity and information on a large scale.

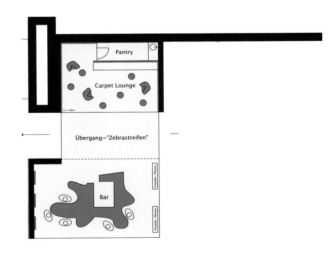

Private Equity Firm

The office reconstruction for a luxury financial services provider completes the interior work in the Bürklein building / Maximilianhof. The implementation of the classical River boat theme with choice materials and a clear-cut design set new standards. Boarded floors with stainless steel inlays, glossily painted walls and doors, coupled with high-quality exotic woods reflect the customer's desire for a unique room experience. The visible steel girders of the roof construction add dynamism to the room, while the balcony along the full length of the building offers a great view of the city.

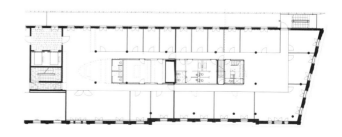

City-Apartment

The city apartment was conceived as a "mini loft", with only the bathroom located in a separate space. The elegant timeless interior design is atmospherically divided and accentuated by different light scenarios. The walls encompassing the loft are silver-bronze metallic framed large areas with white room-high curtains. The "middle block" incorporating a steam sauna, bathroom and kitchen is clearly delineated as an added volume in veneered light oak with a horizontal structure. On the bedroom side it constitutes a work surface as well as a washing stand and integrates a small kitchenette on the living room side. Only the small separate bathroom is primed in the accent color plum.

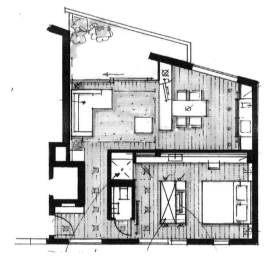

Stadtpalais Potsdam

After a 1995 fire in a roof truss, the largely unchanged 1920s department store located in the middle of a world heritage site of Potsdam's Baroque city quarter had to be refurbished. The listed façade of the steel frame structure on Bradenburger Straße was redeveloped along with the atrium with a painted glass roof. The original natural light illumination had to be replaced with artificial indirect light due to the addition of a floor. The glass panels were manually reconstructed using special glass and decorated after researching historical drawings, photos and color remainders. The new parts of the building carefully adjoin the original historical structure, nonetheless fulfilling modern demands of commercial architecture such as biophysical standards.

die blaue caro * kitchen club

The kitchen turns into a club with a floor sample of the existing tile pattern also covers the walls and the ceiling in various scales. Individual squares of this programmable pattern are extruded and loaded with functions such as a sound system, chandelier, fruit bowl, logo bearer and stag. They provide the infrastructure for the new use. This way the floor sample is more than a simple decoration, but can be palpably interactively experienced and used. In addition, the raster with its multitude of squares represents at its intersections the fruitful outcomes generated within a creative network whose members party and become inspired at the blaue caro. The pattern can be altered, expanded and converted for various events.

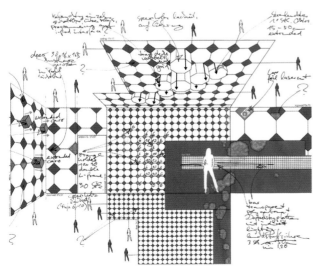

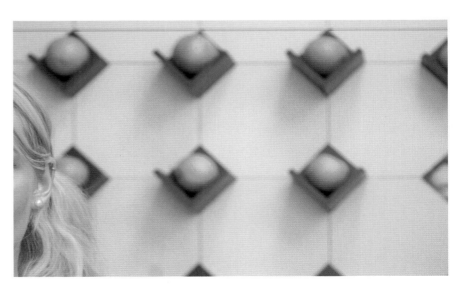

Corporate medical service of the state bank of Baden-Württemberg

The atmospheric mix of glass, light and color coupled with the walnut floors creates a welcome contrast to the neighboring administrative offices. This effect is underscored by the spring-green hallway walls, which point out the special nature of the premises from a distance. The glazed separation walls of the relaxation and treatment rooms are semi-transparent to ensure discretion and to communicate the room function. A red linoleum cross integrated into the floor demarcates the entrance to the corporate medical services, containing two leisure and treatment rooms each, as well as two doctor's office and six application rooms. Due to their separate entrance, the employees can also relax in the leisure rooms outside the regular operating hours.

Jazzclub Bix

The new two-story jazz club is located in the listed Gustav Siegle House (Theodor Fischer, 1912, reconstruction by Martin Elsässer, 1954). A large auditorium for live Jazz performances on the ground floor and an intimate bar and lounge area on the upper level nest into each other. Both have a slightly angled bar to one side, which mirrors the non-orthogonal geometry of the house addition. A continuous wall panel creates a sense of identity and encompasses both the stage and the auditorium. Warm brown and gray tones as well as textile room partitions add density to the club atmosphere. Large-scale prints accent individual wall surfaces and a light object defines the double-height entrance area of the atmospheric room.

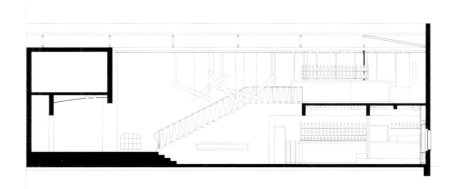

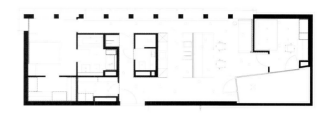

Apartment S

The focus of this residence was to create a continuous open space while maintaining the connection of livable spaces through the use of materials, lighting, and ceiling elements. Once the walls were removed, the home opened itself up from one end to the other. This allowed for a functional progression and an abundance of natural light to flood the space. Piercing through the entire length of the home, a ribbed structure, doubling as a light fixture, threads each space terminating in the dropped ceiling above the fireplace / entertainment wall. A connection of the main spaces was achieved through the path that was laid in the floor juxtaposed wirh contrasting types of wood.

Apartment Sch.

The building is located on a slope in the urban area of Stuttgart with a spectacular view of the metropolis located in the valley. It complies with the high demands of the art loving owners who wanted a stylish setting and sufficient space for their extensive collection of paintings. The apartment extends across three mezzanine levels in the upper floors of a 1980s building. The rigorous restructuring of the building and the light-colored semichina floors applied throughout created a three-dimensional flowing space whose architecture is entirely focused on images and perspectives. The impressive collection of paintings intensely interacts with the materials, geometries and colors of the interior design.

Bella Italia Weine

With her warm-hearted nature, the products of her native home, and most of all, her creative cooking skills, the Sicilian owner of this wine shop and restaurant has introduced a section of Italy to Germany. The move to a new location was intended to increase the seating of the restaurant and improve the presentation of goods. Her previous venue, a small room resembling a living room, held a special charm that should be transferred to the new premises as well. Warm shades of brown in combination with bright colors such as yellow and pink create a pleasant atmosphere. At the same time, the large number of various mirrors arranged on the ceilings and lamps suspended above the tables create a surprising combination of variety coupled with uniformity.

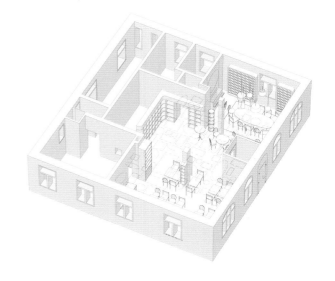

Quant

The concept is about creating a living environment that goes far beyond the average and approaches what living is really about: getting the most out of life. Similar to a loft space, the apartment is immediately tangible as a generous, continuous space. It can be apprehended in its entirety from certain vantage points. All functions are accommodated in freely defined areas, which can be closed off by means of sliding doors and heavy curtains, if so desired. In this way, a whole range of new and beautifully framed interior and exterior vistas become apparent. The bedroom and study form a common zone, defined by a circle of oak, encasing wall, floor and ceiling.

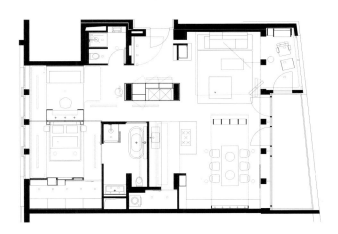

Wittlinger Hahn Stern Health Center

The challenge in designing a suitable interior lay in uniting the necessary high degree of technical integration with a lucid functional layout. The radiology practice is characterized by a high patient turnover, long waiting times due to the complicated diagnostic procedures involved, and an apprehensive mood on the part of its patients. The waiting rooms convey a sense of security, the orientation system is designed to make orientation easy and the technological apparatus remains to a large hidden extent. All these serve to endow the patient with a greater sense of security and confidence in the surroundings.

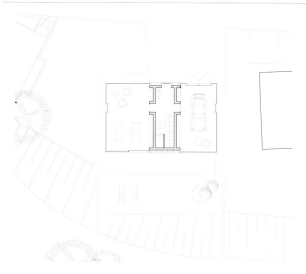

T-Bone House

This distinctive monolithic T-form was the combined result of building regulations and the spatial design of the architect. This produced an exciting mixture of introverted and extroverted forms – rooms that are either largely open or closed – all under one roof. The house accommodates both man and automobile: next to the "room with a view" is the "garage with view". Brown oil shale, under floor heating and built-in closets set the tone in this snug multipurpose space. A long, submerged box forms the base of the T-Bone. Because the house is cleverly positioned at the edge of a slope, there is a perfect transition from the house to the sheltered courtyard garden and the mature orchard.

Mykonos Grace Hotel

The latest, swankily designed four-star destination can be found at the Mykonos Grace Hotel, located on the sandy and protected beach of Agios Stefanos. Committed to the traditional Cycladic formal language, its subtle cube-shaped buildings are dotted all over a slope above the sea. Since the complete refurbishment in 2007 the aesthetic quality of the hotel is on a par with the latest interior design standards of international boutique hotels. The hip reception area with nuances of the Aegean big blue, the elegant pool-side area adjacent to the bar and restaurant, the private outdoor hot-tubs, the refreshing spa and the vibrant fitness room all add experiences to a special holiday or romantic honeymoon.

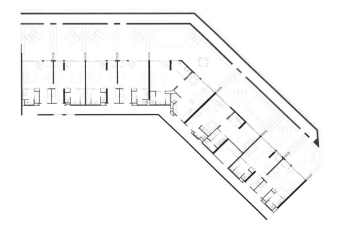

Alexander Beach Hotel & Convention Center

Alexander Beach Hotel is a newly renovated spa hotel in Alexandroupoli. The rooms were enlarged and enhanced by en-suite outdoor lounging terraces with private swimming pools. The interior was partially covered with oak paneling, creating a warm and hospitable feeling. The abstract handling of the design in combination with the unique style of furnishings bestows an additional nuance to the sophisticated, cosmopolitan atmosphere. Careful attention was given to the arrangement of the lighting, often employing indirect sources of light, for a more dramatic ambiance that enhances the warmth of the employed materials. The renovation included the crea-tion of a wellness center with special facilities for warm and cold-water treatments that offer plenty of opportunity for physical and spiritual well being.

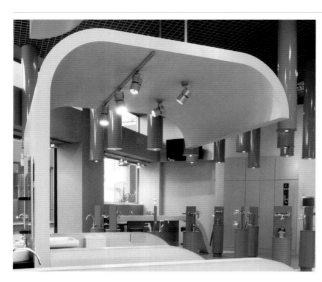

Seydap Showroom

The design concept was based on the element of water considered both as moving wave-form, and as still, calm reflecting surface. The first inspired the major design structures of the interior and exterior space. The second inspired the logotype and the advertising imagery. The logotype is designed as a mere reflection of the name of the company in black and orange background. The orange colour was proposed to escape the strict exclusiveness of water, and also allude to heating, an area on which the company also specialises in its other branches.

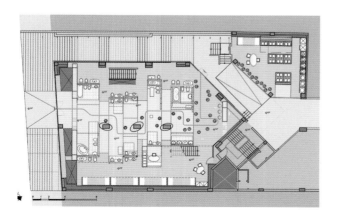

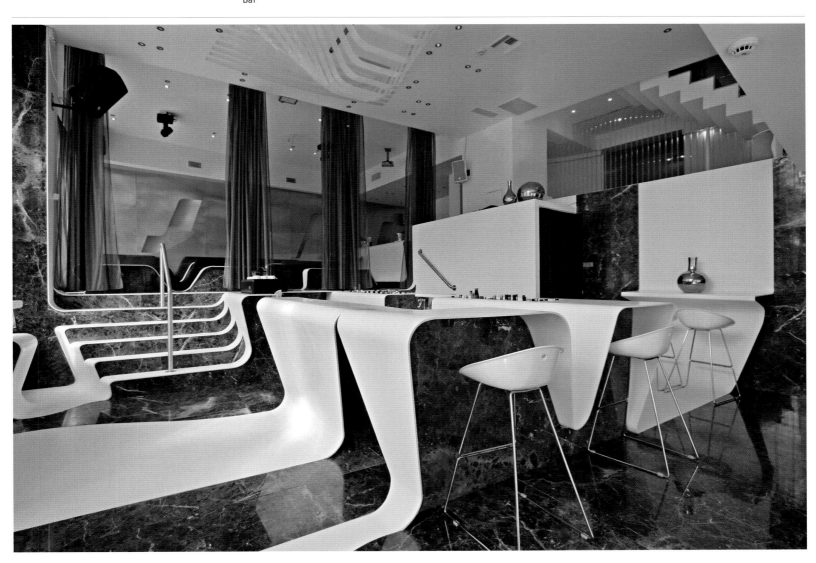

frame bar

The idea was to recreate the usual typologies of chairs, benches, bars stands, tables and coffee tables using forms that melt from one geometry into the other. This was achieved by using advanced parametric design techniques which led to the specification of a series of multi-use poly-surfaces, ultimately constructed out of thermo–formed staron, a corrian equivalent. The geometrical continuity is retained throughout the design, ultimately offering a continuous interior topography that assumes different geometrical specifications in relation to specific programmatic intentions.

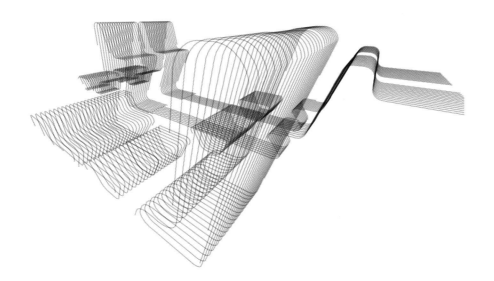

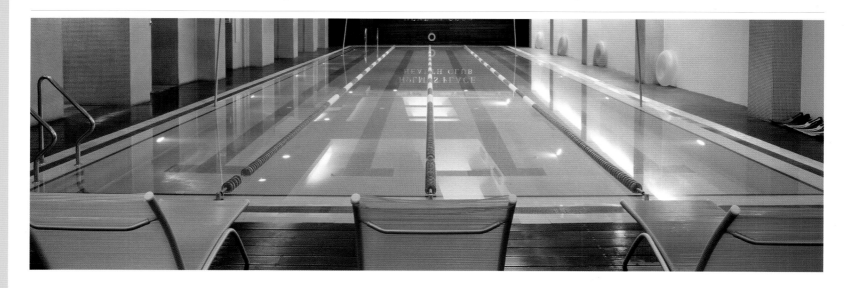

Athens Holmes Place Health Club

Holmes Place at the City Link shopping center is housed in a historic, listed former army building, extending on three levels, and offering a wide variety of services. There are many large surfaces with wooden floors and solid dark oak walls, combined with unusual stainless steel and aluminum constructions. A special feature is the internal staircase of the club connecting the first and second floor, which is made from a metal structure and green glass treads. The wet areas' walls are made of metal mosaic-tessellations, especially resistant to chlorine and humidity.

Technopolis Cinema Complex

The key design concept was to create a characteristic outdoor element linking the various spaces land, guiding visitors through the complex. A series of green, metallic triangular structures were designed. The exterior walls were constructed to be free of openings, comprising three horizontal zones of varying materials. They are solid zinc (upper), perforated zinc (central) and the inner plaster (lower) covered concrete wall. In the interiors materials were used to continue directed movement, guiding the visitor through each space and the connecting spaces. In the main lobby RGB lighting was used, changing color at regular intervals, hence transforming the space in relation to the movement of time, reminiscent of the moving images of cinema.

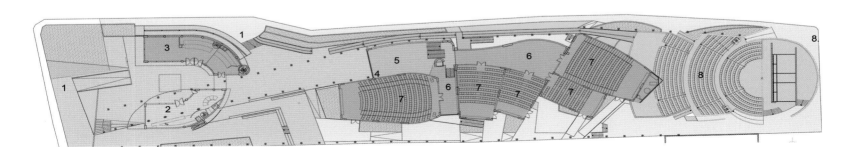

Cyclos C Club

This is the most important circle and hub of exclusive activities in Mykonos and the Cyclades, Cyclos is a multi-functional club with an exclusive membership. The outdoor terrace has a unique design of landscape walls mixed with tropical nature and white walls typical of Mykonos. Cyclos C Club is also a media center connected to the world and directs events transmissions. The indoor space is a multi-functional club with private bars. There is a large projection screen in the club. Contemporary design furniture adds simplicity to the white interior and exterior.

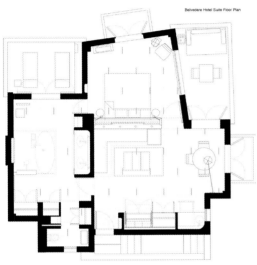

Belvedere Hotel Suite Floor Plan

Belvedere Hotel

Inspired by the Aegean Sea, the project is a three-level space. The materials and design elements used echo those that are native to the sea. Guests enter on the top level, where there is a bar comprised of a live edge wood bar top supported by a marble bar face. Hand-carved marble stones on stainless steel standoffs cover the bar face and are backlit to create the appearance that they are floating. In the Standard Rooms, the Junior Suites and the Belvedere Suites, the designer used classic Mykonian materials of marble and plaster, mixed with a twist on other luxurious natural materials. Hues of whites, warm tans and greens reflect the Mykonian and Aegean land and seascapes outside.

Vedema

Vedema Resort overlooks rolling vineyards and the Aegean Sea. The resort is located in the medieval village of Megalohori on the island of Santorini. Lush gardens contrast with the Cycladic architecture of the resort's 45 fully furnished apartments and villas with private verandas, lounge-dining rooms and romantic beds. Houses are built in the traditional style with an authentic look inspired by the characteristic colors of the Greek islands. Each house is equipped with all necessary amenities and features original artwork by noted Greek artists. The heart of the property is dominated by a 400-years old winery, now a restaurant. The resort also includes several other restaurants, bars, and a spa.

Capri Palace

Capri Palace stands 300 meters above sea level, overlooking the open Mediterranean Sea and the Gulf of Naples. Dating from the mid 20th century, the hotel was recently refurbished. This process involved considerable alterations whilst still maintaining its classical Mediterranean style and conveying a noble and distinguished design which can be witnessed on the palace's stone floor, its archways and the enveloping columns. The interior design is based on white and gold, with fabrics in warm tones. The hotel features 85 rooms, four with their own private gardens and heated swimming pool; five luxuriously furnished suites among which one finds the penthouse "Acropolis" bathed in sunlight, boasting a marvellous jacuzzi tub from where one can gaze at the stars and across the sea.

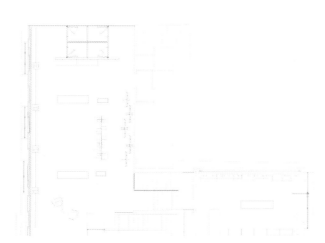

Bruschi

Located in the old town center of Bolzano, the shop expands on four floors and can be accessed through one of the characteristic arcades of the town. The main concept of the renovation philosophy was to differentiate four interiors of the shop by using different kinds of material, expositive typology and lighting system on each floor and to keep at the same time a harmonious atmosphere and style. A sound diffusion system, which is integrated with lighting (created ad hoc), guides customers through a sensorial experience among the various floors of the shop. The ground floor — the real window of the shop — is completely covered with Brazilian green marble slabs.

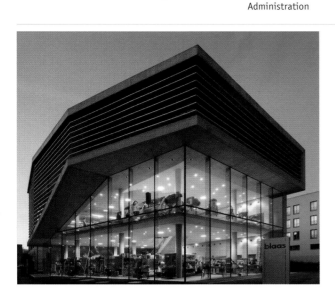

Blaas General Partnership

The company Blaas in Bolzano is specialized in electro-mechanics. On the ground floor of its new head office there is the sales division and on the first floor the exposition area and the repair shop, while all administration offices are located on the second floor. Although the overall impression of the structure is a homogenous and closed building, there is a separation between the public and private sector. The client can perceive this internal division already from the outside. The glass façade on the Northern side provides a maximum of visibility to the exhibition and sales area. The repair offices, stockrooms and offices, however, have their façades exposed to the South, East and West, protected with a sun screening system.

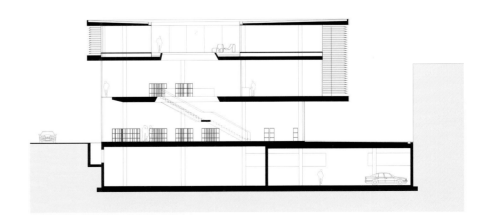

Casa Brixen

The villa's original architecture from the 1960s has been transformed with simple and rigorous additions into a transparent chalet. A glass tower emerges from the lower floor, connecting all three levels, while large windows bring natural light into the basement and allow a view over the mountains. The ground floor living area continues underground, transforming the basement and creating a natural continuity with the garden outside. Light is extended in the upper part of the living room using white marble stucco, while the whole interior decoration is made of traditional wood and stones from the region. This design seems modern but also conserves the rigorous spirit of the typical architecture of this Italian region.

Byblos Art Hotel Villa Amistà

This five-star art hotel was created with the objective to connect Byblos fashion style to the brand's interior design. Its neo-baroque formula unites antique interiors with fashion, design and an important collection of contemporary art, an ideal synthesis for hospitality. Just like the products of the Casa line, the furniture and objects are an exemplary, museum-quality collection. The furniture is designed to address the private and hotel market, offering many different streams such as ethnic, revival and design in order to please international tastes. A wide range of materials is used for the interior design, which is produced by the manufacturer Erre Studio Edizioni in exclusive traditional craftsmanship.

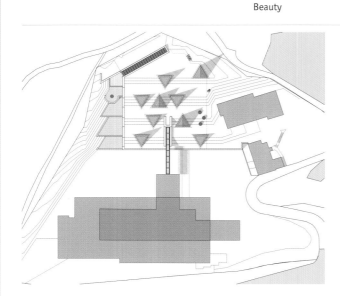

Private Spa

A wall completely covered by gray mirror, extends the length of the room, creating an interplay of reflections which endlessly multiply the space. The resin floor is the perfect surface on which to work out and the fitness equipment with its chromed finish camouflages perfectly with the wall covering. The sliding doors are made with frosted extra white glass. The wellness area consists of a tepidarium, a rainfall shower, a swimming pool and a whirlpool zone. The floor, walls and seats of the tepidarium are heated to provide a relaxing and regenerating effect. The shower is recessed into the ceiling.

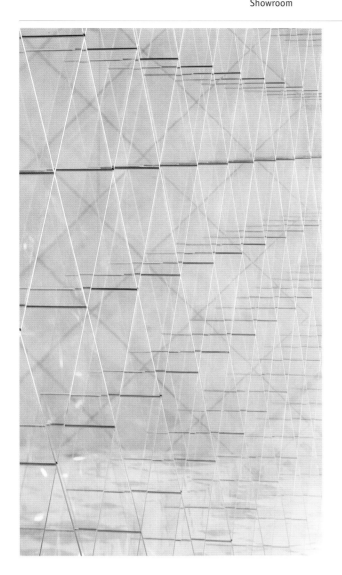

Burlington

The argyle as a design principle consists of a rhombus and a grid structure. The design concept was based on providing room for interpretation of the traditional recognition feature of Burlington. The playful and colourful handling of the graphic pattern element is the identification element and manifestation of the layout principle. The argyle becomes physically palpable and the main feature of the design. The three-dimensionality of the concept results in an intermediary space in which lights and shadows interplay. A color layer, which covers the actual construction, the furniture, and the relief wall like a second skin, provides the opportunity for repeated redefinitions.

Cave

The 'Cave' installation takes inspiration at the Pitti fashion show from geological caves: dark spaces, beams of sunlight entering through crevices, striking shapes of minerals and precious stones, intense natural colors. Ilaria Marelli has given all these elements an abstract look in order to create a fascinating, masculine scene. The shape and surface of the entrance façade are jagged like natural deposits of basalt. Just behind the entrance door, visitors pass through a curtain of transparent strings hanging from the ceiling. Inside the pavilion, further coloured light-cascades cut the dark spaces and reflect on vertical mirrored panels, offering further surprising views.

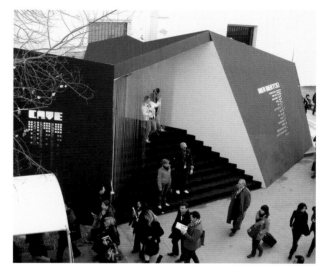

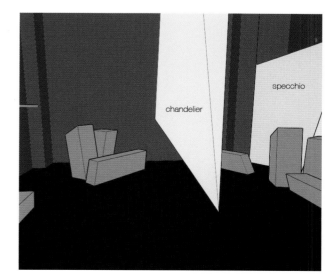

Corte

The "Corte" installation by Ilaria Marelli, the fifth exhibit design for Pitti Immagine, creates the relaxing atmosphere of Mediterranean houses, courtyards and squares by featuring their typical tones of white and blue, architectural and decorative elements and the characteristic painted ceramics and tiles called "azulejos". A wide staircase, featuring a vaulted ceiling, leads the visitors to the elliptical central space, its walls entirely covered with figurative decorations, a reproduction of Lisbon "azulejos", the traditional ceramics painted with rural scenes and mythological figures. Further characteristic elements are placed in the middle of every room, emphasizing the courtyard mood.

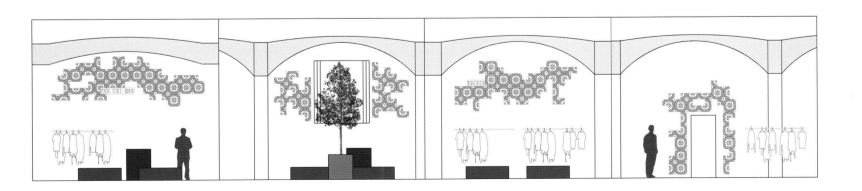

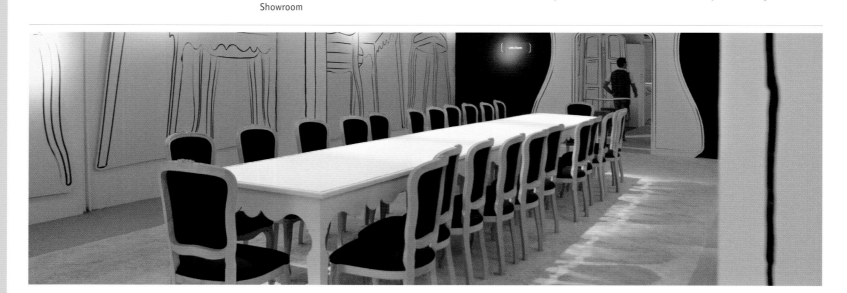

Micro Macro

This project consists of an installation between irony and dream. The out of scale rooms remind of the fairytale of Alice in wonderland or the extraordinary adventures of Gulliver's Travels. The visitors are surprised by objects and furnishings dissociated from reality, represented in an "ant" perspective, projecting enormous shadows. The central installation is made with miniature furniture, ten times smaller than in reality, projecting shadows on the surrounding walls in a size five times bigger than the original. The macro-shadows represent in perspective the micro-objects in the center of each area.

Secret Garden

The suggestive installation "The Secret Garden" shows an impressive and artificial flowered hill, which covers the façade of the Lyceum and acts as the main entrance. The designer chose to color the hills in a sunny yellow and dressed them with white kite-petals, which move in the wind like beautiful field flowers. Inside the pavilion, the central area transforms into a big green lawn with little yellow hills on which to sit and rest as if the visitor has unexpectedly entered a park. The kite-petals are discomposed and re-arranged in vaporous white clouds which move freely in the sky-ceiling like dandelion particles.

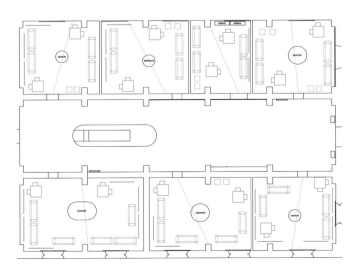

Luisaviaroma

The three-story shop is characterized by the use of white and indestructible materials such as concrete, steel, Corian and thick tempered glass. The space will be used for events, exhibitions and fashion shows as well as in its primary function as a store. In order to enable the transformation from a shop into a venue for special events, the clothing racks are designed as freestanding units that can quickly be moved. Claudio Nardi carried out a radical restructuring, creating new spaces and volumes. A myriad of monitors, LED lighting and a glass terrace are only some of the many features that make this place extraordinary.

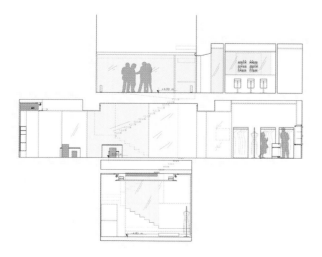

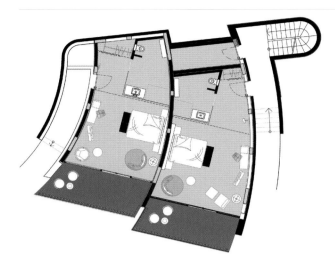

Riva Lofts

This group of buildings was a small factory in 1880. Today the nine suites are decorated in the style of French studios, blending a metropolitan lifestyle with a welcoming and domestic atmosphere. The interiors, all distinctly unique in size, shape and style, boast a well-defined and recognizable character. Fusion is the leading theme behind the structure's conception: pure and contemporary, the warm atmosphere in these distinctive spaces is due to a series of recovered historic elements – modern antiques, 1950's furniture, old and new materials, wood and Corian, and examples of sophisticated design. Riva Loft is made up of nine suites, all with independent entrances and well-equipped kitchens, which range from 30 to 100 square meters in size. In spite of its location close to the old city center of Florence, the Riva Lofts 'home for guests' is particularly quiet and peaceful thanks to its location in an area of parks and gardens.

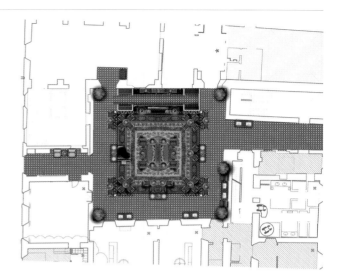

Four Seasons Hotel Firenze

After seven years of meticulous renovation, Four Seasons Hotels and Resorts opened its second property in Florence, Italy, on the edge of the city's historic center. The hotel consists of two protected renaissance palaces: the 15th century Palazzo della Gherardesca and a former convent from the 16th century, Palazzo Conventino. The interior offers frescoes, bas-reliefs, stuccoes and silk wallpapers that have been carefully restored to reveal vivid detail dating back over five centuries. Original Florentine art and craftsmanship can also be found in several of the hotel's 117 individually designed bedrooms, suites and bathrooms.

Romano

Romano is a shoe store located in the historical center of Florence. The idea of the project was born from the tartan textile design. All the walls were created in the weaving pattern of tartan design. The base of the wall was made of stucco to generate effect of a warm and organic feeling in different shades of white and gray. From the horizontal lines of the textile design were born the three-dimensional shelves and seating benches. The idea becomes more evident at the back of the space where the design is printed on metal panels and covers the whole space of the small resting area.

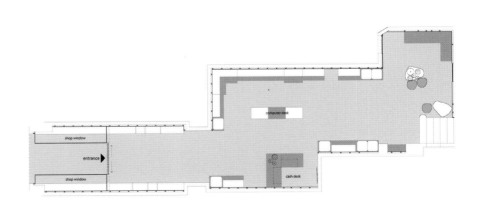

San Paolo Parish Complex

The new parish designed by Fuksas Design has two main architectural elements: the first element, the church building, consists of two rectangles inserted into one another. The second, also rectangular shaped but long and low, is home to the Pastoral Ministry. Both volumes are connected through pyramid-shaped elements. Spirituality and meditation are joined together by natural light entering horizontally and vertically, drawing a dialogue with the sky. The sculpture "Stele-Cross" in cement and white marble by Enzo Cucchi and the 14 Stations of the Cross by Mimmo Paladino complete this composition.

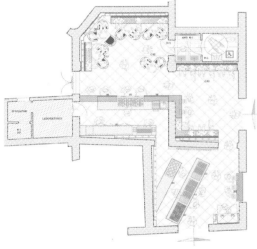

La Buvette

The confectionary area of this café and shop is characterized by a counter made of cement and iroko wood with a glass showcase to exhibit the pralines almost as jewels. A huge white chandelier dominates this entire zone and the back counter which is equipped with lighted shelves. The café area is furnished by a black chandelier and a modern counter with aluminum panels, lighted from the bottom. It is divided into two parts, one with a white corian top, the other with a glass. The refreshing area is cozy and elegant: the tables have a white glass top, the chairs and the wall sofas are white, light lilac and beige. The black and white graphics on the walls recall the village as it was years ago.

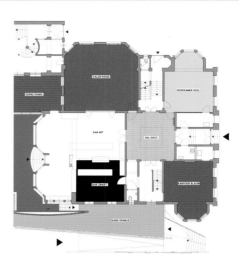

Therme Meran

The Therme Meran are located at the heart of the old South Tyrolean resort on the banks of the River Passer. The architect's aim in Merano was "to create a natural oasis in the heart of the town" and "to employ shapes and materials to evoke memories of the primeval strength of water". Recreation, harmony and relaxation are among the main aims for the Merano Thermal Baths, featuring a total of 25 pools and a refined sauna area. Cozy warmth and a unique flair are provided by a first-class sauna area. Among the state-of-the-art facilities are a Finnish sauna, two steam baths, a sanarium, hay bath, caldarium and an outdoor log cabin sauna.

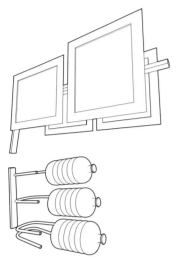

S.P.AQUA

Water is the source of life. This exhibition design has "water" as its starting point and inspiration. Each display unit consists of three supporting elements realized with large bottle racks usually used for water transportation, on which are welded metal profiles connected by a central joint providing balance to the structure. The same metal profile holds the photographs that are protected by a thin Perspex sheet. The exhibit design creates a sense of lightness, transparency and simplicity. The weight of the water becomes an essential element, without which the structure would lose its balance. The displays were also designed to be easily dismantled, moved to a different location and re-installed.

Twin Lofts

Designer Frederico Delrosso divided one single house into a twin loft. Both halves share the same elements and have identical structures, but the interiors were created with different spirits. Delrosso used materials and colors like the letters of an alphabet: to write similar, interlocutory or opposed phrases, but always with a coherent grammar. If the staircase is the strong element in loft A, thanks to its volumes and the raw material with bare welds, it is dematerialized in the other loft using crystal for treads and white painted iron. Hence, this impressive project successfully combines similarity and contrast.

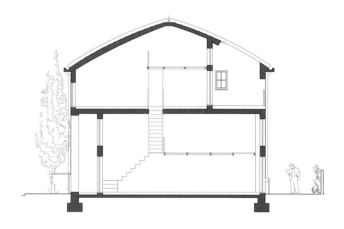

Showroom DuPont Corian

The "Corian® Design — Milano Store" applies several materials and products by DuPont in its design and decor. Among these, Zodiaq® (cut in large size tiles) for the showroom floor; Corian®, for a large, backlit and curved panel (about 21 meters long by 1 meter high with surface decoration via sublimation and carving), mounted at a height of about 2.5 meters, as decorative and display covering for some walls and built-in furniture and for the three internal and external store window frames. In addition, laminated safty glass SentryGlas® Plus was used for the three store windows and decorative safety glass SentryGlas® ExpressionsTM for an interior glass wall.

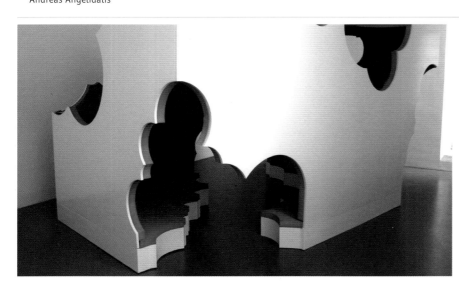

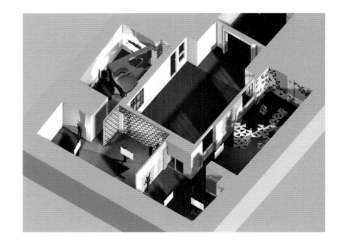

Superneen at Galleria Park

Superneen curated by Nina Vagic was an exhibition of Neen works at Galleria Pack in Milan. The designers' contribution was to convert the space into a "Neen World" environment. They treated the gallery as an apartment and converted the pavilions into furniture for that apartment. The exquisite artworks of Neen stand in sharp contrast with the simple interior design. The design gives prominence to the artistic atmosphere, at the same time provides visitors with a profound understanding and strong impression of Super Neen's work.

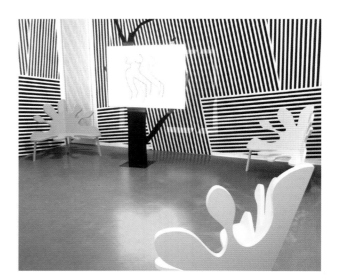

Atomic Spa Suisse

Atomic Spa Suisse is a long way from the pristine minimalism of many hotel spas. On the reception ceiling, the designer placed several "mirror bubbles", half-spheres of plastic, coated in chrome. These bubbles are a strong motif throughout the scheme, linking the design of each of the areas. Several large, sinuous tree-like structures made of expanded polypropylene appear to support an undulating, cave-like ceiling studded with hundreds of the same mirror bubbles that are used in the reception and corridor. In the pool the mirror-bubble edges are lit with blue LEDs and sensationally reflected in the swimming pool, which is lined with white pearl mosaic.

New Urban Face

New Urban Face is a mixture of past, present and future, showing a balanced view of architecture, fashion, design, culture, and human relationships. According to designer Simone Micheli, it represents "an urban living room, fostering human relationship and the exchange of ideas, and at the same time it represents an interactive space to highlight Milan's excellence." He designed the furnishings and experimented with lighting to execute a modern vibe. Mirrored walls and highly reflective surfaces engage visitors as part of the design of the space. The existing archaeological excavations of the previous space are covered, but not hidden, under modern steel, stone and glass floor elements.

Showroom Tucano

The design of Tucano in downtown Milan develops basically around two major themes: on the one hand texture, representing the intrinsic quality of the products of the company, which uses tough technical yarns with specially spun fibres. On the other hand, the crossing of lines in space derives from the idea of movement through the streets by people who use notebooks and other electronic accessories protected by Tucano products. The sales space is endowed with an urban atmosphere: through the choice of rather coarse materials, such as sheets of natural steel for the walls, the flooring similar to stone pavement, the veneers of the furnishings with materials that from outside look almost like plastic, the shop appears as the natural continuation of a metropolitan street.

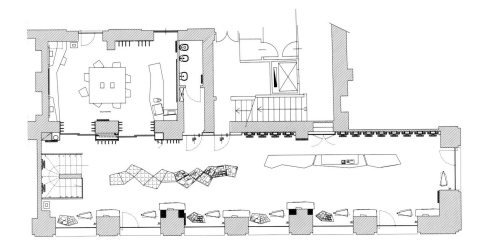

D&G Headquarters

The new D&G Headquarters in Milan contain the showrooms for the collections, the offices, a restaurant and a series of image spaces, in a total area of 5,000 square meters. Two buildings dating back to the 1920s and the 1960s have access to three streets and are combined into a complex with five floors above ground as well as two basement levels. The project is based on an architectural principle of great rigor and was realized with the use of natural materials like white Namibia stone, glass and unfinished steel sheet.

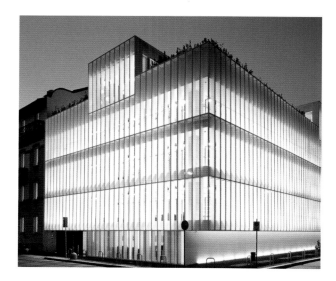

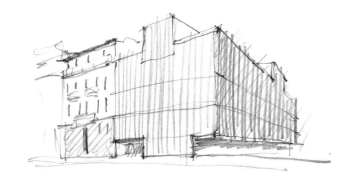

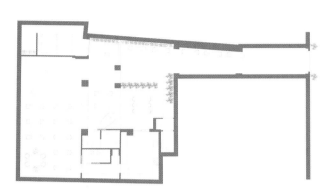

Home-Made Delicate Restaurant

Since the idea for Home-Made Delicate Restaurant was to design an authentic home, the interior, exterior and garden were created according to this concept. The owner realized her visions with the help of architects, designers, landscape specialists and prominent suppliers. The result is a homey but at the same time supremely stylish location, right next to the epicenter of Salone del Mobile in Milan.

169

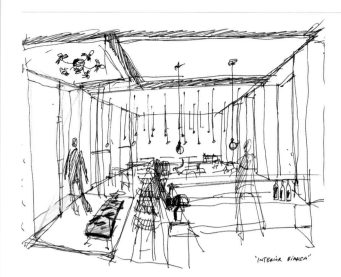

Bianca

The leitmotif is white, expressed in various forms and materials. Light bulbs descending from the ceiling give a pure light to this bright and glowing place. The designers of the chairs placed around the glass tables are those who founded design: Panton, Eames, Jacobsen. All nuances of the color white appear: the white resin floor where one can see the brush marks, the iced white of the bar counter and the table tops which are made of glass with a satin finish, the compact whiteness of the plastic chairs, the soft white of the wall panels, the white material of the blinds and of the acoustic panels and finally the warm white of the bone china, the Corian of the exterior signage.

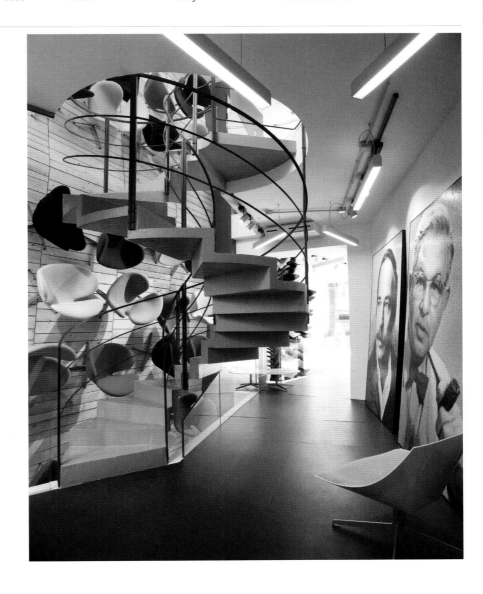

Fritz Hansen

A major challenge to Stefano Tagliacarne was to overcome the spatial irregularity of the showroom, composed of three levels of different size and shape. Tagliacarne links these three levels by the means of a big red column and a wood clad wall, both developing from the bottom of the basement to the top of the first floor. The wooden wall itself, set up in a spectacular and attractive way with "Series 7" chairs designed by Arne Jacobsen in 1955, becomes an extra exhibition area and a visual guideline from the entrance throughout the whole space and levels. The entrance at the ground floor connects to the first floor by a concrete spiral staircase, dedicated to the staircase at Copenhagen Radisson SAS Hotel.

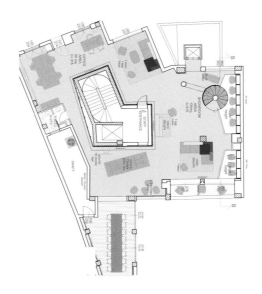

Tokujin X Moroso PANNA chair

In collaboration with Moroso, "PANNA chair" was presented at the Salone del Mobile 2007. The space installation consisted of a display of Tokujin's experiments and studies in fibers for the past 4 years. Tokujin presented a large-scale installation by using 3 million transparent straws. He incorporated the essence of nature into his design as a mean to communicate with people. Just like clouds, snow, or beads of water, straw is transparent by itself, yet displays depth and the color white when numerous numbers are piled up together and their transparency is condensed. The straw installation might exemplify the realization of unsubstantial things, in other words, making the impossible possible.

STRAF hotel&bar

A vintage 19th century building houses the new modern design hotel STRAF. Its smart interior was designed by the architect and fashion designer Vincenzo De Cotiis. The concrete and black slate with scratched mirrors and gauzed glass gives the hotel a very modern look. It offers 64 rooms and suites combining two design philosophies, which seem contrary but are nevertheless harmonious: extreme hi-tech functionality with a minimalist feel is mixed with a warm, intimate atmosphere. The rooms are designed with elegant, innovative materials like quarry-rough slate, burnished brass and concrete, along with furnishings especially designed by Vincenzo De Cotiis.

New Headquarters Ermenegildo Zegna

The structure overlooks the street from a long glass tunnel which opens into Via Stendhal through a narrow foyer. The long tunnel has four levels with footbridges connecting the showroom area to the office building. Zegna's headquarters has a showroom for each of its collections, the commercial and public relations offices, and a presentation area on the ground floor. All the functional spaces are grouped around an inside courtyard terrace, which is shaped like the ceiling and presents an inside view of the building's different activities. The external front is only partly glazed and treated with reflecting materials. It utilizes the inclined plane shapes to reflect the surrounding industrial scenery.

Casa Milano

A three-level loft in the heart of a formal industrial area of Milan was transformed into a home where rustic elements are combined with contemporary styles. Every object is interesting alone and in its interaction with other objects. The project wants to represent the owner's history and personality through architecture and the interior design concept, combining classics from the 20th century with works of artists designed for this particular space. The spaces are dedicated to different moods, being either focused on the outside as meeting spaces or meant for moments of privacy and tranquility.

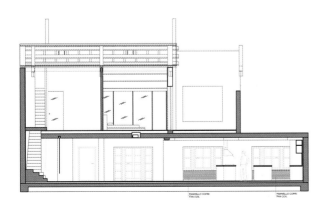

Dietro la Vigna

Meaning "behind the vineyard", this nursery follows certain features of the existing site to amplify its peculiarity and unique qualities. The main hall, where most of the learning activities take place, faces the vineyard, offering a unique opportunity for the children to be in constant contact with the landscape, and receives a substantial amount of soft light from the north. All internal spaces follow the concepts of promoting learning and stimulating the sensorial experience of architecture, whether a broad or a narrow room, a high or low ceiling, a dynamic or fixed space. In each space, pedagogical concepts cohere with architectonic solutions to determine the children's behaviour and awareness.

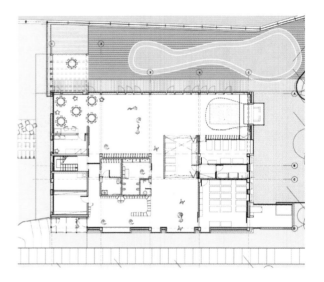

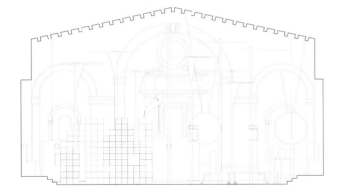

BEEC — Historical Archive and Library of Palermo

BEEC — Historical Archive and Library of Palermo The Sant'Elena and Costantino Oratory that flanks the Palazzo dei Normanni in Palermo, was constructed at the end of the XVI century. In the past it served as the center of Confraternita of Madonna di Monserrato, the religious cult imported from Spain. The interior design of the library is that of a grand installation in a restored space. The project retains the structure of the old building and tries to preserve the original atmosphere so that the future users breathe a certain spirituality. The architects have proposed a different utilization of the existing space, not a simple re-use of the old building. Finally the project succeeds by interpreting Palermo's culture and architecture's "variety" and by its ability to fascinate anyone who gets close to it.

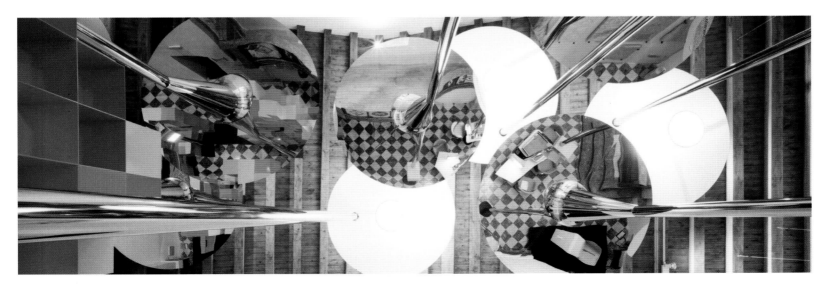

Glass box in the columns box

The construction lot at the edge of Palermo was to be used in such a way as to distinguish it from the industrial building. For this purpose, the existing structure was to be altered as little as possible and the available elements utilized. The project was implemented as two interlaced "boxes". One of them is a grey cement building with beams and columns that creates a neutral space. The second glass box contains the offices and was positioned in the center of the other box. The main element is light – warm and focused on products in the building, and white and technical in the offices. The surprise factor is thus guaranteed.

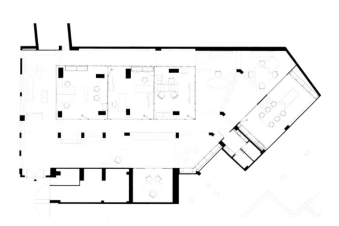

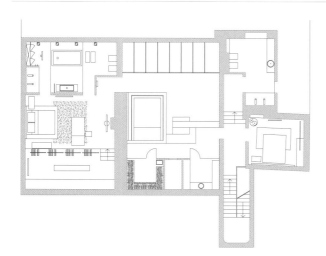

Cambi's Apartment

The apartment takes up the three top floors of a landmarked 17th century palazzo, but the interior is far from antique: the original furniture has been replaced by a minimalist style in shades of gray. Most of the original oak floor was kept, replaced in parts with gray granite tile. In the living room, walls painted a lighter gray soften the rigorous assembly of black leather oversize sofas and ottomans on white shag rugs. A white porcelain chandelier and a dark granite tabletop dominate the dining room. This is a high-tech apartment with extensive media and electronic equipment, but it has a soft soul.

Vyta Boulangerie Italiana

This bakery was built inside a railway station, the symbol of speed and progress, and therefore shows a contrast between tradition and modernism. This was the theme of the interior design for the bakery: the traditional image of the bread shop is reduced progressively to its essential features. The familiar colors of oak wood harmonize with the pale colors of the flooring and the ceiling, while the multi-functional counter is the heartbeat of every shop and in this case also an essential exhibition structure. There is a large decorative wall consisting of a paste creation symbolizing the surface and the fragrance of a bread crust. Aesthetics and functionality are combined and make this bakery unusual in its offer and design.

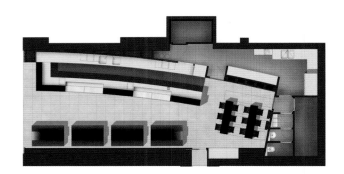

Palazzo delle Esposizioni

The objective was to transform the Palazzo delle Esposizioni into a large cultural center. The project increases the value of the existing space, re-designs its functions and emphasizes the possible uses. Each level has an independent entrance, rendering the various display spaces autonomous. Furthermore, the project increased the commercial functions by adding a bookstore, a design store and a cafeteria. Another new feature is the small theater, a multifunctional, 180-seat space that can also be used as an educational facility. The large greenhouse, demolished in the 1930s, was reconstructed in the course of this project. This completely transparent structure now contains the roof garden restaurant.

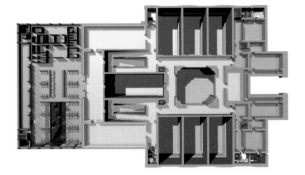

Via Giuia

Restructuring of a Renaissance palace that reinterprets the same exotic marble in ancient Rome and Renaissance. A shadow line traces the highs of where wall decorations would normally have been positioned in a Renaissance palace that unfortunately were not found under the layers of paint. Every element is been reduced to a minimum visual impact, a removable skirting board of the proportions used in the Renaissance hides all technology. Doors do not have handlers and tablets supported from the walls contain electronic light switchers and security necessities and AV diffusion.

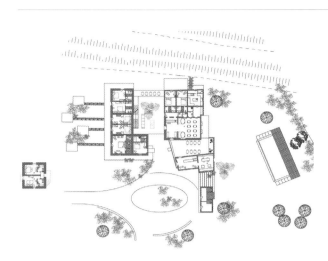

Caol Ishka Hotel

On the bank of the Anapo river, only two kilometers from Syracuse's historical center. Contemporary design meets the charm of an old Sicilian Masseria: in a warm mix, materials, designer furniture and antique pieces have all been blended into a rustic environment. The garden consists of a wide lawn beside the pool giving way to the surrounding nature with bamboo, wild grass and spontaneous vegetation. Whereas the outside exhibits a traditional feel, the inside features white and natural oak beam roofs that alternate with white ceilings; warm colors for walls and floorings in colored resin and hardwoods. Bath-rooms are spacious with designer basins and large walk-in showers. Oversized doors have been crafted by local artisans with various finishes: bisazza mosaics, mirrors, and gold leaf.

FORMAT - The Mulitmedia Library in Trentino

The media library in Trentino's university district is a meeting place, a place of study and a promotion of the audiovisual materials. The entire building has a modern style, matching the highly technical equipment displayed. The ground floor spaces have a strongly graphic character, using black and white to evoke the cinema. In the specialized library, volumes are gathered and organized on metal industrial shelves. The video room is characterized by long and thin white surfaces, while the central info desk is illuminated from the back, standing out against the dark floor in shiny resin.

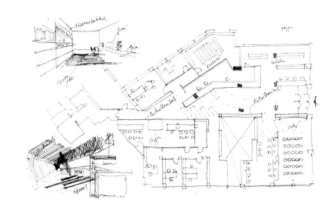

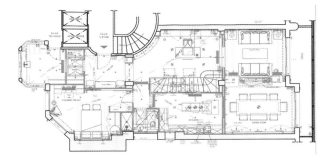

Duplex Monaco

The owners of this 200 square meter maisonette in Monaco desired to optimize the space by completely renovating the apartment. Their choice of materials concentrated on marble and polished wood in warm tones. D&K Interiors design concept followed from these demands, creating atmospheric spaces with indirect sunlight and high-tech materials. A complementary interplay of interior and architecture in a comfortable and elegant atmosphere has been created through harmony of colors and materials as well as furniture selection.

Office 00

All three boardrooms and a lounge are executed in an overall design concept. Large round lampshades, spray painted gold on the inside, seem to cast light and shadow oval marks throughout the whole space. This playful pattern of golden ovals contrasts with the angular cabinets and desks, which are executed in black stained ash wood. The lounge area has, in combination with the white marble flooring, these same light/shadow patterns that cover the bar and benches in silver fabrics. This area can be used for presentations or social working, with an integrated flat screen in the bar and data connections in all pieces of furniture.

Home 07

This single-family apartment for four people is situated in a stately building in southern Amsterdam. The original structure, with rooms for staff, a double hall and long hallways with lots of doors has been transformed into a spacious, transparent dwelling full of light and air. A kitchen in combination with cabinets from floor to ceiling has laser-cut front panels, all spray painted white. This pattern results in a dynamic mixture of open and closed cabinets, the holes also function as integrated handgrips. The transparency of the object's skin gives depth to the volume which is complimented by furniture like the Grcic chair one. An atrium with open staircases brings natural light from a large roof light into the living area. Along the open staircase a wall of two stories high is covered with clear pine wood, and connects the two levels. Upstairs the master bedroom is situated next to a large bathroom with a finish of structured tiles from Patricia Urquola, glass, and wooden cabinets.

University Library of the University of Amsterdam

A library has been turned into a "home" in which to study. A growing number of students, between 1,500 and 5,000 every day, visit the University Library in order to study and pick up their digitally ordered books. Despite future plans for a new building, the university wished to have a new, temporary interior design for the 2,500 square meter space that would comprise study rooms plus 235 extra workplaces, a canteen, the information center and an automated check out area. The designers wanted to achieve a space like a white page of a book, in which the students themselves would play the main role. In red cabinets with 1,105 red crates, piles of books wait for their borrowers. This is the heart of the University Library.

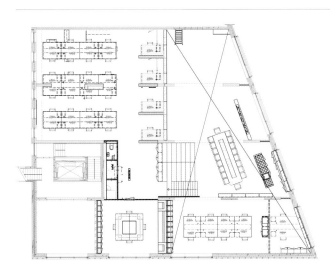

Post Panic Amsterdam

The biggest priority of this project was functionality. On the one hand, separate areas to house Post Panic's different departments and facilities were required, while on the other the feel of an open space was to be preserved. Post Panic wanted to create an environment within which it could work for clients, feel inspired and pursue its own internal projects. The space had not only to reflect the company's personality and creative attitude but also provide a functioning work environment and inspirational space. Mentjens' conceptual approach guarantees that the different atmospheres come together as one world. This dynamic, inviting environment surely offers Post Panic all the required room to play.

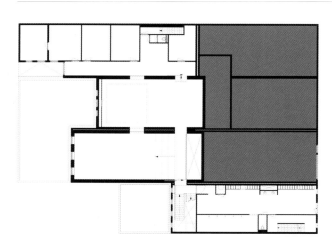

Club Sportive

In the city center of Amsterdam four houses from the 17th to the 19th century were redeveloped and converted into a wellness center. Each of the four buildings was given its own color and material – stucco, cement panels, wallpaper, and wood – to provide distinct individual atmospheres while moving through the different buildings. In the massive old warehouse, where no sound insulation was necessary, the stucco ceilings were removed to bring the characteristic heavy wooden beams back into view. In the back, a stairwell was created by removing 2x2 beams, bringing daylight to the ground floor and revealing the typical warehouse façade on the inside. The reception, locker rooms and sauna are located in this building.

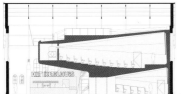

Cinema Het Ketelhuis

A freestanding, bulky structure rises through the interior of a converted boiler house on the site of the former Westergasfabriek gas works in Amsterdam. The inner volume contains two 50-seat film auditoria at ground-floor level with a larger, 143-seat auditorium above them. The connection between these two levels is provided by a suspended steel staircase which climbs on the outside of the volume. Apart from the first landing, which receives additional support from a tension rod, the staircase is secured only by mountings at the top and bottom. The strips of wood visible from the outside are of larch, and form a cladding which smoothly envelopes the bulging form of this huge piece of furniture, wrapping around the three auditoria to form a compact volume.

Heineken The City

Launched in the brewer's home city of Amsterdam, the store comprises six buildings where special products and services are sold in the spheres of music, fashion, travel and events and, obviously, beer. The project aims to highlight Heineken's international network, and the brand's foreign and domestic sponsorship activities. The design of Heineken The City claims to be "revolutionary", full of the latest technical devices, including speaking mirrors, 3D television screens, an ice wall and interactive pillars. This store is the first in Europe to be 100% LED-lit. Heineken The City targets Dutch consumers and will be open seven days a week.

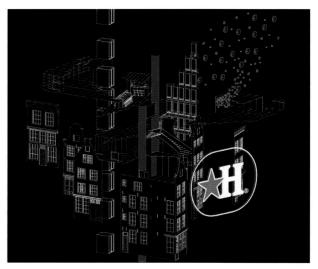

LUTE SUITES

LUTE SUITES consists of seven monumental houses. Acclaimed Dutch chef Peter Lute has teamed up with star interior designer Marcel Wanders to create an unusual collection of luxury suites overlooking the Amstel River. Transformed from 18th century workers cottages into bastions of high contemporary design, each suite has a different look with its own character and surprising details. Two multifunctional boardrooms for private dining and stimulating meetings link the suites to the renowned LUTE restaurant with its sophisticated French-oriented cuisine. For private boat trips, a charming 1920s designed LUTE canal boat can be rented with private chef.

ROC Care & Health

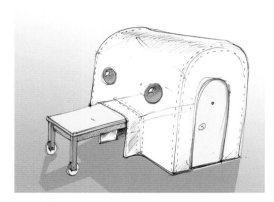

The designers were asked by the ROC Professional Training School in Apeldoorn in The Netherlands to design the reception area of the Care & Health Department. The idea of care has been visualized in a humoristic way using different interior elements. A protective shelter in the shape of a large box with a seemingly swung open cover forms a relaxation area. The interior surfaces of the shelter are covered with fabric reminiscent of oriental carpets. Tidy made-up beds become chairs. The reception desk is formed by soft mattresses and an informal meeting space is created by simply protecting a table by a sick bay tent. In their sum, these elements create a funny kind of hospitality as a result of their juxtaposition with hospitals.

Luxor

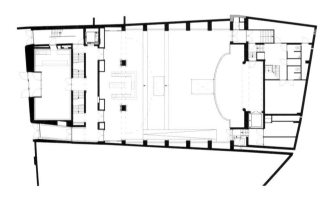

In 1915, Luxor was the preeminent movie theater boasting premier technology. This was also visually communicated by featuring a variety of luscious architectural styles on its façade. In 2008, Luxor was converted to a contemporary multi-use center. However, the original elements of interior design and architecture were restored or reconstructed. New spaces and elements (balcony, basement, elevator) were added, others replaced (LEDs). The expanded function affected the building's physics and technology: noise insulation, light and sound system, infrastructure for food and drink services were successfully integrated while continuing to use old infrastructure. The building's second skin houses air conditioning technology and helps maintain strict environmental and noise regulations.

VilaSofa

The designers used the idea of a warehouse as metaphor for speed, the conceptual solution consisting of a combination of warehouse aesthetics and home aesthetics. This resulted in materials such as plywood usually used for crates combined with high-end glossy finishes. The symbols used in transportation and packaging have been metamorphosed into decorative elements that form room dividers, arranged to organize the space and routing. Finally there is a big wall suggesting the idea of a magical villa.

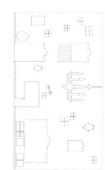

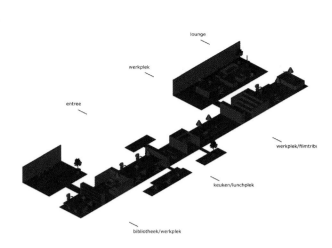

Office 03

Since the advertising agency Gummo wanted to rent the space only for two years, i29 convinced them to adopt the concept "reduce, reuse, recycle". They developed a theme that reflects Gummo's personality and design philosophy – simple and uncomplicated, yet stylish with a twist of humor. Everything in the office conforms to the new in-house style of white and grey. They used second-hand furniture and whatever was left over from the old office and spray-painted everything with polyurea hot spray – an environmentally friendly paint – to conform with the new color scheme and give a new soul to the old furniture. The new office is a perfect case study of a smart way to fill a temporary space stylishly and at minimal cost.

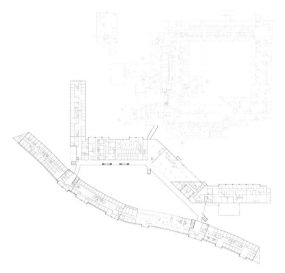

The New Martini Hospital

The design for the Martini Hospital placed the new building next to one already halfway through its 40-year lifespan to be eventually replaced by a new building. Furthermore the function of the building can also become totally interchangeable in the design phase and when the building is in use. A nursing department can be converted to an outpatient clinic or offices, for example. Extensions can also be randomly attached to the façade to gain extra floor space allowing the accommodation of bigger departments. The only fixed elements are the service shafts, which will always remain at the center of the block.

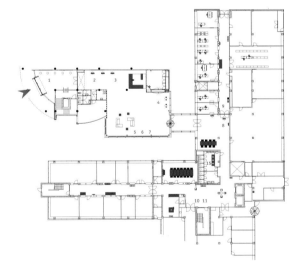

Publieke Omroep

In spite of the limited budget available, it was possible to create a powerful concept. The interior design is timeless with colorful accents. In 2006 COEN! redesigned the television test picture to symbolize the National Broadcasting Channel. The well-known test picture was translated into colourful art forms on wall panels and window accessories throughout the media building. Based on the same design, a series of 16 colorful giclées were produced, which when taken together form the complete test picture. Each giclée is available in a limited edition of 50 prints. Each print is signed, numbered and framed in aluminum behind glass.

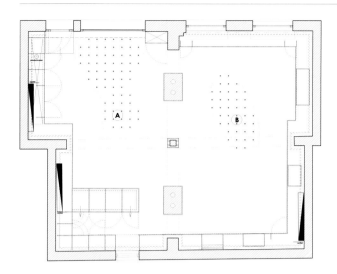

Kymyka

The central presentation is literally borne by two areas of steel tubes. They act as fragile pedestals on which the mainly high-heeled shoes are displayed like exalted treasures. The construction is as simple as it is ingenious. The tubes themselves are firmly anchored in a fixed grid in the sprung floor, while the shoes are attached using strong magnets. The space is entirely enclosed by low, multi-functional console tables. All the shop functions are contained in these: storage space and display cases, as well as cut-out seats and technical facilities such as the meter cupboard and heating. Only the sales counter itself protrudes into the space like a peninsula. All interiors are tailor-made, with careful attention devoted to ergonomic details such as the opening direction of the cupboard doors, the correct seat height for trying on shoes, and even the accessibility of the concealed wiring.

Fabbrica

Every detail combines industrial sturdiness with soft colors or decorative elements. Designers chose not to intervene with the authentic industrial character of this 19th century warehouse so they left all the structures in their original state. The walls, for example, were left intact; in several places large glass panels were placed in front of them covered with Italian wallpaper, the patterns on which seem to "float" in front of the wall. Lovers can sit in a train structure that floats in the center of the space. The logo of Fabbrica is based on a font in which the point on the "i" resembles the beautiful shape of a handmade pizza, but one can also see a full moon, as it enlightens Fabbrica at night.

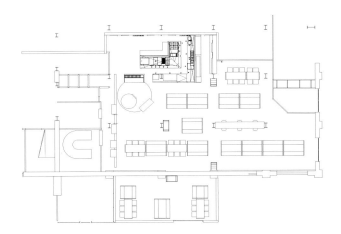

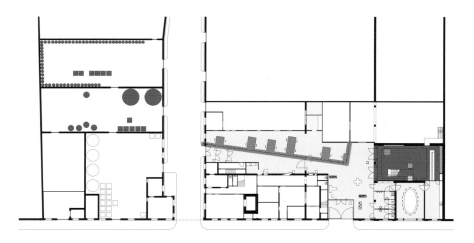

De Kuyper Royal Distillers

The new arrangement for the reception area of the office was designed to appeal to contemporary tastes – the world of chic cocktail bars frequented by a young, successful, dynamic, international, trend-setting and sophisticated clientele. The visit is also an instructive experience, where people can get acquainted with the distillery's history and sample the latest products through sight and taste. Visitors follow a route along a thirty-meter display cabinet through the old distillery with copper stills and wooden vats in an atmosphere of history and craftsmanship. Finally, visitors find themselves back in the reception area, which has metamorphosed into a completely different space – the Future Spirits Bar.

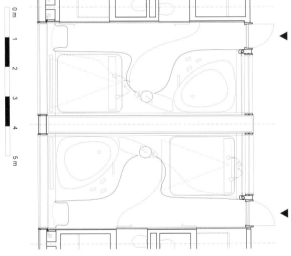

Risor Hotel

It is the first design hotel in Norway. A salt-water aquarium divides two hotel rooms, with an electric adjustable glass screen in the middle, which can be opaque or transparent. An alternate version features an electronic aquarium, featuring a versatile low resolution screen for interactive electronic art and inter-room communication for the new generation. The floor is inspired by forms of the Risor peninsula, where jetties have formed huge pot-holes for swimming, and waves have polished the rock silk smooth for sun-bathing. The floor, bed and bath form one continuous bathing-sleeping landscape — a private spa.

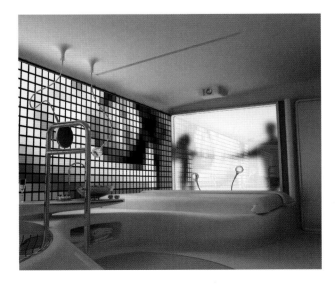

White House

Situated in a rather dense suburban setting, the house dynamically combines sheltered areas for privacy and open ones with interesting views. The central space of the house catches the morning light among the pines in the east, and the western sun on the horizon of the Oslo fjord. The house is clad with painted wooden panels both inside and out. Walls and ceilings on the first floor are finished in oak, while floor and walls of the ground floor consist of exposed concrete casted on site.

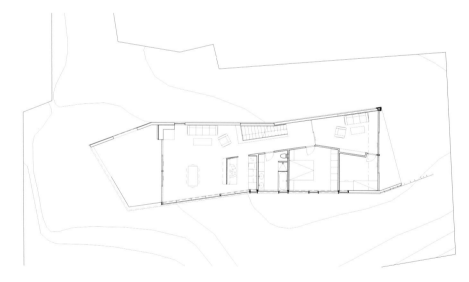

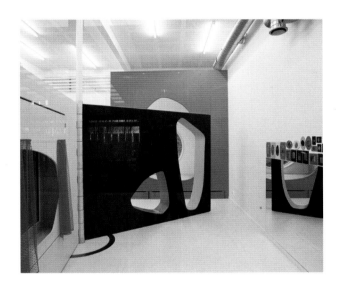

Kindergarten Somereng and Fjellvegen

This kindergarten concept is organized in a number of linear zones from a series of roofed outdoor terraces and an "indoor street" with water-play areas and a winter garden feel to intimate reading nooks and mezzanines. These zones enable a soft transition from the exterior to the interior spaces - from the exposed wide landscape to the private and quieter zones. The rooms themselves offer a variety of functions: simple moves can transform the size and feel of each space. Adjustable walls contain a variety of playing elements: pull-out furniture, climbing walls and puppet shows. The concept is an exploration of a child's imaginative world with themes of transition, conversion and surprise.

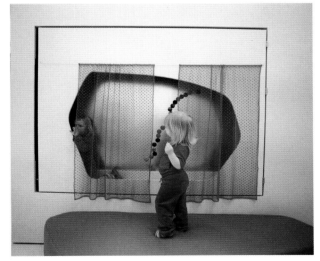

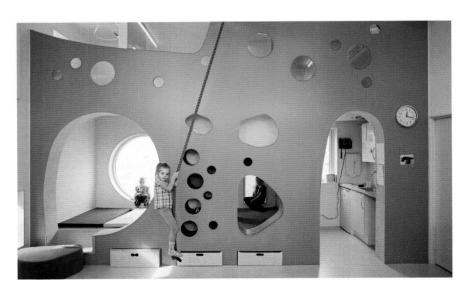

Andel's Hotel Krakow

The design develops the core principles established by the previous Andel's style and comfort, with respect for the specific requirements of the traveler in this part of the world. The design and detail makes reference to the locality, using the best locally sourced materials. Warm, textured, riven stone lines the rear of the reception, contrasting with burnished metallic shells enclosing the restaurant. The shells interlock to locate and define zones, establishing set routes and views through the building, while allowing space to flow freely. The bars are lined with locally sourced stained glass in saturated colors with warm stained timber.

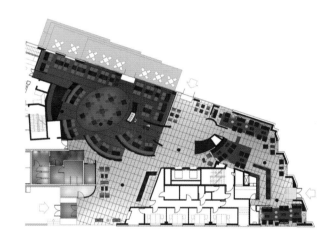

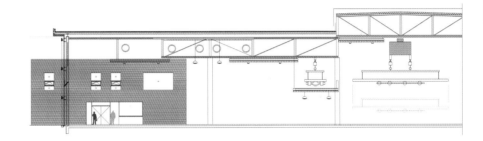

MAN Assembly Plant

Heavy-duty trucks destined for the Central and Eastern European markets undergo final assembly at this plant. The factory premises are divided in a modular fashion into supply; assembly, logistics and accessory manufacture functional zones in accordance to the production flow. This makes it possible for all functional elements to be expanded individually in the future. The central factory gate is executed using dark gray brick and services all delivery, employee and customer currents. Assembly takes place in a compact, equally expandable hall. The paint shop and auto finish areas are added to the side as independent units. Material choice and details together project an image of precision and accuracy as well as genuineness and sturdiness.

Multikino Golden Terraces

The Golden Terraces, Poland's best-known commercial center, is also the most spectacular, stylish, elegant and chic cinema in the heart of Warsaw. A total design has been created, covering the entire complex and all image-related aspects of visual identification like the logo, cinema guides, popcorn boxes and other graphical elements. There are three levels: The main foyer and seven auditoria, the Velvet Bar and the "35mm" music club. Thanks to modern technological solutions such as one of the biggest screen in Europe, "Christie", a world-class digital projector, and the "Martin Audio" sound system, all placed in the center of impressive design arrangements; one can fully experience the magic of the cinema world.

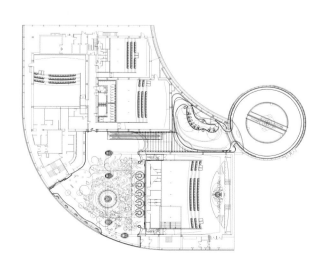

Pharmacy Monteiro

The intervention area is part of a small palace built in 1882 in Esposende (in the north of Portugal). The intervention space comprises two contiguous spaces which have different characteristics, geometries and coverings — a smaller room with no natural light and low quality coverings and a larger main room which has a sculpt ceiling, surfaced granite walls, and solid wood floor covering, and from which several doors make the connection to the exterior. The background supporting area (lab, ordering conference, storage and bathroom) occupies the small room. The various activities are organised in a liberalized way in an open space and the color white was chosen to increase the luminosity of the space.

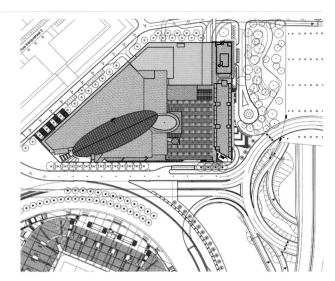

Dolce Vita

The shopping center is an elliptical, vertical atrium space that rises from below the ground to break through the roof of the building. Each of the elliptical walkways that project into the space of the atrium is a bolted, cantilever, steel-and-glass structure. Underneath these translucent glass walkways are upward-facing lights (responsible for giving the translucent glass floors a mystical shimmer) and downward-facing lights (providing adequate illumination for the floor below). At the top of this elliptical space is a "folded butterfly" ceiling of perforated metal panels that provides a gossamer effect and allows views beyond to the trusses that support the ceiling.

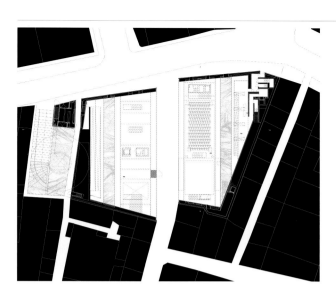

Centro de Artes de Sines

The building is situated at the start of the main street which links the town to the sea and marks the traditional entrance to the historic center. Diverse activities, capable of generating an exceptional array of services, are combined in the building: exhibition rooms, a library, cinema-cum-theater and a documentation center. The wide-ranging program calls for the whole plot to be occupied, enveloping the street below the main ground level and adapting its exterior volume to the monumental scale of the adjacent castle walls. The four modules have decks hung from a bridge-like structure which guarantees a continuous view across the building's interior, including the Center's activities in relation to the daily life of the town.

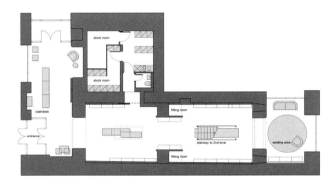

Red Plaza Boutique

Located in the center of Moscow at the Red Square, this luxury shop reflects the historic building in the shape of its rooms. Huge arcades, an old shop façade in timber wood and heavy stone walls are set in a contrast to the designer's elegant concept with black walls and ceilings, backlit glass walls and patinated brass panels. For the merchandizing tables and the cash desk, the designers chose white marble and stainless steel. A gallery had to be built in the large main room to provide additional space for the men's collection. An impressive stair made of patinated brass and illuminated glass steps invites visitors up to the men's level.

Bosco Pi

With the idea that the world is becoming very visually and info-savvy Karim Rashid created a "technorganic" seamless fluid ambience. A large digital pattern, reminiscent of a traditional Russian embroidery pattern of old cross stitching techniques defines the space itself as a large graphic art piece through which one walks. The pattern is an ever-undulating wall of sound waves, data, and information that embrace and envelop the shopper. The space is filled with bright colored objects – blobjects – expressions of dynamics, depth, motion and emotion; hypermodern and the by-products of the tools provided by digital technology. The sensually shaped display elements are designed around an extensive grid of columns and have functions and presences that define particular diverse shopping experiences.

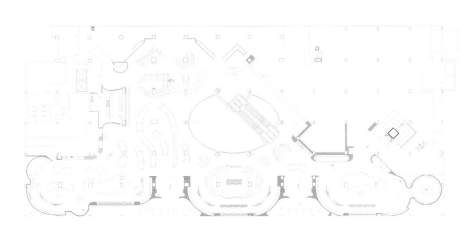

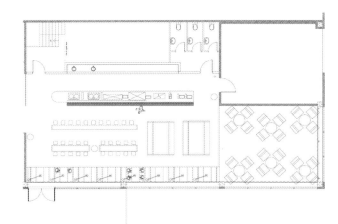

Teaspoon

SHH created a bold and striking new design concept for Russian tearoom operator Teaspoon, with the first outlet now open in the newly built O'Key shopping mall in southern St Petersburg. The Teaspoon menu is based around a range of speciality teas, along with savory and sweet pancakes. Each pancake is made to order and so the client brief asked the designers to underline the theatricality of the preparation process, whilst customers await their order. The designers used different colors and styles to decorate the walls of the space. Bright orange is the dominant color – even the light features are orange – and the chairs are designed to be both comfortable and fashionable.

Duet Sports Centers

The Duet Sports Centers chain is a clear example of a living club, focusing its interior design on a deeply human level. With distinct motifs of graphic representation, these centers avoid all conventionalism. These clubs utilise a unique chromatic and image motif that reflects the type of activity that takes place there, with visual and intuitive information giving life to a colorful and calm environment of great visual richness. Enhancing the visual impact, the designers created an sense of uniformity in the color scheme: two corporate colors categorise the areas by gender: masculine (blue) and feminine (orange), with two complementary colors that point to zones of collective use.

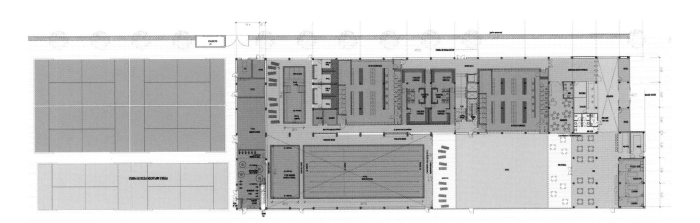

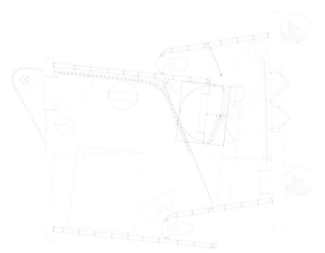

Chic&Basic Hotel

The new structure retains the regimented classroom layout while aiming to create little idyllic oases which give the sensation of belonging to a wide-open space. In each room the shower, wash basin and toilet will be housed in a well-defined nucleus around which a distinctive design for each individual room is based. The walls to each of the rooms have been built in accordance with the new design while respecting features from the original structure, its plasterwork and painted decoration, but without actually adhering to the same layout. Cornice strips and wall festoons cross the new divisions, sweeping in and out of rooms, evoking their origins in more generously spaced quarters.

Showroom Barcelona

Thread, the basic element of the dress, creates space in this showroom. The intervention forms a transparent space that it is generated using light. It is delimited by multiple transparent threads which vary in their appearance throughout the day due to different light reflections. It resembles an ethereal vertical sculpture created by "sewing" the space through an artisan process. The vertical woven textile acts as a diluted glazed wall, suggesting inner and outer space without defining either. The boundary remains diaphanous, permeable and dynamic. A complex and delicate process was completed to realize the project. Three thousand nylon threads were placed five centimeters from each other on a suspended structure 13 meters in height.

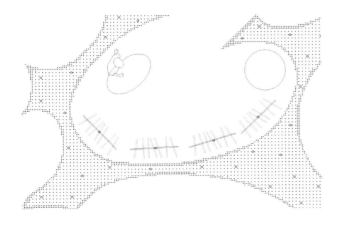

Hotel Me by Meliá

The tower stands out in the Barcelona skyline like a metal needle; a "jewel", with red, blue and green glass distributed at random along the façade like a giant stained glass window. At night the tower turns into an urban lantern, a luminous diagonal symbol. The interior design is based on the generous views from each room, like a giant screen overlooking the city. This screen is articulated by a series of smaller screens resembling television sets that form a "wall of images". The result is a building clad in a protective skin of thick sheets of anodized aluminum - dense, stiff and corrosion-proof.

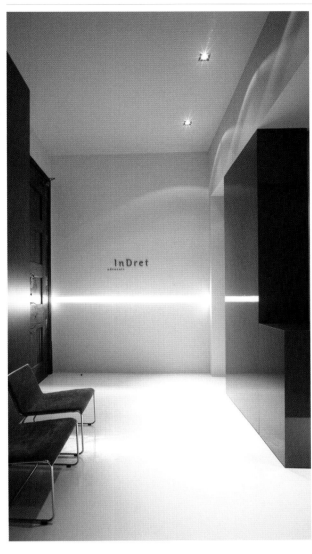

InDret

A floor of an early 20th century building in the historical center of Vilafranca del Penedès, was renovated to house the new central office of InDret. The building's principal façade had a noble look, while the other side opened to an unattractive back yard located 1.60 meters below ground level. This court was renovated as well. A great longitudinal 60 cm wall forms a structural axle, determining the location of the bathrooms for men and women. Featuring smoked glass mirrors, these bathrooms resemble cockpits, and are designed as two "suspended" boxes located below the rest of the building.

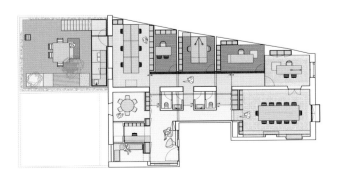

Barcelona Meeting Point

The stand is a representative space and a symbolic place where wills, intentions, criteria and actions are expressed by an allegoric language, avoiding the accumulation of logos, slogans, images and texts present at almost all stands at BMP. Dwellings built by Layetana will someday be somebody's home. This is why the stand is designed as an interior space of a house, a light void that could be approached from the exterior. The house is the limit of a unique space created by forms and objects. At the stand, the limits are defined by tridimensional lights that reproduce iconic elements, the parts of any home. A Layetana logo is displayed on one of the walls together with a small present, consisting of light sticks, which visitors can take away.

Museo Nacional de Ciencia y Tecnología

This project combines two different functions – a dance school and a museum for which the architects designed a single volume. The basic shape contains the school while the outer section, in the space between the form and the limit, contains the museum. The architects changed the function of the dance school, turning it into the service area of the museum. The entire exhibition area space is structured in six different heights that can be perceived simultaneously. This space will operate as a versatile environment for many different activities. The roof is turned into a technical floor from which the space for each exhibition is adapted.

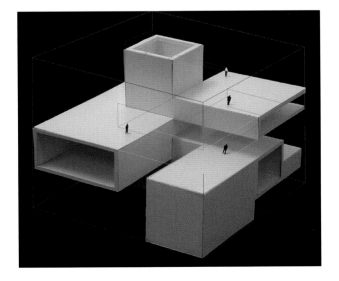

Showroom UME iluminación

The new space is intended to be an environment in need of "luminous objects" to take effect. The leit-motif of this company, as can be read in the phrase, "there are no shadows that cannot beat the light," is evident in the exhibition space, marked by generous heights (after demolition of the old false ceiling), areas of darkness and contrasting elements: glowing fluids converted into graphs that run on the walls, or the lights themselves reincarnated in autoiluminados satellites, the undisputed protagonists of the staging. The proposed overall design extends across the graphic identity of the company, renewed by the hand of Medusateam.

Hospes Palacio de los Patos

The original building was constructed in the late 19th century as an urban palace. Its recent transformation mainly focused on connecting the existing old structure with a functional-modern new building. "Two buildings - one single soul" was the motto of the renovation. The palace with its presumed feminine style is reflected in the alabaster and glass façade of the "male" new building, dominated by clear shapes and lines. Both parts are distinguished by a wealth of light, while a green belt arranged on two levels completes the multiple award-winning fusion of th two buildings that only seem different at first glimpse.

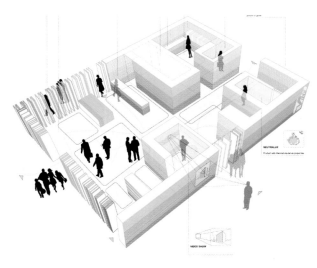

Vitro Pavilion

Fast and disposable architecture built with rubbish – 25,000 pieces and 170 tons of glass were used for 35,000 visitors during 100 hours. The Vitro Pavilion was conceived, developed, built, and destroyed in less than 6 months. Glass as an indestructible material was used in a temporal exhibition, built with the main purpose of being destroyed. The exterior shape of the pavilion was a perfect geometric form, orthogonal and flat, while the interior was an amorphous space, like the molecular structure of glass, regular and flat outside but heterogeneous inside. This geometrical system allows a larger interior perimeter and creates more exhibition space, with differentiated spatial ambits where uses get mixed.

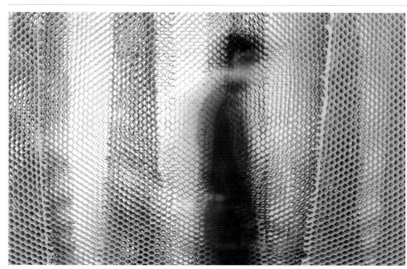
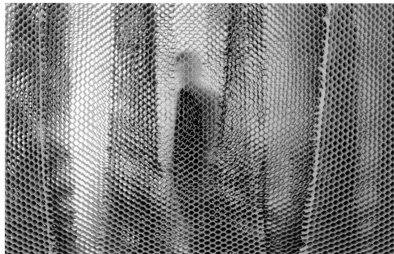

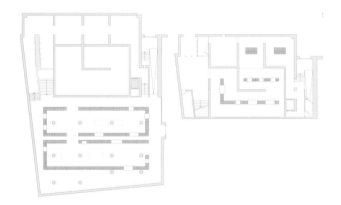

Susana Solano Exhibition

The project aims to scale the space to the size of the objects to be displayed here, providing order and rhythm to an exhibition which aims to be intimate. The models of public sculptures done by Susana Solano are treated as jewels that relate to each other visually as they do historically. A single system is designed to suit two spaces with opposed spatial attributes, allowing for a single reading of the exhibit. A unique envelope ought to unify spatial perception while solving by its layout the display of the pieces. A fragile, translucent, white, almost sacramental envelope is build to receive a number of sturdy and powerful pieces. The reference is clear: the paper lamps used in fairs, made out of a fragile honeycomb paper, with its volume build up on air and inventiveness.

Reina Bruja

In a corridor-like, subterranean space, divided by columns the combined use of light, color and curves gives this club a constantly changing appearance. Lighting is the key, the designer has used an LED technology to drench the walls, dancefloor, and even the washrooms in a dazzling flood of color that changes constantly in time with the music. The curved lines play a very important role and the furniture such as the red leather sofars and the flowing white Corian conters, also designed by Tomas Alia, adopts different geometric shapes.

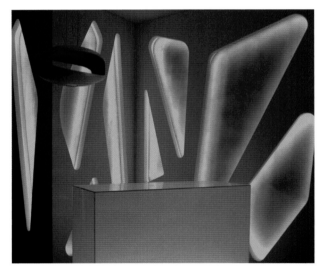

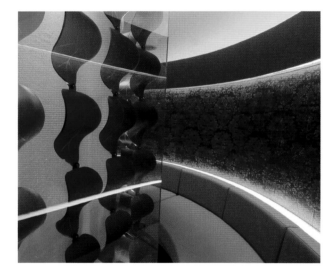

Hotel Puerta America, Level 1

The hotel development comprises 14 floors in total which 14 designers have been commissioned to design one floor each. Hadid's response to the clichéd hotel bedroom is to develop a new dialogue between the complex and continuous nature of merging forms and textures. This seamless fluidity represents a new language of domestic architecture – created by new developments in digital design and enhanced manufacturing capabilities. Inside the rooms, the floor, wall and furniture constitute one continuous surface or skin, making them pieces of art. Every single element, whether the walls, bedroom door with its LED signs, sliding door to the bathroom, bathtub or vanity unit, is rounded in a single curved sweep.

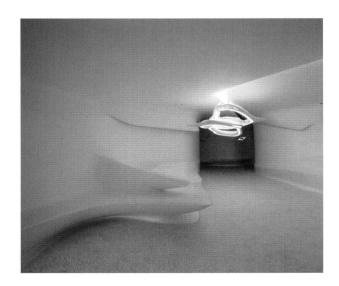

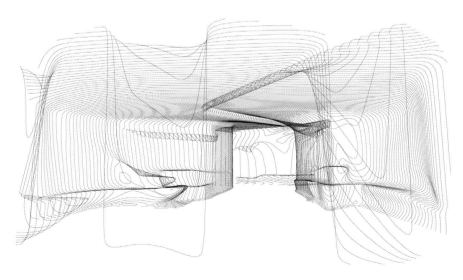

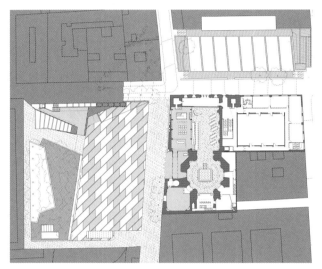

Cultural Center in Lavapiés

The ruins of the old church located in Lavapiés, one of the oldest quarters of Madrid, have been re-purposed for a library, and a new building has been built which consists of an auditorium and meeting rooms. Combined with stone and wood, the red bricks play an essential role. Resting on the ruins, this contemporary section mainly houses the reading rooms. Inside, the old brick walls have been preserved and restored. Light penetrates deep into the buildings, and this is stressed in particularly by the shaft of light between the old building and the new one highlighting a concrete staircase. The project illustrates how continuity and ruptures in history, techniques and aesthetics can create a new and harmonious unity.

Hotel Puerta America, Level 4

A different architect/interior designer of international standing was commissioned to create each floor, turning the hotel into a vertical juxtaposition of contemporary architecture. In the rooms of the fourth floor, a long meandering sheet of stainless steel becomes the main organizing element of the room. Moving along the back wall, it starts as a desk, turns into a headrest then a seat. It "crashes" into the glass division wall and mutates into a bathtub and finally the shower. The folded glass wall that divides the bedroom from the bathroom has also become another product of distortional forces. The two pieces of furniture seem to have crashed perpendicular into a single pane, transforming it into a prism that breaks light and presents views in ever-changing oscillating configurations.

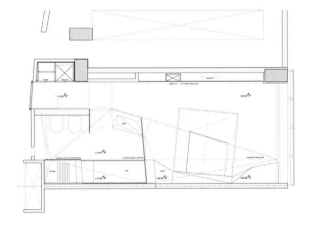

Hugo BOSS

BOSS Orange offers casual collections for men and women. The interior of the store is a contrast- rich interplay of authentic natural materials combined with high-gloss paint, white finished metal and brass surfaces. This combination creates an strong contrast for "radical chic". Colored walls with finely etched graphics form a beautifully accented impression. The ground floor functions with its two entranceways and the 65-square-meter surface area, as an opener to the ground floor. After walking up the stairs, with the wire netting handrail, the visitor arrives at the first floor, where two fashion boxes with integrated changing rooms and a lounge area with vintage furniture are located. Hanging racks enframe the room.

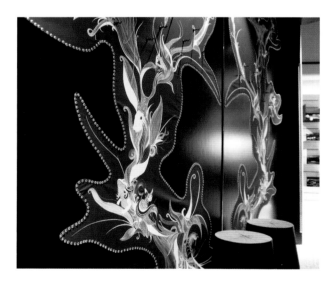

Sergi Arola Gastro Restaurant

A cool and elegant new restaurant stands at the heart of Madrid. This gourmet restaurant is organized around a space set on two levels: the high street level where the main dining room is placed, as well as a private lounge for eight diners, and the lower street level, housing the cocktail bar, as well as the wine cellar with capacity for 1000 bottles. The kitchen, fitted with the latest technologies, stands on both levels. The private lounge has the privilege to view the fun and frenzied activity in the kitchen through a glass wall (transparent / frosted). From the fringe of the main dining room passing through a suspended passage visitors reach an elevator which leads down into the very exclusive wine cellar.

Kindergarten in Murcia

This kindergarten is dedicated for children of up to three years of age. The façade, as opposed to the usual building's façade, is composed with the interior of the classrooms; so, the meaning of inhabiting a space is contradicted here by allowing the exterior activities come into the interior. The program is divided into two types of spaces: the "existential areas", classrooms or dining room, learning spaces, play and social areas for the children; and the "soft areas", which are the rest of the functional spaces: lobby, kitchen, storage, sleeping rooms and bathrooms. The interior is composed of three semitransparent boxes, which function as bathrooms and kitchen, with a rather ephemeral material. They are understood as furniture, almost mobile.

Puro Hotel

This city hotel resulted from the restoration of a residential building in the neighborhood of La Lonja, the former port of Palma de Mallorca, one of the principal areas of medieval trade in the western Mediterranean. The concept was based on the theme of 'the art of travelling' or 'knowing how to travel'. The team of architects and interior decorators interpreted this by trying to harmoniously bring together the essential traits of some of the big cultures in history. The Mediterranean sensual flair is represented by the proper building, while Oriental serenity is present in the wall decorations, roofs and materials of the areas and rooms. The materials of the decorative objects and furniture are clearly accentuated by the magic and exoticism of the Arab-Hindu culture. Light, water, fire and the landscape are constantly present.

Nursery School in Pamplona

The building is organized as a series of four parallel bodies in which fully built and empty areas are alternated. A body with administration services is located at the west of the site and filters the traffic noise from this side. The empty central space is illuminated through a skylight that emerges above the rest of the building and a third body houses the children's areas, including classrooms, workshops, refectories and bedrooms. Lastly, the external backyard is conceived as a prolongation of the classroom spaces through the opening of large windows. Diverse colors and textures (concrete, rubber and grass) create suggestive and varied playing spaces for the children.

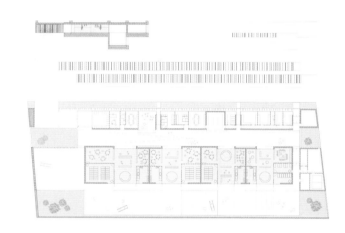

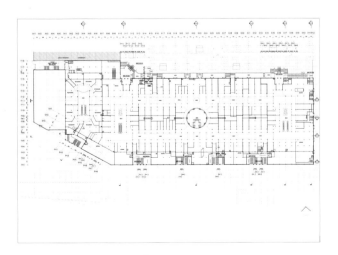

Plaza Norte 2

Situated in a prosperous suburb 19 kilometers north of Madrid, Plaza Norte 2 has become one of Madrid's most important shopping environments. The retail, non-hypermarket-based project is part of a large master plan with over 200,000 square meters of commercial space. The scheme has been designed as a "race-track" retail layout on two levels, with a classically themed interior build around a central glass dome. The concept incorporates a two-level restaurant atrium situated adjacent to the cinemas. The 226 retail units are designed to provide maximum flexibility for renting occupants.

Corral del Rey

Amalgamating Mudejar designs, the 17th century Casa Palacio, Corral del Rey, situated in the heart of Seville a few minutes away from the Cathedral, in the old quarter of Barrio Alfalfa, has been meticulously restored into a private luxury hotel. Striking a fine balance between historic charm and modern design, the architectural features include original Roman marble columns, wrought-iron balcony railings, terracotta tiles, and wooden carved beams. A blend of old and modern, inspired by sensitivity and imagination, the fine art work is accentuated by a subtle Lutron controlled lighting scheme. The well-appointed bedrooms, situated around a central patio, are decorated with classic Nicole Fabre fabrics. The combination with pale olive green cabinets and stylish oak paneled floors provides an understated modern touch.

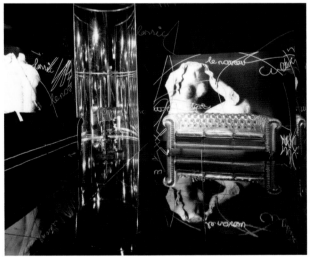

Abdón & Lucas

Abdón & Lucas, one of the main producers of furniture upholstery in Spain, presented its new collection at the 2006 Furniture Exhibition in Valencia. Barbosa Space Project designed an exhibition mixing photographs of classic pieces of Rome and Greece, taken with the permission of the National Archaeological Museum, with contemporary graffiti outlines. Barbosa contributed a new meaning to the existing pieces in the catalogue. The used materials, coming also from other industries, the weaves and the most exclusive skins, next to sumptuary elements like Swarovski crystals, materialized and gave form to these exclusive products.

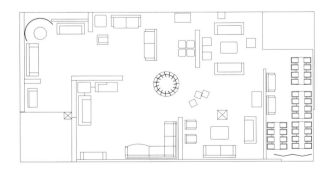

VillAnn

VillAnn is strongly oriented towards the western seafront. All that separates the exterior from the interior is a single ten-millimeter tempered glass pane. The house is made of concrete that has been cast on site. Thick sections made it possible to vibrate the concrete between the reinforcement bars to the smooth form of plywood. Brushed and lightly white-glazed Douglas fir dominates the floors, joinery and tables inside the house. The floorboards are 30 centimeter wide and as much as 14 meters long. The pool has been cast in black concrete and the water runs over the edge on the western side.

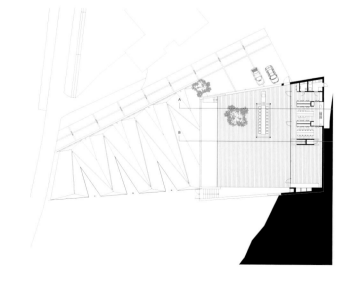

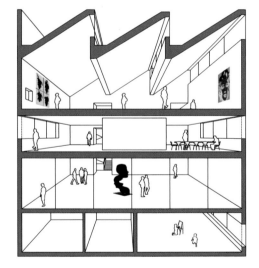

Moderna Museet

A new art museum, a public and cultural building, was considered to represent a rare opportunity to create a new node within the city. The museum is located in a former electricity plant with a newly added extension. The new volume marks the arrival of the new museum in the city and houses the main entrance and reception space, as well as a cafeteria and a new upper gallery. Inside, the building was spatially reconstructed. Two new staircases allow the visitor to move in a loop between the grand turbine hall and the upper exhibition rooms.

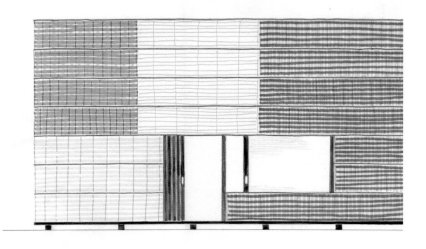

Kvadrat Sanden showroom

The Kvadrat showroom is structured using textile walls made of separate "tiles" assembled together via an ingenious folding system. The North Tiles system was conceived specifically for the textile showroom program. It aims to highlight various textures and materials featured in Kvadrat's collection by dressing the space with sensuality and warmth. It grants certain flexibility and guarantees a wide range of possible transformation. This system is the realization of long-incubated ideas about constructing soundproofed spaces with textile. Conceived similarly to fish scales, North Tiles can take on infinite shapes, both organic and geometric. The highly modular system allows the consideration of multiple applications for building autonomous and soundproofed locations.

Rica Talk Hotel

Offering 248 rooms, a restaurant, a VIP lounge and a conference center, the Rica Talk Hotel is one of Stockholm's most spectacular buildings. The hotel is inserted diagonally into one of the existing fairground halls. The surrounding landscape infiltrates the building complex. Its pixel-patterned glass façade is derived from reflections of a water surface. From the interior the screen-printed glass façade forms a lace curtain. Black amorphous islands integrated in the epoxy floor and colorful carpets form meeting zones in the congress center. The interior design includes natural materials and craftsman-like treatment of contemporary materials applied in new ways.

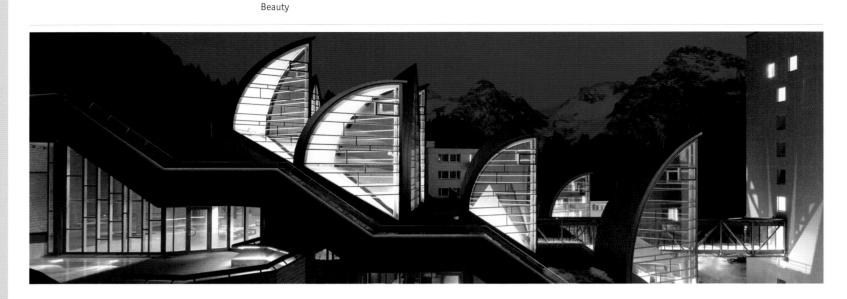

Wellness Center "Tschuggen Berg Oase"

Tschuggen Bergoase Arosa offers the extraordinary geographic configuration of a natural basin sur-rounded by mountains. It is a place with a constant contrast between human beings and nature, empha-sized by the powerful landscape in which the ancestral fight between human beings and mountains is evident. The site of the newly built Bergoase consists of a free space and park at the foot of the moun-tain next to the great hotel. The architect's concept consists of building without building, asserting the presence of the new through the added parts (artificial trees as metaphor of the nature) and combining the huge area with the functional program. The cover of the lower spaces is designed as a stage marked by geometric planted shapes that arouse the visitor's curiosity.

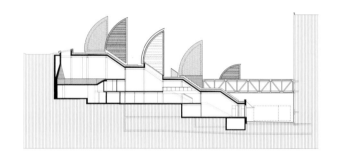

→ Ushi Tamborriello Innenarchitektur &
Szenenbild

→ Leisure &
Beauty

→ 2005

→ Baden

→ Switzerland

Photos: Courtesy of the architects

Hamam Trafo

The Hamam, which promises us a refuge from the outside world and a journey to the inside, is located in the landmarked Trafo building. On their journey to the inside, guests are accompanied by colors and surfaces on which the darkness apparently has been deposited in several layers. This includes mystic earthy surface on the walls in different shades of gray and green that clearly show signs of their processing and whose colors reflect those of the steel bearing structures of the landmarked industrial hall, as well as room-high glass walls that control views and insights and that bathe the area in green light. Filtered several times by colored glass and meshed textures, the outside light only enters as a dim memory into the central room of the premises, allowing the floral pattern of the floor to occasionally light up profoundly in the half-light.

D&G Dolce&Gabbana Time/Jewels

Designed in line with the brand image inputs given by Stefano Gabbana and Domenico Dolce, the out-standing feature of the trade fair stand of "D&G TIME" and "D&G JEWELS", is a presentation surface installed on the walls and ceiling consisting of more than 110,000 RGB LEDs, on which brightly colored video animations are shown with a powerful musical accompaniment. The combination of color and movement, stressed by the pavement made of mirror, gives the impression of a concert stage on which the exhibits, presented in two transparent glass cubes, practically function as main characters. Even in the upper floor lounge, visitors can still experience the fascinating light show. The metal framework of the stand allows the light to spread and be reflected unrestrictedly.

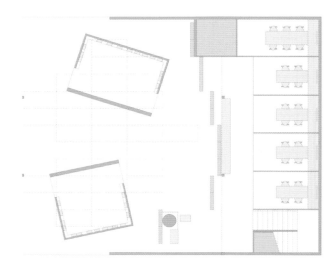

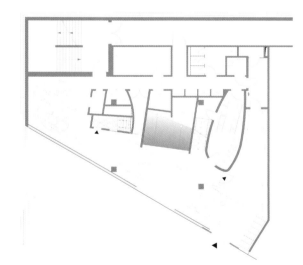

Kinderland Westside

The "Kinderland Westside" is located in a shopping center and is designed to occupy about 100 children for up to four hours. This task is accomplished with a varied play landscape extending over two levels. The Kinderland design is inspired by the Savanne. In reference to the many animal illustrations, the two levels depict the animals' habitat. For instance, the entrance to the cloakrooms is conceptualized as a "canyon". In contrast, the green hued reading area creates the impression of a bird's nest in the treetops. In the main section with the crafts area there is a bench with a softly contoured edge of a riverbank, surrounding a sky blue "waterhole".

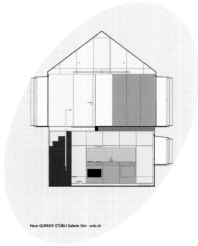

Haus GURINER STÜBLI Galerie Ost - eob.ch

Guriner Stübli

The Guriner Stübli is located in Bosco Gurin the highest village of the Canton, at 1,506 meters above sea level. The architecture of the house features typical characteristics of the alpine region wood and rock, integrated in the façades. The basic design idea was the innovative use of "boxes" as elements injected into the old space, using minimal interventions. On the ground floor is located the kitchen with the living room. Bedrooms, bathrooms and storage are on the upper floor, with a multipurpose space under the roof.

Tivoli Lodge

The traditional exterior belies a chic and contemporary interior with more than 700 square meters of living space and sensational views from the south-facing windows towards the highest peaks of the Engadine. Tivoli sleeps up to 16 guests in superlative style, with two master bedroom suites, four further bedrooms, plus four more single beds in a delightful children's bunk room, if required. It is perfect for relaxing too, the spa complex houses a relaxation area and hot tub, not to mention a sensational Indoor pool, complete with jet stream and a waterfall tumbling into the shallows.

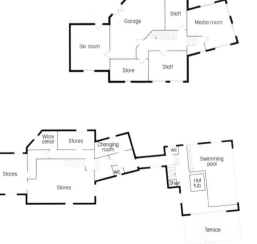

Single Family House

This crimson object in the densely constructed single-family district of "Im Lenz" resembles a sculpture that has been retroactively placed in a garden. The building structure resembles a temporarily constructed tent, distinguishing itself from the surrounding, mostly traditional homes. The structure was reduced to projecting concrete plates and a few load-bearing walls. The resulting concrete frame constitutes the thermal mass of the building and is heated in winter. A thermally insulated lightweight construction is placed on this frame. Its untreated OSB plates characterize the style of the building's interior design.

Clubgolf Sempachersee

The architects were to design two new buildings in connection with enlarging the course – the clubhouse and restaurant building and the new maintenance building, which are grouped around a centrally located kitchen. Each of the two restaurants has three large viewing windows, forming a sequenced 180 degrees panorama view. The mirror over the bar constitutes in effect a fourth window, multiplying and refracting the panoramic impressions. The large entertainment hall is dominated by a single over-dimensional window, forming an almost 20 meter long, wide-screen panorama over the snow-covered Alps.

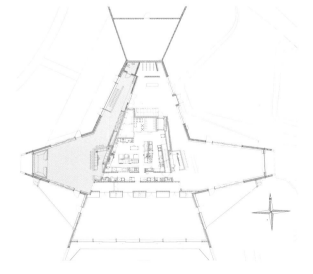

Hôtel de la Poste

The project is well integrated in ist location and reflects its general character. Historically, this site is characterized by the complementarity of the urban environment of the Rue du Bourg and the rear court-yard and garden space. The project, which highlights the redevelopment of the gardens of the adjacent city hall, extending them to the former car park just in front of the Hotel de la Poste, has given rise to the further project of constructing a pavilion in the park. The project plays on the relationship between mineral and vegetable aspects, which has inspired a new structure seeking to complement the mid-18th century Hôtel de la Poste.

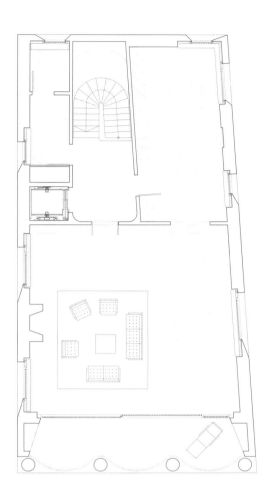

Chesa Lumpaz

Chesa Lumpaz is a modern, contemporary and luxurious 900 square meter villa, set on five floors connected by stairs as well as an elevator. It features the most modern systems in home comfort, entertainment, spa and wellness. With a professional full-time service team and a private five-star chef. It has four large double bedrooms, each with en-suite bath/shower rooms. Adjacent to the two double bedrooms on level two, is a children's master bedroom, including a large double bed, bath, shower and a separate smaller bedroom for a nanny. Chesa Lumpaz offers modern amenities and the highest standards of luxury.

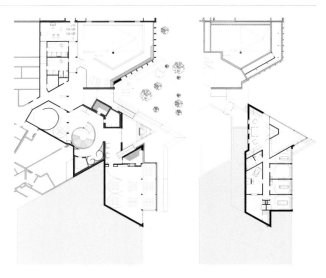

Seminar and Wellness Hotel Stoos

At 1,300 meters above sea level on the sunny high plateau of Stoos situated in central Switzerland, the 1,100 square meters wellness & spa center was created as an addition to the existing hotel. The architect's goal was to enable the guest to sense and experience the beauty and uniqueness of this mountain region in the setting of a decidedly modern and warm interior design. Fantastic views, materials from the region and associative connections with the features of the surrounding environment, such as the typical wooden shingle frontages, mountain lakes, the alpenglow and mountain flowers, should awaken feelings for the beautiful surrounding landscape.

Chalet Pierre Avoi

Located in the secluded Plan-Praz area of Verbier lies Pierre Avoi; a chalet that has mastered the juxtaposition of comfort and style within breathtaking surroundings. The chalet sleeps 12 guests in six bedrooms. The interior has been lovingly designed by the owner using natural mineral walls and striking pieces of art. The open plan living area features a roaring fireplace and floor to ceiling picture windows. The west side of the chalet boasts uninterrupted views of endless snowy fields, which can be enjoyed from the Jacuzzi, or from the large decked terrace.

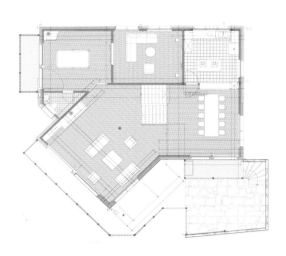

Chalet Grace

Chalet Grace sits in a prime location, in the exclusive Petit Village with breathtaking views of the Matterhorn. Built to an exquisite finish, Grace features double-height floor to ceiling windows on all three levels and a dramatic beamed interior. It has numerous south-facing balconies capturing the inspiring mountain views. Accommodation is luxurious, spacious and light, offering five en-suite double or twin bedrooms. It also boasts a luxuriously seated home cinema, a games room with a pool table, a spacious glass fronted wellness center including a sauna, shower room, massage room, Pilates/yoga space, outdoor hot tub and shower.

Omnia Hotel

The interior design takes its cue from 20th century American modernism established by Europeans who settled in the United States. The design concept could be summarized as a Continental-American dialogue. The interior of the Omnia, in the true modernist tradition, consists of a highly edited and natural color palette. While the Omnia is a hotel, the goal was to create an atmosphere where the guests would feel "at home." The interiors are meant to create a calm background to the breathtaking views of the landscape and the village of Zermatt. While the design and furniture are based on cross-cultural references, the materials are very much of the Valais.

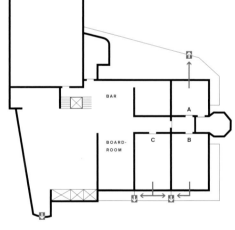

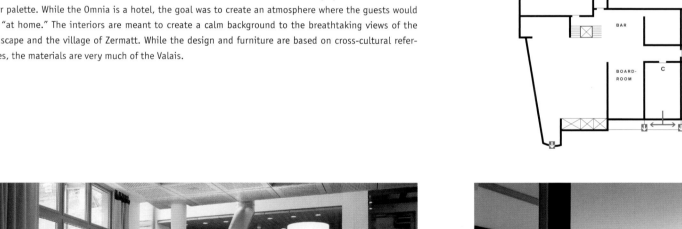

Google EMEA Engineering Hub

Google's new EMEA Engineering Hub cultivates an energized and inspiring work environment that is relaxed but focused, and buzzing with activities. The new Google office is about functionality and flexibility in the personal workspace, and choice and diversity in the community areas, creating an environment that holistically supports the Googlers in their work and well-being. The research undertaken by the architects extended beyond purely functional aspects, and provided information about the Googlers personality types, representational systems, values and motivational factors.

Kaufleuten Festsaal

The ballroom in the businessmen's complex was erected in the 1920s by the business administrators' social club. The 350 square meter-room has been authentically restored and modernized, and hosts a range of events. The acoustically polished ballroom includes a bar, stage and gallery, and the reception area is buffered by a foyer. The historical space is now being revived for banquets, and for use as a lounge or bar with a dance floor. An impulsive composition using modern materials, intense and warm colors and an individually adjustable lighting concept have been combined with monument preservation details, leaving the historical ambience recognizable throughout the space. For example, the characteristic horizontal wall organization reverberates in the entire room.

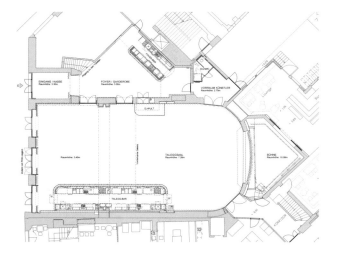

Fathom

Zeff has fitted out this vessel with some of the most luxurious interior fabrics and materials. Fathom accommodates eight guests in four cabins including one oversized master bedroom suite stretching from port to starboard. Engulfed in white silk from floor to ceiling the master bedroom offers separate dressing areas and a bathroom with marble walls, soothing river-rock floors and custom bronze fixtures by J.D. Beardmore. The other three guest rooms feature en-suite baths and internationally inspired decorations (e.g. Indian, Thai) tailored with exotic materials such as bamboo, leather panels and red handmade rice wallpaper.

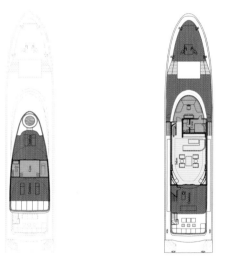

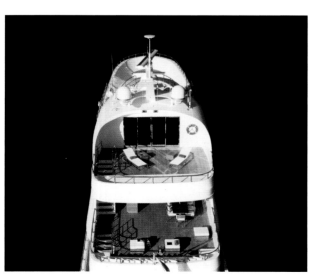

The Dome Spa

Located in an area of natural beauty also known as the Turkish Riviera, the Kempinski Hotel The Dome lies directly near the beach. It offers various relaxation options for its guests look in. The Dome Spa embraces one of Turkey's largest spa and Thalasso facilities, including extra large outdoor pools and an outdoor Jacuzzi. Spread over 3,600 square meters, The Dome Spa offers facial, body and Thalasso treatments as well as a variety of saunas, a heated indoor swimming pool, a heated seawater pool and a genuine Ottoman Hamam, all laid out in exclusive, refined settings. In 28 carefully appointed and equipped treatment rooms and sections, guests can enjoy a true oasis of relaxation.

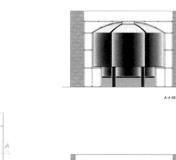

A-A KESIT

PLAN

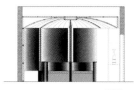

Bodrum House

The idea of creating shadowed open spaces came from strong climatic influence in defining the physical environment. Different effects of the sun during different times of the day transforms the interior spaces. Simplicity, the dominant concept in the whole house, was the starting point for creating a calm and quiet atmosphere. Different types and colors of wood were used, combining simplicity with different details and materials, turning the house project into a "home". Cutting the joints of the ceiling, walls and the floor, gave the opportunity to perceive each important element separately which meanwhile strengthened the effects of fullness and emptiness in the whole space.

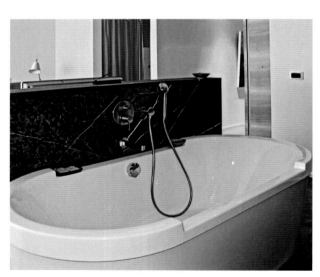

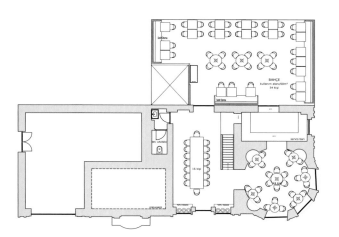

The House Café Corner

The building shapes a busy corner at two busy streets. As part of the Te vikiye Mosque that was built in the 18th century, the original bricks of the wall and engravings in the canopy are protected and enriched by different textures and colors. The already existing concept of the small House Café chain was adapted to this space, fusing the contemporary design with the historic. The canopy has an interesting style as the Castiglioni Taraxacum lamp is coming through engravings.

The House Café Kanyon

This project is an integration of the Kanyon mall's original architecture, the House Café brand identity and Autobah design approach. A site-built structure made of steel and glass, which functions as a transparent box to contain the cafe, is carefully planned and designed to fit the valley-like architecture of the mall. It is placed on a walnut platform to add warmth to the cafe's interior. Although an extension, the structure bears its own strong design identity while blending in with its surroundings.

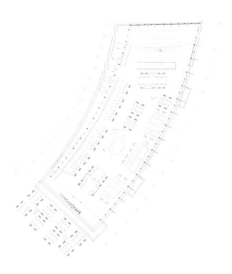

X-ist Art Gallery

The gallery is situated in the basement of an apartment in Nisantasi, with five bedrooms and a living room. The designers wanted to create an open art gallery with white walls that would allow the paintings to stand out. For that reason, they created one big main exhibition area and a closed back office area. Epoxy was chosen to create a cold atmosphere that contrasts with the paintings. Although the art gallery is in the basement, there is a small courtyard in front of the main exhibition space that allows sunlight to enter and attract the attention of passersby.

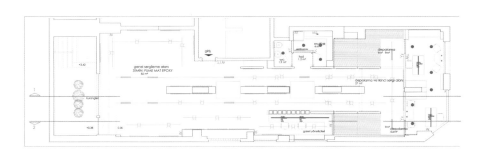

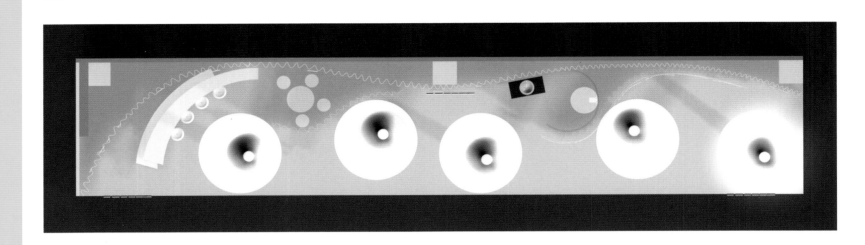

Brezza Exhibition Stand

The stand was given an elegant look to fully express the nature of the exhibited shiny mosaic tiles. The organic forms, which were closely related to the Kütahya stand, were covered in tiles forming several colorful flowers, displaying the capabilities of the material. The white color used for the stand allowed the colors to pop out even more. The dignified look of the stand was underlined by the tall, white, velvet curtains that provided a background for the tall, linear layers of mosaic tiles displayed in front. Specialized spaces such as the meeting room and a bathroom display were created by the curvilinear movements of the curtain.

Garanti Zone Lounge

Zone is a private airport lounge in Istanbul Ataturk Airport, designed and built by GAD in 2007 for the American Express & Life card holders of Garanti Bank. Zone is 580 square meters and consists of an entrance area, lounge area, a business center area, and two bars, one for drinks and the other one for an open buffet and bathrooms. The main idea behind Zone is to create a comfortable and colorful environment for visitors before their long fligts. They can enjoy food and drinks before the flight, use the business center, watch television, play billiards, and their children can enjoy the Playstation in a special room designed for them.

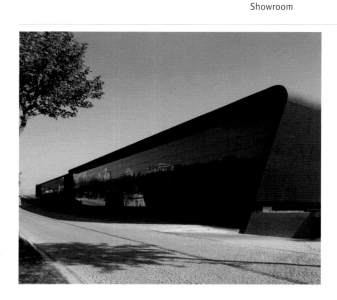

Prestige Mall

Prestige Mall is a building in which structure and form correlate with each other. Shiny materials and illuminated surfaces, exposed concrete and black plaster give the feeling of grace, purity, humility and infinity. The proportions of matte black plaster and shiny glass create a balanced esthetic and allow the building to appear almost camouflaged. The curved horizontal lines of the building bring a sense of flow and dynamism. Reflective surfaces carry on inside to create never-ending illusionary perspectives.

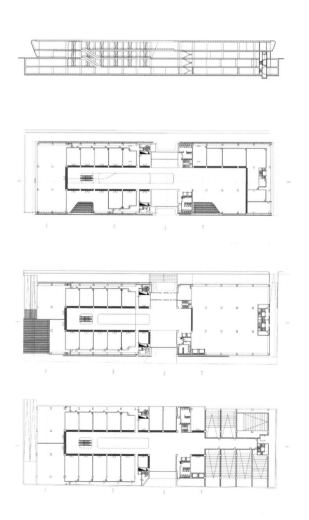

Habif Mimarlik Office

Through looking the answers to the question of what kind of environment people would most like to work in, the architects aimed to create a very calm, serene, tranquil, luminous and warm environment for the Habif Architecture Team. This was concretized by designing big wooden study and meeting elements without any separations.

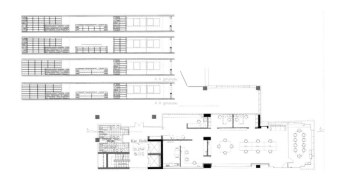

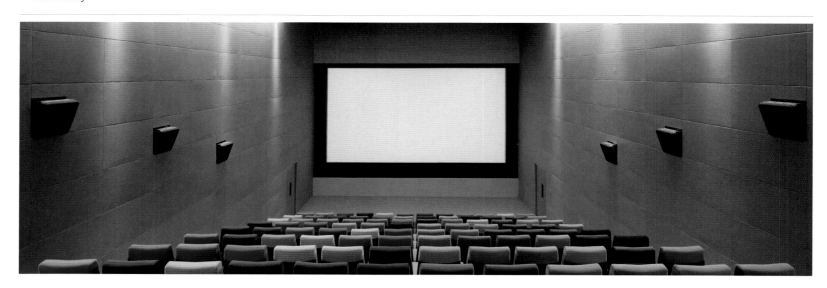

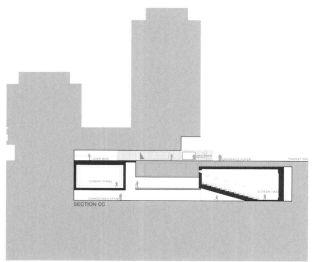

Light House Cinema

In refurbishing the Light House Cinema located within the Smithfield Market, the architects took care to integrate a variety of screen sizes to ensure a diverse cinematic program and to be able to extend runs of popular films for longer periods. The architectural challenge of this project was to combine the insertion of four cinema volumes into existing basement voids while creating an informal circulation route. Each of the four volumes has a consistent color coding which expresses the thematic diversity in accordance to the spatial structure and size of the rooms. Walls, furniture and floors were designed to optimize the cinematic experience while maintaining a unique character.

Wales Millennium Center

The Wales Millennium Center was to be a landmark building befitting its location, cultural importance, and its status as a Millennium project. The design of the building draws on references from the industrial archaeology, geology and heritage of Wales. Its simple composition and limited palette of materials disguise a complexity of internal organization. The Theater at the heart of the project presented the greatest challenge: it was to be both a beautiful room and excellent acoustically. An all-enveloping single perimeter skin unifies the space and places the audience on 'floating' tiers within a single volume. The seating balconies were treated as physically disconnected from the walls and appear to grow out of the shaft formed by the technical control rooms at the back of the auditorium, like boughs growing away from the trunk of a tree. The balcony fronts have variegated hardwood strips, laid in horizontal strata and tailored to meet acoustic requirements.

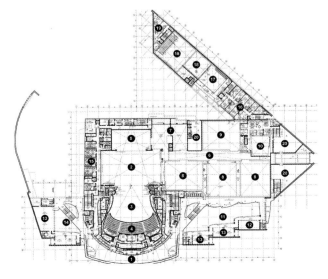

Hurst House on the Marsh

Hidden away on the far southwestern corner of the Welsh coast, Hurst House on the Marsh is a haven of boutique luxury. Originally a 16th century dairy farm, it sits in the heart of 26 acres of marshland, but its recent overhaul by de Valero Design places Hurst House at the forefront of modern hotel interior design. 18 bedrooms and a spa located within stunningly renovated outhouses enclose a large courtyard, while the main house and restaurant overlook an organic kitchen garden and the marshland beyond. Many of the original buildings were listed, presenting a challenge to the designers who aimed to create a hotel of the highest standard of comfort and service whilst preserving the full character of the ancient structures. A new swimming pool/Jacuzzi, spa treatment area and restaurant extension formed the final and most ambitious phase of the project, which began in 2002.

Hotel Missoni

In the 8,630 square meter building in Edinburgh, Matteo Thun & Partners worked on 129 rooms, seven suites, the bar, restaurant and conference facilities in close collaboration with Missoni. The name of this prestigious Milan fashion house conjures up images of a skilled use of many tones and shades: a minutely applied, perfectly controlled riot of color. Used in tone upon tone and tone against tone, the Missoni approach to color gives its products an unmistakably strong character of their own that is instantly recognisable the world over. The designers developed a method to melt Missoni's approach to their products with the interiors of this outstanding hotel. The quality of the preparatory thinking, the choice of materials and the final result are every bit as painstaking as Missoni's own selections of color schemes.

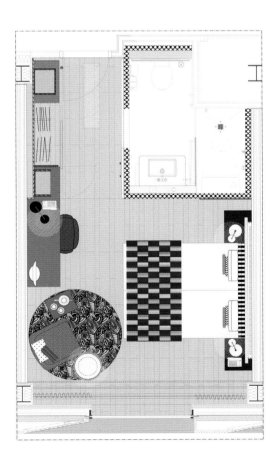

Lucky 7 Canteen

The brief was for a pared back interior with an under-designed feel that would be quirky and lived in and target both the office workers and the pre-clubbers. Finding a way of complementing the refined period detailing and proportions with the worn feel of the design was crucial to the project's success. Budget was also a key issue and Surface ID had to create several features at minimal cost, including the cast concrete lamps and graffitied log wall. The design pays particular attention to detail through the use of textures and materials including exposed wood and brickwork, mess hall benches, concrete panels, long wooden tables and distressed wallpaper which gives Lucky 7 its unique character. The finished product is both raw and inviting yet maintains a certain refined, faded elegance reminiscent of its former glory as a grand townhouse.

The Olde Bell Inn

With parts of the inn dating back to 1135, The Olde Bell is steeped in history. Rather than sacrificing its oak-beamed medieval heritage, Ilse Crawford chose rather to re-invent it and imbue the interior with a rustic elegance that is still quintessentially English. Chunky farmhouse furniture, oak floorboards, woven wool blankets and natural tones combine to create a cosy, comfortable feel to what is also a strikingly modern interior. Hand-made rush matting even adds a grassy rustic aroma to the rooms. The bathrooms are fitted with drench showers and elegant claw-foot baths. The rooms themselves do not dominate The Olde Bell Inn; rather it is the common spaces that are the heartbeat of the hotel which functions almost like a village in itself. While the main building provides space for the overnight guests and locals, auxiliary buildings are available for private gatherings.

Black Lamb House

Black Lamb House is a Grade II listed house in an ancient Sussex village next to a Norman church. The first half of the house was built in the 17th century with a later addition in the 18th. This 2009 extension uses many of the old elements of the house to inspire the new ones. 200-year-old oak beams were sourced, ancient sinks brought in from Europe and doors with original glazing were found. Fireplaces were salvaged from both the UK and France. Newly lime rendered walls and beamed ceilings sit happily with the latest under floor heating and insulation. Most of the interior furnishings consist of antiques or salvaged items, even down to the use of vintage fabrics for the curtains. Ironmongery, tiles and even the French doors were all reclaimed from other buildings. The unpainted, lime rendered walls and stone fireplaces gave the interior a well-worn feel from the moment it was finished. The result is a modern functional home set amongst the history of an ancient building.

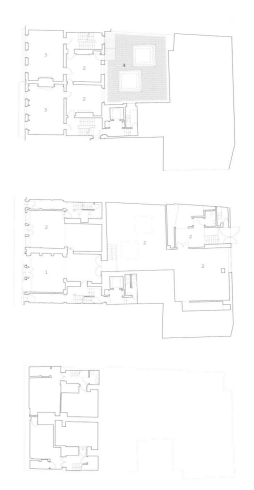

Raven Row

Raven Row, a new contemporary art exhibition center is embedded in two of the finest 18th century silk mercers' houses and a 1972 concrete framed office building in Spitalfields. Originally built in 1754 the Grade I listed buildings have been added to, converted, neglected, ravaged by fires and repaired over two and a half centuries. The latest intervention by 6a Architects weaves through the buildings to create a new architectural narrative of spaces, surfaces and textures that binds the past with the new in a contemporary whole. The project includes contemporary art galleries within a new semi-basement and a series of 18th century Rococo rooms over three-stories with additional studio space, offices and apartments for artists in residence above.

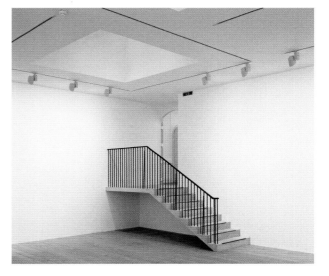

Emperor Moth

Katia Gomiashvili commissioned Ab Rogers Design to create a new store in Mayfair for her Moscow-based fashion label. Clothing itself comes alive when we wear it, moving with us as we walk, run, or dance. How can we bring it back to life when it hangs on the rack in the shop? The designers began with the idea that a still image can seem to be in motion when it is fractured, repeated and extended on all sides. They created a multi-faceted mirrored tent to occupy the space. Any object placed on display – and any visitor – can suddenly be seen from a variety of angles simultaneously. The studio created a series of animals – a crocodile, a peacock and a wild boar – to keep the clothing company in the mirrored tent. A series of life-size puppets wearing the Emperor Moth clothing dance throughout the shop, animated by motors and pulleys. Entering this space is a kind of transformation. Even a slight movement suddenly takes on an air of drama and dynamism. Each splash of color becomes a new mosaic. Each light becomes a new constellation.

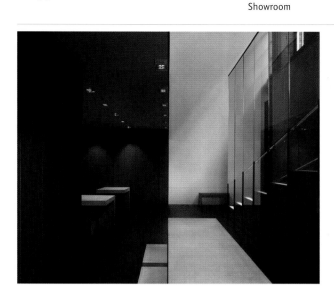

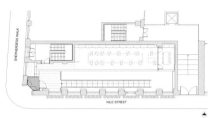

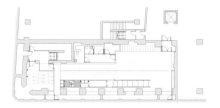

Kvadrat HQ

The new UK headquarters and showroom for Danish textiles company Kvadrat was designed by Adjaye Associates in collaboration with Peter Saville in the former premises of a Victorian factory. The showroom is a light-filled, double height, lower ground space with an office on a mezzanine floor. Part of the floor was removed to create a dramatic, singular hall-like space with a spectrum-coloured glass balustrade following the length of the staircase. The space will be used for events and a place to showcase art, design, and moving image creative endeavours which Kvadrat actively supports. It was also essential that Kvadrat was able to display the artist/designer special projects that it commissions. The feel of the space, however, is more reminiscent of a nightclub than a corporate entertainment space. The rustic wooden staircase at the entrance leads down to a basement dominated by muted grays and blacks. Textiles are on display here in cabinets that disappear into the wall leaving space for social events.

King's Road Anthropologie

Originally the site of a billiard hall and garage, Anthropologie stripped the buildings back to structure and reinstated all of the decorative glass details, wood storefront, and skylights. Passing through the main entrance highlighted by colorful encaustic concrete tile and chandeliers, the visitor arrives in the former billiard hall. This space with its high vaulted ceilings and decorative steel trusses has been finished with a reclaimed maple parquet floor. In the center of the space is a steel vignette, comprised of recombined components of a vintage French shop front. A large cascading stairway flowing through a portal of reclaimed barn wood forms a gentle transition between the billiard hall and garage. The garage floor is polished concrete to reflect the nature of the former space, while beautiful saw tooth skylights flood the space with natural light. The industrial feel is balanced by the colourful and eclectic artisan plaster vignette walls that surround the space.

Hearth House

The Hearth House is a redeveloped Edwardian semi-detached house in North London that provides a new home for a family of five. Untouched since the 1940s the old house enjoyed a generous provision of space but was dark, spatially unvaried and saturated in the residue of the previous residents. The new house has a range of differing spaces, whose individual characters are defined through a variety of architectural effects. A triple height space, lit from above by an operable roof light, brings direct sunlight into the north-facing spaces. At its base a warm poured concrete hearth and stair provide a center for family life, perfect for clambering and reclining. The pattern of the reclaimed chevron parquet flooring is repeated in the surface of the concrete, encouraging domestic and historical associations. Nooks, internal windows and screens ensure the family can easily enjoy the more public areas of the house whilst maintaining their own desired level of privacy.

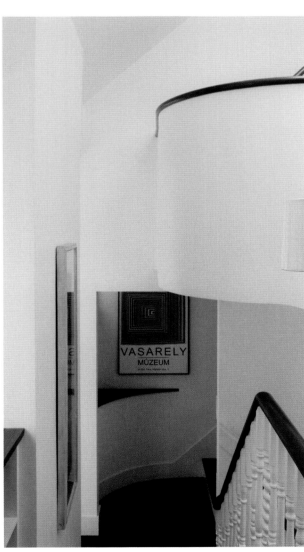

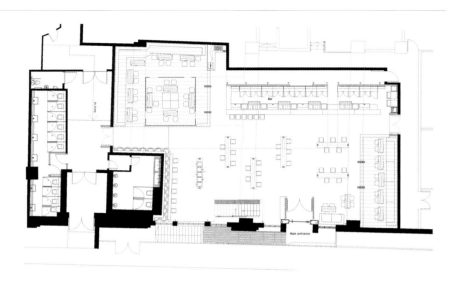

Carbon Bar

This destination venue, at the distinctive Guoman Group hotel, features an exceptional interior inspired by industrial architecture bringing raw Shoreditch chic to the West End. A unique fusion of concrete, brick, steel, mesh and leather contrasts with outsized Chesterfields, beveled mirrors and sketches of 21st century industrial living on the walls. The design maximizes space, privacy and the ability to be seen all at once. It includes a Chain Room, with chains suspended floor to ceiling to create a semi-private function room; a Champagne Bar with a five-meter high champagne wall; a 14-meter bar created from concrete blocks; and a DJ booth unusually located above the bar and floating mezzanine. The bar's toilet walls are adorned with mock blueprints that explain how to handle 20th century tools. The ladies' washrooms ironically feature scribbled instructions on how to handle heavy-duty machinery, while the gentlemen's toilets display instructions from operating manuals for ovens, irons and household objects.

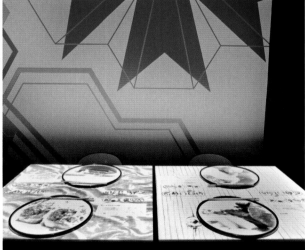

Inamo

Inamo is a 310 square meter restaurant and bar, offering customers high-quality Asian fusion cuisine. It also offers a new paradigm in the way food is ordered, with menus projected onto tabletops, allowing diners to order food and beverages interactively, to change the ambience of their individual table, to play games or even to order up local information and services, such as booking a taxi. 'Cocoon' projectors are set at the same height throughout within the suspended high-gloss black ceiling. When customers sit down, white spots for plates appear along with a customizable 'e-cloth' for each table. The concept behind the restaurant was ambitious and difficult to implement; great consideration was given especially to the lighting levels and proportions to enable the restaurant to function throughout the day and night. It was also vital that the design had an overall strong sense of identity as a space, neither overwhelming nor being overwhelmed by the technology at its heart.

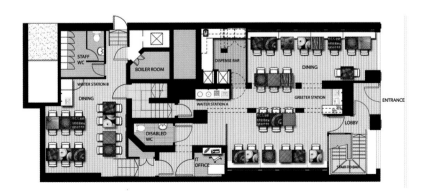

London House

The first floor plate was removed leaving a double height box (10 meters squared). A new steel armature was inserted, stabilizing the box and hanging a mezzanine (4 x 10 meters). The minimalist impression is developed through concealed lighting throughout the house; the ceiling to the mezzanine visible to the ground floor is covered in black lacquered panels with slits of light running through to the extension, giving the unusual impression of illumination escaping from a single, solid block of light. Douglas Fur lime-washed broad planks extend throughout the ground floor, whilst black oak used on the mezzanine, in harmony with the extension ceiling parallel to it, emphasizes the overall warmth in the design.

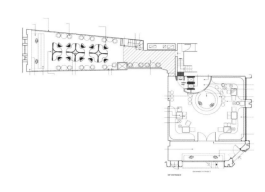

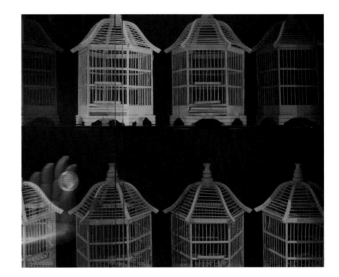

Electric Birdcage

Electric Birdcage, an edgy, fantasy space hidden inside an old bank, is a surreal world of giant black polymer panthers, imposing black stallions and a merry-go-round bar. Fluorescent pink stucco ceilings and giant hand seats combine with neon wicker furniture and root tables scattered across a distorted Fibonacci checkerboard floor, which extends up the walls. Iron birdcage chandeliers dangle from the pink ceiling and the DJ himself is housed in a birdcage. Stained glass windows and dim sum add to the bizarre world of the Electric Birdcage. The extravagant interior, fusing sophisticated party venue, funhouse and late-night cocktail bar demands a reaction. With a capacity of 300, Pan-Asian food served all day and cocktails served all night by staff in retro airline dress, Electric Birdcage represents an experimental foray into an eccentric new world of interior design.

Paramount Bar

Paramount Bar is the latest of London's exclusive members' clubs. Design Research Studio was invited to create something very special, to differentiate the club from stiff competition. The design concept is inspired by the architecture of the building, a Brutalist aesthetic in geometric forms. Shapes found in the concrete of the building façade are reintroduced to the interior through the design of custom items such as bars, wall paneling and furniture. Hard-edged materials such as concrete and stone were widely used to create a blend of 1960s retro and futurism. Located on levels 31, 32 and 33 of this landmark building, the design ensures that the spectacular view remains the key asset for the club. This is done by directing all internal light away from the windows and using matt finishes wherever possible.

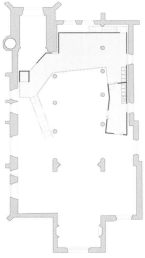

The Garden Museum

The brief for the redesign of the museum asked for a new gallery space where temporary exhibitions could be housed in secure and environmentally controlled conditions. In addition, the designers created a dedicated place for the museum's permanent collection, which was previously often displaced by temporary exhibitions. A belvedere within the existing building houses the temporary gallery on the ground floor and the permanent collection on the first. This arrangement empties the nave of exhibits, enabling the museum's diverse cultural programme of lectures and debates to take place alongside the exhibitions. The belvedere is a freestanding structure made of Eurban, a pre-fabricated and lightweight but very strong timber material. The timber walls are left unfinished and recede into the background, allowing the exhibits to dominate the interior space, while the windows and doors are strongly colored and protrude through the raw timber. Strongly colored furniture adds a further layer of detail to the mute timber form.

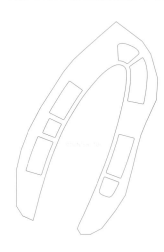

Home House

Zaha Hadid Architects' first London interior for two decades explodes within the Georgian restoration of the ground floor at Home House. The furniture installations, in saturated Georgian colors, flow through the bar, entrance, and reception rooms to create an interior landscape of sculptural islands. The sinuous forms follow the fluid geometries of natural systems and distortions. James Wyatt's original programmed spaces are recalled in the functionality of the composition's fluid and fresh forms. The islands float between history and future, inviting a dialogue between past and present, elasticity and solidity and craftsmanship spanning three centuries. The bar environment is dominated by the bar itself, a structure occupied by the members and guests who become part of the experience. A greater degree of warmness and intimacy was achieved in the lounge, which was developed as a horizontal field of disparate objects formally integrated into an ensemble.

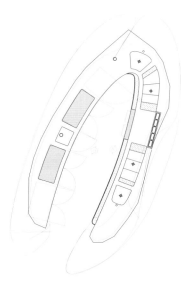

Rough Luxe Hotel

Rough Luxe is the antithesis to conventional hotels with air-conditioned constancy, marbled flooring, polished finishes and bland colors. It is a fascinating blend of urban archaeology, partially sanded surfaces, bare floorboards, chipped paint and rough edges mingled with gloriously opulent contemporary wallpaper and modern art plus top quality furnishings. Early on in the refurbishment, layers of wallpaper were peeled away to reveal decoration ideas from centuries ago. This intriguing 'archaeology' of interior design was kept and remains tangible in every room of this narrow town house. Breakfast is served in the basement dining room next door to the original 1960s utilitarian kitchen; guests sit around a table made of wood salvaged from Brighton Pier beneath an imposing ceiling photo of a Renaissance dome. The nine intimate and comfortable rooms with their original light fittings and door fixtures beguile with their period charm and obvious wear and tear.

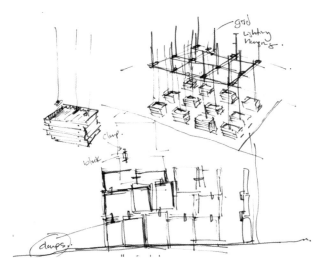

Shop&Show

Coinciding with London Fashion Week 2009, Tracey Neuls created a temporary "shop and show" in Kensington. Her collection of shoe designs past, present and future, were showcased and sold for a period of three weeks. The shoes were hung from vertiginous towers made from hundreds of reclaimed vintage drawer units. The drawers were also arranged vertically and clamped together to form shelving. Amongst the shoes lurked an array of objects, muses and everyday, overlooked paraphernalia which inspires much of Tracey's work. Like Eileen Gray last century (to whom she has been compared) she is a designer who consistently shuns mainstream preoccupations with fashion, instead melding her instinctive, material sense with a concern for timelessness. Shop&Show offered a rare glimpse into her creative process.

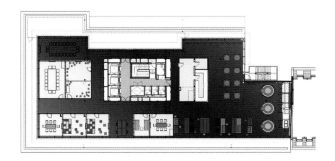

ENGINE

The challenge was to create an environment that would appeal to many tastes while respecting individual brand identities. A dramatic element is the floating auditorium at entrance level, designed for presentations. The "talking points" in the building include the seating pods on the fifth floor with Corian shells and Barrisol light ceilings where employees can interact in a series of conference and meeting rooms ranging in design, size and style. Imaginative solutions include 'mini auditorium' seating systems and a room clad entirely in cork (with matching cork stools) for quick temporary interactions.

Haymarket Hotel

Kit Kemp has fused modern and classical references in this landmark building, which was designed by the master architect John Nash. The lobby is a clean airy space featuring a stainless steel sculpture by Tony Cragg and large black and white paintings of the London skyline. The conservatory and library have their own particular style with handpicked antiques and objects as well as original paintings by a diverse range of modern artists. The vast and impressive Shooting Gallery, 18 meters long and five meters high, has walls covered in dramatic de Gournay wallpaper featuring jungle landscapes in grey sepia tones. It is furnished with an eclectic collection of furniture including 1970s lucite tables and lamps and pictures by Oliver Messel. Downstairs, the pool area is more bar than spa. The sleek swimming pool is edged in stone, surrounded by acres of grey oak and has a ceiling covered in hundreds of fiber-optic lights. Martin Richman has installed an ever-changing colorful light installation.

72 Rivington Street

72 Rivington Street, Shoreditch, houses design agency YCN. It includes a gallery area, library, shop, office, studios and roof terrace. The ground floor gallery is defined by irregularly shaped mobile objects; a playful kit of parts including plinths, vitrines, shelves, and steps configurable to the changing requirements of whatever is happening that day. The objects fit together like a three-dimensional jigsaw. Black chalkboard surfaces serve as special announcements canvases, playfully providing a solution to a practical problem. A concealed mirrored door leads upstairs where an elegant polypropylene coated plywood ribbon forms desk surfaces at a variety of levels, folding to create threshold archways within the space. Ready-made steel drawer units penetrate the shuttering ply plinth for storage and staggered plywood boxes with various widths of whiteboard door visually disintegrate the surface of the walls whilst also acting as an adaptable labeling system. A fun and flexible creative work environment.

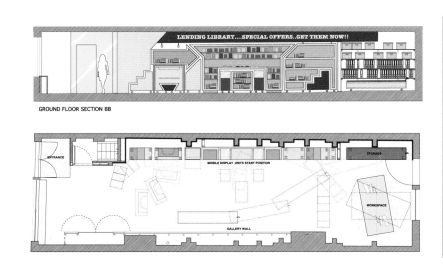

GROUND FLOOR SECTION BB

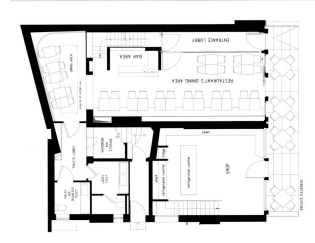

Delicatessen Shop Olivino

Olivino is a delicatessen shop complementary to the newly opened restaurant Olivomare, with which it shares the appealing aubergine coloured shop front as well as a graphic taste for its interiors. It is of rather small proportions, if only the part accessible to customers on its left side is considered. At the entrance a staircase protected by a full height frameless glazed partition leads to the storage in the basement and is adjacent to a perimetrical wall entirely covered by a cladding finished with a double layer (white and black) of thick opaque laminated plastic, on which has been engraved a decorative pattern of variously oriented bottles and glasses.

The Zetter

Pivotal to the design of The Zetter is a new five-story atrium, around which walkways to all of the 59 rooms are situated. This atrium allows light and air to flood into the building, naturally illuminating and ventilating the circulation and public space on every floor and reducing the hotel's dependency on artificial ventilation systems. This principle is carried into each guestroom where the new sliding sash windows allow guests to ventilate each room naturally and controllably. The use of water has been carefully considered in the building. A borehole was drilled directly below the hotel to tap into large water reserves trapped in the chalk strata under London.

Manchester Square

SHH was asked to create a "high impact, 21st century office interior with a strong personality" with more in common with a gentlemen's club than a traditional office space. Although the property was made up of a classic (and Grade II listed) Georgian townhouse, the client was very open to a sense of contrast for the scheme, favoring a highly contemporary treatment. The generous per capita space was exploited with very individual rooms with differing personalities, achieved with varied color saturation and differing degrees of formality. Bespoke lighting and art underline the individuality of this project, including two statement contemporary chandeliers, made to order and designed by Michael Anastassiades and four wall projections by artist Hugo Dalton. The artist produced a series of sketches of ballet dancers morphed with floral motifs, which were then laser-cut onto stainless steel discs and fitted into ceiling-mounted projectors.

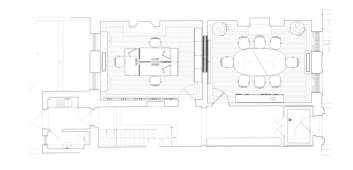

Modular Lighting Showroom

RHE took advantage of his client's proclivity for the extraordinary to design this showroom. The open space of the original showroom was broken into smaller spaces by the introduction of six sculptural walls, all of different heights and forms, custom made using fiberglass with a shiny gel coat. These walls wrap, slice and enclose the areas, creating a narrative journey, enhanced by the hi-tech theatrics of Modular's lighting and dimming systems. RHE then took these walls and punctured them with a veritable menagerie of animal cut-outs, an idea sparked by the exquisite photographs in Modular's cult catalogue. These apertures allow the viewers a small glimpse into other zones of the showroom.

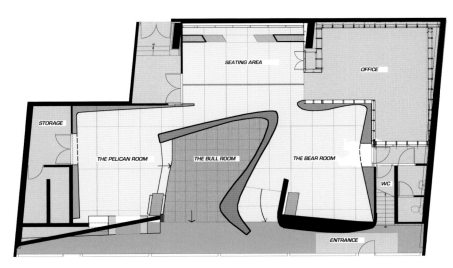

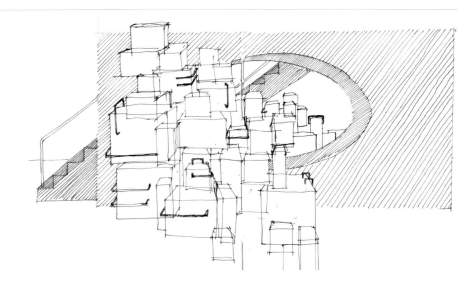

Sneaker Department, Dover Street Market

London's legendary Dover Street Market has just revamped its basement by giving it a clean new look. As part of this transformation, Faye Toogood was asked to design and install a new sneaker department that could sit alongside Rai Kawakubo's personal vision. Faye wanted to create a raw but elegant space and chose to work with plaster, concrete, copper and rope. She was not aiming for a glossy, highly finished look but rather to reveal the nature of the materials themselves and their inherent imperfections, or inherent beauty. A series of stacking building blocks made from plaster were designed to help re-configure and change the way the space is used. The purity of the white plaster contrasts with the roughness of the rendered concrete walls and a series of interlocking copper pipes provide a strong industrial element to the design as well as providing plinths for the more practical purpose of displaying multi-coloured sneakers. The space is lit by bulbs on rope by Christien Meindertsma.

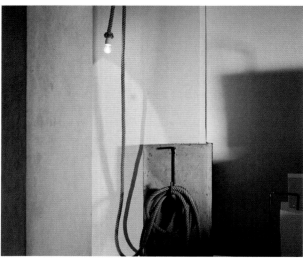

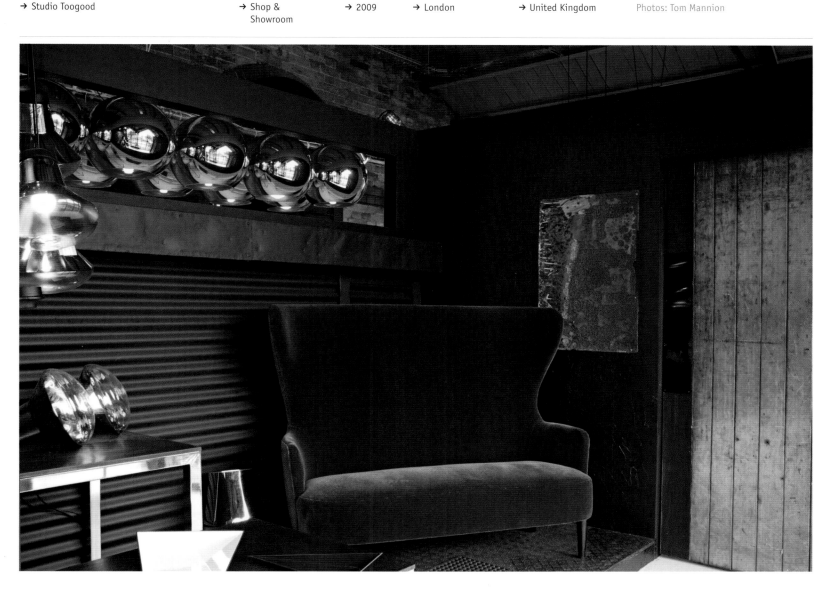

Tom Dixon Shop

The new London Shop is part of Tom Dixon's new office complex in Portobello Dock, Ladbroke Grove. The interior showcases Faye Toogood's distinctive approach to design that disregards convention in favor of something altogether more brave, joyous and impulsive. Over 1800 square feet, the new Shop permanently displays the full Tom Dixon collection alongside Tom Dixon by George Smith upholstery pieces. The showroom is conceived as a stage set representing Tom Dixon's industrial aesthetic, with windows and walkways linking individual room sets within the warehouse. Visitors can explore the showroom by peering through these windows and doors into each room. The design is inspired by materials used in Dixon's designs, including copper, cast iron and wood.

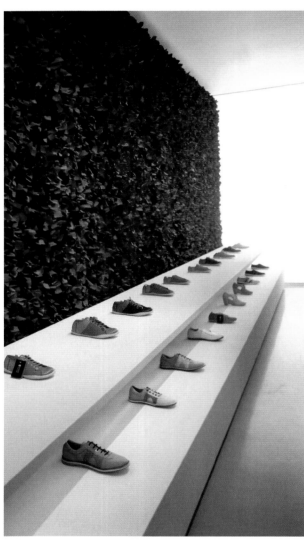

Camper Store

Plants, flowers and other elements found in the natural world can please us with their ever-changing appearance. The idea for this new store, which incorporates such beautiful and miraculous principles of nature, is derived from the installation presented in New York in 2007, where approximately 30,000 sheets of tissue paper were used to cover the entire space and create a scene reminiscent of a snowscape. On designing the new store concept for Camper, the leading Spanish shoe brand, Tokujin Yoshioka contemplated how to create a new style by embracing both Camper's brand identity and his own original design concepts, following on from Camper's previous collaborations with distinctive international creators. The red flower blossoms with an emphasis on the corporate color are in full bloom in the store. It expresses the nature of the tissue installation on a more permanent basis.

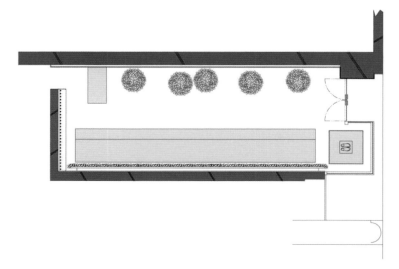

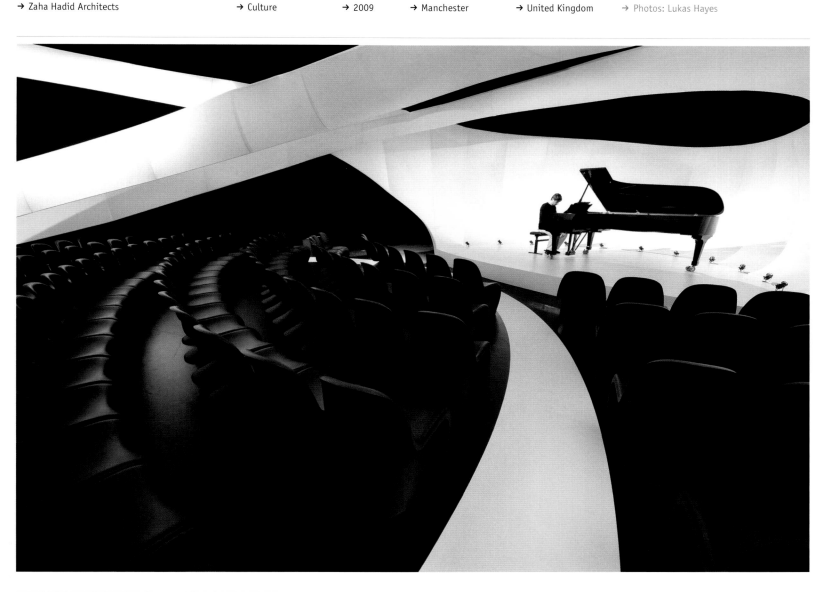

JS Bach Chamber Music Hall

This unique chamber hall was specially designed to house solo performances of the work of Johann Sebastian Bach. A voluminous ribbon swirls within the room, carving out a spatial and visual response to the intricate relationships of Bach's harmonies. As the ribbon careens above the performer, cascades into the ground and wraps around the audience, the original room as a box is sculpted into fluid spaces swelling, merging, and slipping through one another. The ribbon consists of a translucent fabric membrane articulated by an internal steel structure suspended from the ceiling. The surface of the fabric shell undulates in a constant but changing rhythm as it is stretched over the internal structure. While enhancing the acoustic experience of the concert, the ribbon simultaneously defines a stage, an intimate enclosure, and passageways. It exists at a scale in which it is perceived as both an object floating in a room and as a temporal architecture that invites one to enter, inhabit and explore.

Carton House Hotel

Representing a new breed of luxury hotel, Carton House Hotel successfully combines an original paladin 18th century mansion with an impressive hip new 147-bedroom hotel wing. The design concept included the conversion of the existing house to be incorporated into the hotel, as well as the construction of new elements including a bedroom wing, a large ballroom, conference facilities, a spa and leisure center, as well as extensive support and in-house activities for the hotel employees. The architectural solution discreetly integrates the new hotel into the landscape, connecting the 21st century wing with the 18th century house and outbuildings via lightweight glass elements and corridors.

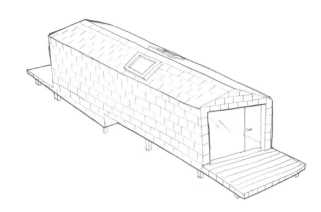

Kent Chalet

The beach chalet pared down to the essentials: eat, drink, sleep, and view. London-based Danish designer Nina Tolstrup of Studiomama wanted a weekend retreat to escape life in Shoreditch, so she bought a small plot of land on the shore in Whitstable, a seaside town located in northeast Kent. The 36 square meter structure is located in the middle of a row of 25 tiny cottages, sits on galvanized steel stilts, and is clad with cedar shingles. The interior is sawn softwood; and the focus is the sea view. A sleeping loft accommodates Tolstrup and her husband, and her two children sleep in bunks.

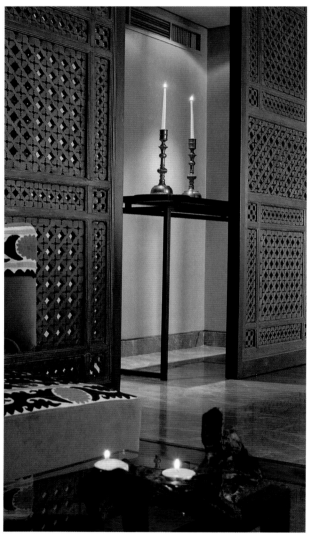

Apartment With A Nile View

A private apartment is located in a large apartment block in Cairo, with a panoramic view of the Nile and the city below. The concept was to transform this conventional space into a place with a unique identity. This apartment was designed for a client with quite specific lifestyle needs; it is the home of a well traveled and busy professional man. It incorporates an interest in cultural architectural references and the necessity to accommodate a modern European lifestyle. Here a fusion of both cultures creates a new design language, a language which forms a balance between functional demands and the esthetical experience of the apartment.

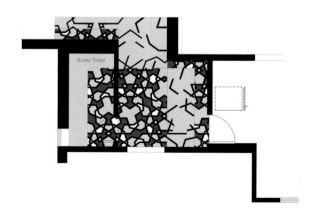

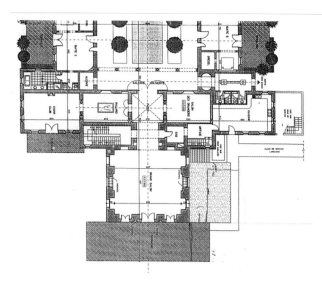

Ksar Char-Bagh

The library features two sculptures and paintings. The courtyard pays homage to the Alhambra with its carved plasters, marbles, murmuring water and perfumed scents and the spectacular swimming pool as a huge basin surrounded by giant palm trees. Everything here is involved in the architecture, the materials and the light, a labyrinth of salons, corridors, staircases, high vaulted and painted ceilings, terraces and large windows opening on the gardens. The walls are made of marble powder with pigments and clay, painted plasters with white and earthy colors, the floors of stones, and desks with a touch of marble.

303

Bahrain World Trade Center

The Bahrain World Trade Center (BWTC) stands as an icon of sustainable design and includes the first installation of large-scale wind turbines into a commercial building. As well as offering 50 floors of premium office space, the BWTC also houses the boutique shopping facility MODA Mall, providing nearly 16,500 square meters of high end retail space. The shopping mall has been designed in keeping with the iconic nature of the BWTC, incorporating sweeping staircases, impressive glass domed courtyards and relaxing water features. Inspired by a distinctly nautical theme, each tower of the BWTC is visually anchored to the ground by a curved concertina.

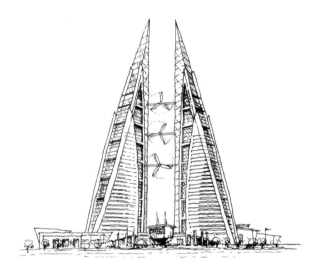

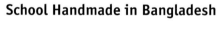

School Handmade in Bangladesh

The entire project includes the building of a school as a representative public building, the building of two-story houses as a model for rural living as well as the design of the outside areas. The ultimate goal is to gain and disseminate knowledge and information for optimising the use of locally available resources. The improvement of the building techniques is as important as the economic aspects and the creation of a regional identity. In order to create jobs and to build up a capacity for producing sustainable architecture it is essential to include local workers in the building process. Training through "learning by doing" should help the local craftsmen to improve the standards and condition of the rural housing in general.

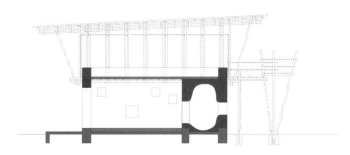

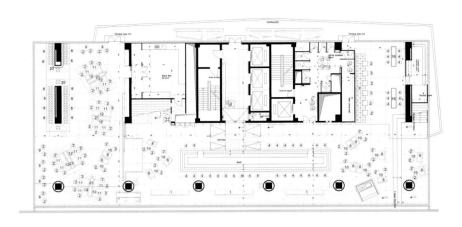

Klubb Rouge

A decorative lighting creation with very unusual technical and aesthetic characteristics – 650 irregular Murano glass spheres, blown and shaped by hand and arranged in four rows with 22 cascades each for a total of 88 (in reference to Chinese numerology in which 8 is a lucky number). The exclusive hand working of the glass is accompanied by state of the art lighting technology – 8,000 LEDs and 250 spotlights powered by fiber optics provide diffuse atmospheric lighting. With their different intensities and transparencies according to the thickness of the glass, the spheres are modeled individually in appropriate sizes and shapes to create a play of perspectives and reflections, shimmering like fluctuating bodies along a soft wave. Throughout the vibrant length of the work, the spheres are mirrored in a steel plate which reflects and expands the chromatic effect from top to bottom.

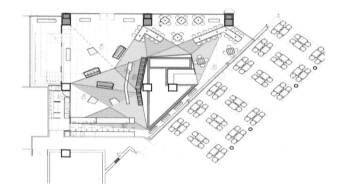

Fauchon Beijing

Fauchon is a large retail design project that is spreading gradually throughout the world. It is presented as the "house of luxury culinary goods". Originally, Fauchon was established in Paris, on the Place de la Madeleine, in 1886. Quickly it became the most exclusive place for food in Paris. Now, its products are sold throughout the world in more than 400 places. The new "house" is divided into three main rooms. The gold room is the bakery, the silver room is the restaurant and the black and white room, the largest of all three, is the fine grocery store. The entrance lobby and circulation spaces are pink.

Eric Paris Salon

The remodeling of Eric Paris Salon started with the need for a connection between the newly acquired second floor space, which will house the hair cutting stations in the future, and the existing salon entrance, retail space and reception located on the ground floor. GRAFT introduced a continuous fluid staircase, linking these two spaces together and creating a vertical 'cat walk'. This main vertical circulation becomes the central spine which branches off and connects the different functional areas throughout the salon. The manicure and pedicure stations are set off as galleries for clients to admire the other roaming customers.

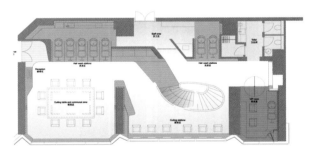

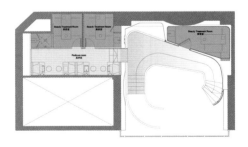

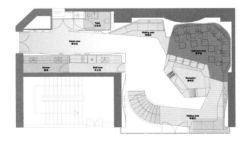

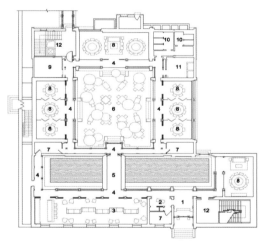

Beijing Whampoa Club

Beijing Whampoa Club is situated in a reconfigured traditional Chinese courtyard house amidst a cluster of modern high rises on Beijing's financial street. Upon entering the restaurant and traveling through the corridors, one is surrounded by a completely white space. Solemn and serene, the purity of the space draws attention to the Chinese construction details rather than obscuring it with colorful imagery, as in history. The white corridors provide rest for the eyes before their transition to the various decadent destinations. In contrast with the white corridors, the bar is all black. Here, the traditional Chinese screen has been replaced and re-interpreted with a custom-made pattern.

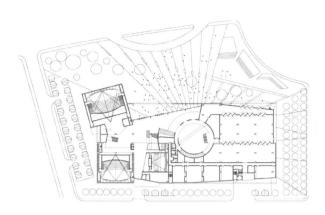

China National Film Museum

The China National Film Museum in Beijing came into being as a joint venture of RTKL and the Beijing Institute of Architecture Design and Research, and stands as a tribute to the history and accomplishments of the Chinese film industry. It was part of a ten-monument cultural improvement program initiated by the city for the 2008 Summer Olympics. The design applies a synthetic approach, offering a design language which expresses local experience and maximizes self-sustained integrity, flexibility and environmental friendliness. The museum totals 30,000 square meters and includes exhibition halls, film technology and temporary exhibits, administrative facilities, an IMAX, a 4D theater and a multi-function hall.

Felissimo

Everything used to display the clothes is reduced to pits and plug-ins. Up to 1000 pits are arranged on the walls and on the floor. All furniture and decorations like clothes-hangers, tables, cabinets, flower vases and posts are inlaid with steel tube plug-ins which can freely be applied to the pits. The pits are connected to the power supply, which makes it possible for lighting fixtures to work. The plug-in of the circular light tube is used to rotate the face-in plug-ins by 90 or 180 degrees; the manner of the node is simple and clear. As a result, the space quality is greatly improved by simply altering the way finished products are laid out and displayed.

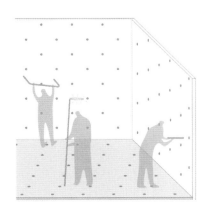

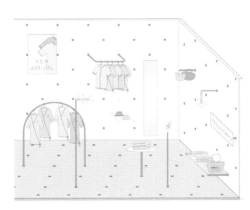

Kid's Republic

Kid's Republic in Beijing is composed of an event room on the ground floor and a picture book store on the first floor. The event room is a rainbow space connected by 12 colored rings with different perimeters. Activities like story telling sessions and animation shows are periodically held here. The section gaps in the floor, wall and ceiling are processed as illumination or display cases, as well as a stage and auditorium. Seven colored ribbons begin in the hall and continue up the stairs to the bookstore. On the first floor, the children can enter a world of picture books.

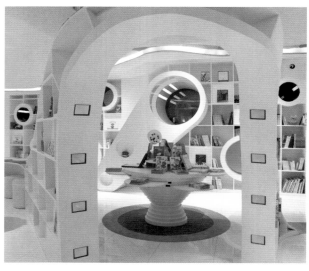

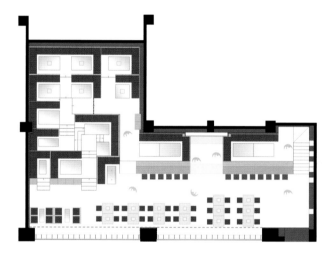

Steps Café

The main feature of the futuristic interior is a very long projection screen: 1.9 x 17.3 meters. The seats are arranged in theater like steps and balconies in order to ensure that all consumers in different position can see the projections. The images created by VJs are projected on the screen by 6 projectors. The light and shadows from the screen in turn reflecting on the armrests, desks, chairs, cups and trays, changes the visions inside the space. The topic of the square to be found everywhere corresponds to the image of the pixel-the smallest unit of the image. The squares with different sizes from 200 mm x 200 mm to 800 mm x 800 mm were used for example on grounds, walls and ceilings.

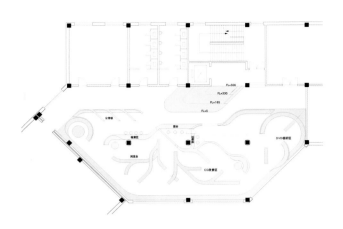

Cultural Exchange Center Branch in Changchun

One corner of the Changchun Library of Jilin Province is a culture exchange center founded by the International Exchange Foundation that is devoted to the introduction of Japanese culture to Chinese people. Changchun, a city with an extremely high percentage of Japanese language learning, is a city that really loves Japanese cartoons and popular music. In order to create a relaxation space with easy access to visitors for party use or personal ease, SAKO Architects designed it with a focus on trees. All designs in the room are characteristic of a forest, attractive and charming, with people seated or leaning on the branches and hiding between them.

Red Box Karaoke

Various tones of gray and magenta were chosen as the key colors to provide a darkened envelope and to create the right mood for singing pop songs. Glossy and matte finishes were applied on ceilings, walls and floors in different zones to create illusion and mysteriousness. The corporate color of hip magenta tone was superimposed and washed on various gray surfaces by glowing room directory or concealed lighting. Spatial rhythm was created by the transformation of intangible musical elements (e.g. rhythm, tempo and pitch) into tangible spatial elements of geometries (lines and circles) in various treatments of the envelopes of karaoke rooms of different sizes.

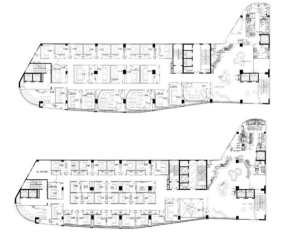

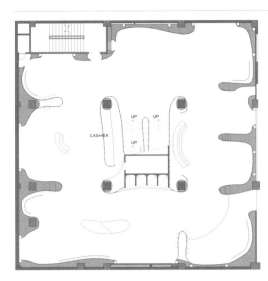

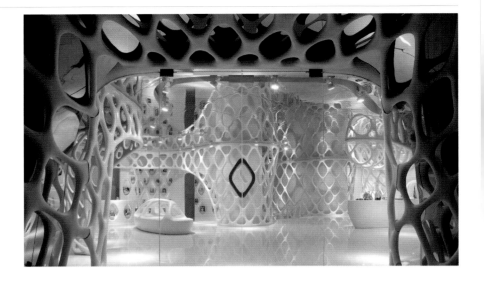

Romanticism 2

Instead of defining space with elements such as floors, walls or ceilings, this concept was based on the idea of clothing space with a skin, able to bridge the functions of space partition and furniture, trying to express the idea of "Clothes-like-space" or "Space-like-clothes". The organic net extends across the entire space, being absorbed from the façade into inner rooms and then changing its shape smoothly until the first floor wraps it up. Close on one side to the stairs, the net expands to the basement. The net changes its shape, becoming partitions, counter, chairs, furniture and even railing. Acting as a third skin, the net has a similar organic structure, of "bone", "flesh" and "skin". Mirror-finished stainless surfaces were used in the ceiling of the first floor, creating a visual impact, with illumination overflowing from the low ceiling. Objects reflected on these surfaces appear to be in the water, simulating a reversion effect of a water surface above the visitors' head.

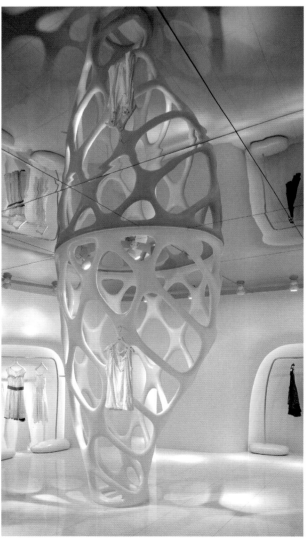

APM – Millennium City

The concept and design of this destination center could very well become the norm for cities facing space issues, a 24-hour culture and the need for "third space" – something in-between work and home. APM is more than just a mall; it is a breath of fresh air. Covering an area of 60,000 square meters, with 52 escalators, 18 restaurants and six cinema screens, APM is a destination specifically targeted at the youth and with a strong regenerative mission for its surrounding neighborhood. Its architectural design creates strong links with existing transport networks, provides ample and dramatic event space, and creates a vivid and expressive stage-set that celebrates the vitality of commerce.

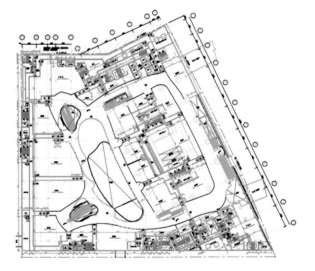

Bossini

This major brand revamp exercise in association with Alan Chan Design was first implemented in Bossini's 10,000 square meter flagship store. The redesign, which was rolled out across all shops in Hong Kong and South-East Asia, greatly enhanced the shopping experience by providing a stronger brand identity and a clearer display strategy, which succeeded in not only retaining existing customers but also appealing to a wider customer base.

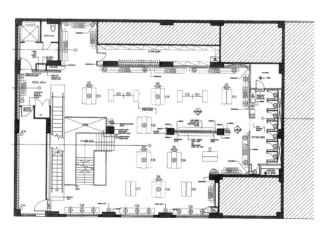

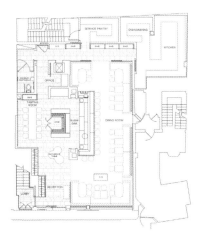

East Asian Games

The exhibition for the East Asian Games (EAG) was created for the Sports Federation & Olympic Council of Hong Kong to promote public awareness about the 5th East Asian Games which were held in Hong Kong in 2009. It uses bold primary colors to delineate display areas which are heralded by arches cantilevering into the open space above the badminton courts. In addition, a series of light boxes with powerful images of renowned Hong Kong athletes emphasize the content and route of the exhibition.

HKJC, OMP Happy Valley

The Hong Kong Jockey Club wanted to offer their staff a genuinely new facility that balanced healthy living, training, information access, and relaxation. The guiding philosophy was to integrate knowledge, health and fitness in a corporate environment. The result was OMP, or "Our Meeting Place", which comprises a modern canteen with a specially devised healthy menu, a fitness center, a library and a music corner. The resulting design emphasizes a casual, contemporary ambience that helps to enhance the employees' sense of belonging. All of these are contained in a three-story rectangular space with each floor characterized by its own distinct color scheme.

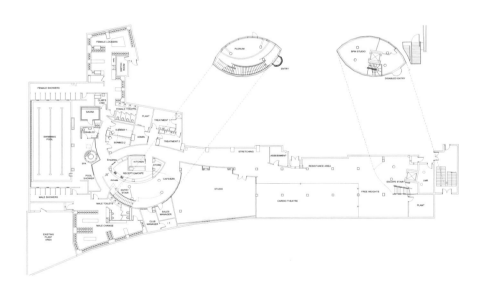

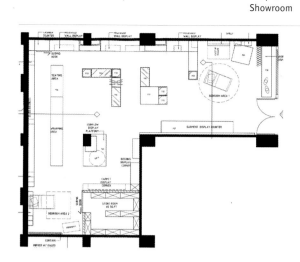

Kaloo Prince Building

For this truly international project, Axiom Oval Partnership was asked by the international French retailer of soft toys and baby items in around 35 countries to create a design concept and implement it across stores worldwide. A distinctive retail environment embodying the company's brand values of "love, care and happiness" was created and successfully implemented in their Paris, Munich, Madrid, Istanbul, Tahiti, La Réunion, and Tokyo stores. Entering into the second stage of the worldwide project, through a different form of design, the shop located in Prince Building carries a stronger message.

Boutique Office

Barrie Ho Architecture Interiors has created a boutique style gallery office which is reserved for multi-functions such as exhibitions and cocktail events and is equipped with multi-lighting levels catered for different events. The inclined black textural tile wall intensifies the strong-sense perspective towards a reception counter, where Asian style settings are placed as a waiting area, creating a noble and graceful area. The Directors' Rooms are conceived as "Glass Boxes" along the Hall of Fame and are elevated for accessible storage, embodying the multi-function concept. In between the two elevated "Glass Boxes", a peaceful and luxurious VIP lounge performs as an accented space for visitors.

Second Floor Plan

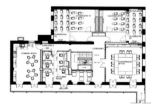

SKH Ming Hua Theological College

This project is the restoration of the 110-year-old Ming Hua Theological College. The design styles and materials were chosen to fit the project's original style. Spaces for classrooms, chapel and conference room were redesigned and restructured for the best use of space. The veranda, windows, staircases, all the doors and the main entrance were revamped for the best aesthetics, comfort and practicality. Furnishings were all chosen to match the historical architectural features of the building. Concealed lighting was employed to enhance the character and atmosphere without disturbing the original outlook and its unique style.

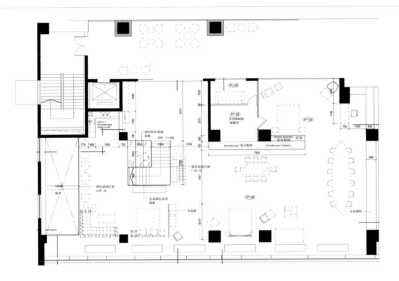

Zstore

The designer here tactfully connects reality wirh design, and makes the 743 square meter show room into a fashion furniture gallery space. The two floors of the store are designed with square French windows, the upper of which is decorated with different brands of outdoor art posters to attract the attention of passersby. Walking into the store, visitors are confronted with a display of furniture which breaks the traditional crowded display in a furniture store. In addition, the display shelves made from lamp-posts are attractive, displaying various artistic seats, just like art galleries.

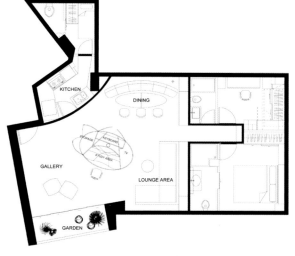

360° Apartment

Johnny Wong and Miho Hirabayashi of FAK3 have created a home in Hong Kong for Joanne Ooi, creative director of Shanghai Tang, which took the concept of open multi-functional spaces to a whole new realm. Wong and Hirabayashi have developed an iconic elliptical entertainment cabinet that can rotate 360 degrees and sits as the central focus of the apartment. On its two longer sides, it houses a set of keyboards and a customised study desk; the two shorter sides accommodate storage and a television. Fitted with industrial strength bearings that can support up to two bons, the walnut wooden cabinet rotates with the push of just one finger.

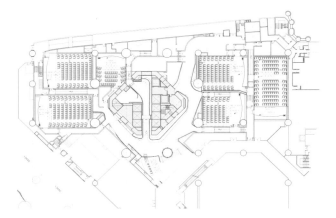

AMC Pacific Place

James Law made this cinema a programmatic building for his Cybertecture. He fuses luxury and astute technology in state-of-the-art architecture. For example, the ticketing box is no longer enclosed in a conventional glass box, but is more akin to a modern sculpture or a chic hotel lobby, protruding outwards to skillfully incorporate the ticket dispensing technology. The walls comprise sculptural, organic shapes molded together to form a U-shaped corridor; the aerodynamic ceiling has a metallic coating witch carries a river-like pattern throughout the foyer of the cinema. The cinema's design has been configured so that from the moment patrons arrive, they are transported to a totally new experience.

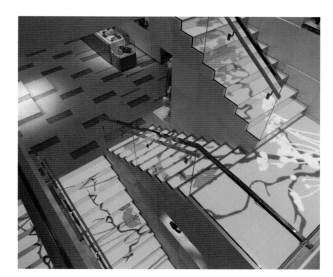

Louis Vuitton Flagship

The store is accessed through two entry points, from the street and from the shopping center levels. The main stair volume, designed as if carved out of a solid block of stone, organizes the project by connecting three distinct levels. The sandblasted glass treads of the stair feature built-in LED panels containing video images on each walking surface, including video representing an airport arrivals/ departures board to connect with the busy Hong Kong traveler. Customers can experience these video images individually with each step. Customers at ground level can also view the reflected images from the mirror on the ceiling.

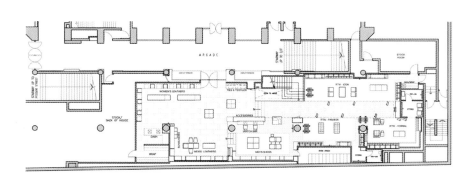

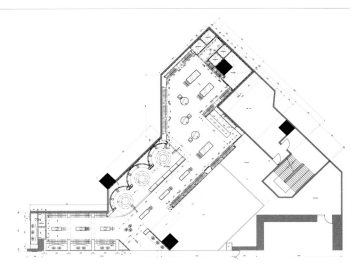

i.t in Hong Kong

This project is for the interior design of the number 1 multi-brand shop in Hong Kong in trendiness and in business. It is the renovation project of the shop designed seven years ago based on the concept of "the future". Since the shop contains highly stylish products from all over the world, the designer tried to produce the design concept by creating a modern feel and an easy-to-enter atmosphere with the maintenance of the high quality function. The theme that the designer conceived was "the classical modern style". To that end, the designer emphasised originality by using materials creating especially for the shop, through ordering custom-made wallpaper and using a carpet in the original pattern.

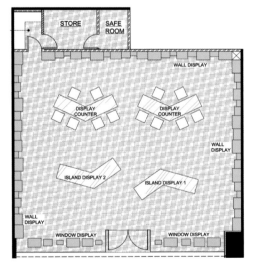

DJS

DJS is a new jewellery label launched by Chinese Arts & Crafts selling diamond and jade. It is a branding exercise to offer new retail experience of a jewellery store targeted at a middle class consumer group in the local competitive market. The interior & C.I. design strategy adopted was to make use of the common natures/chemical structures of the stones and cut shape "facets" of diamond and jade to generate a unique identity for the brand. To achieve this, the interior design made use of the metaphor of interpreting the retail space as a glowing gemstone to contain the two different types of prestigious merchandises for the customer to explore.

La Rossa

Stylish red and pure white are the skeleton of the design direction. Flower graphics around the home form a very warm atmosphere for this three-bedroom sea view unit. A red television cabinet acts like a red carpet, to serve as a foil to a contrasting tree wall. This makes this square living room a romantic place. A tree-like bookshelf in the study is not only functional, but also become a focus of the unit. Its gray square boxes and big red translucent flower on the door create a dramatic contrast. In the master bedroom, bedding, wallpaper and the wardrobe doors are covered with flowers. This continues the floral theme of the whole design.

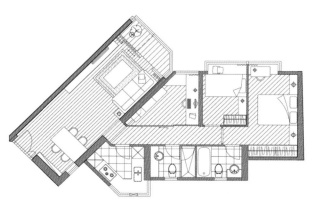

Mangrove West Coast

To generate a strong impression for all visitors, the designer chose "flower" as the theme of this flat. Floral graphics and patterns can be found everywhere, on walls, glasses and accessories. The fresh feeling is reinforced by the bright red and white color combination. Red cushions, chairs, and artwork become the focus of the flat. Flower graphics create shadows and add layers to the plain wall. Bird graphics in the corridor also act as a guide to the bedrooms. The "flower" continues in bedrooms on beddings, artworks and wall graphics. They create a refreshing and warm atmosphere.

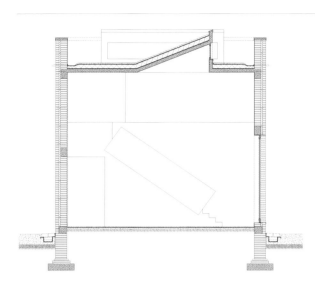

Brick House

This project is the evolution from a prototype of a local courtyard house, where the layout of two brick houses establishes the interesting relationship with the surrounding landscape. The red bricks produced in the nearby fields are still used as the main structure and construction materials. Three different textures of brick skin were used for the façade, where an interlocking pattern leaves perforations between bricks, producing shadows along wall. Arranged in rectangular patches and punctuated by the occasional portal or window, the geometric pattern of brick skin, along with the openings, creates a surface of abstract geometric shapes, reflecting the opening logic of elevation.

Sato Restaurant

This project was for a Japanese family restaurant group to open its first Chinese branch in Shanghai and to start its branding and design its space. This restaurant group already operates at 217 locations in Japan. Primarly, the designers wanted the restaurant to be accessible for ordinary Shanghai people in their daily lives by providing food at reasonable prices and good service. In addition, the designers valued an open air atmosphere, so that passersby felt invited to step into the restaurant. For this reason, the designers worked under the theme of "Consistent Art" in order for further projects to be able to deploy the same style and quality after their success in Shanghai.

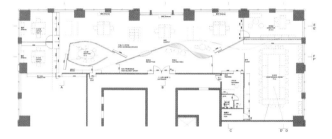

Swissnex

Originally the idea was to open the ceiling to gain more height; the room height was 2.4 meters. But the canals, cables and the huge air conditioners had taken up almost all ceiling space. The strategy became to make the space higher only where it was possible, and all ventilation in and outtakes could be hidden in inner sides. The interior is divided into two spaces, public space and private working space. The two parts permeate into each other. There is a curved partition wall in between, the public side is in Swiss red, and the office side in calm white; the curve floats and shapes a waiting space or a discussion corner, and continues to a meeting at the end of the space.

Metropolitan Chic

For this project, the use of design and materials is controlled and the spaces are separated clearly. The hallway divides the two sides of the space. The living room faces the kitchen, and the master bedroom the guest room or the study room (the small room is either for use by guests or as a study). Extra decoration was avoided in this case. The wall is embedded with steel bars creating a strong contrast of materials and details of design; CDs are hidden in the spaces inside. Spacious visual effects of lines, uneven surface and lighting are used on the ceiling to separate spaces.

Muse Club

Muse is a club that occupies three different spaces overlooking an atrium in the newly redeveloped Tong Le Fang factories in Shanghai. In a neighborhood where new nightclubs abound, Muse had to differentiate itself by asserting an architectural identity through inventing a spatial experience unlike all the others. Drama here is achieved not simply by appliqué or ornamentation, but an experiential theater that is at once monumental and sensual. The insertion of a cocoon takes center stage both physically and metaphysically, serving an array of functions in terms of spatial organisation, yet always acting as a reminder of the transformation that every club-goer secretly desires.

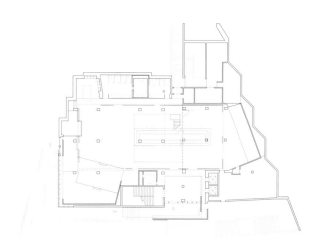

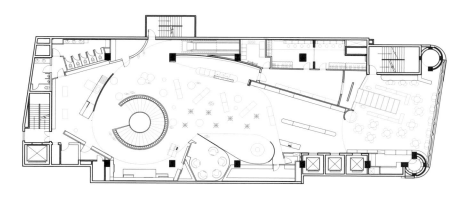

Barbie Café

The flagship store holds the world's largest and most comprehensive collection of Barbie dolls and licensed Barbie products. The design encompasses Barbies of the past, present and future. For the façade the architects combined references to product packaging, decorative arts, fashion and architectural iconography to create a modern identity for the store, expressing Barbie's fashion sense and history. The central feature is a three-story spiral staircase enclosed by eight hundred Barbie dolls – everything literally revolves around Barbie. To accommodate the different ages and atmospheres, a simple and striking palette was chosen: black lacquer, white accents, pink upholstery and curtains. Throughout the retail areas, the architect plays with the scale differences between dolls, girls and women.

Park Hyatt

Located on the top floors of the 492 meter high 101 floor-high Shanghai World Financial Center, which is also known as the 'Vertical Complex City', the Park Hyatt Shanghai towers above the Lujiazui business district in Pudong. Designed by Tony Chi, the hotel radiates an exclusive ambiance. From its dramatic entrance hall on the ground floor up to the reception on floor 87 and the Sky Residence on the 93rd floor, the hotel offers the perfect setting for business travelers and vacationers. On the 85th floor, the hotel offers its guests a water temple and an infinity pool next to a Tai-Chi square and a wellness studio. The Sky Residence on the 93rd floor is the world's highest restaurant and event venue. Each of the 174 guestrooms and suites of the hotel offers a panoramic view of the Huangpu river and Pudong.

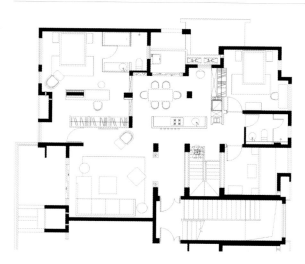

Natural Organic Space

The central body line and the horizontal active line on the ichnography separate the ground floor into a few main areas; in one half is the living room and in the other half a bedroom. The designers did not want any obstacles to obscure the view from the public area and tried to expand the vision of this area to its ultimate size. The doorway extends to the end of the hallway in order to combine with the dining area and move its extension to connect with the kitchen. The lower side of the television wall in the living room is left with an open hole, a breathing tunnel in the visual prospect that connects the living room with the study area in the master bedroom.

Café Mochamojo

The designers had the idea that in essence, the experience hinged on period evocation. By reorienting the entire concept towards the exuberant, visually exciting and easily recognizable 1970s, they drew from retro references and interpreted them in a contemporary context. By researching art, graphics, color palettes, finishes, furniture, wall treatments, tiles, window dressings, interior styles, lighting and more, a library of sorts was created to be referenced for inspiration. A collage of Roy Lichtenstein pop art clad on adjacent walls defined the access to a faux fur lined alcove that exuded excess and decadence of the age. From retro washroom tiles to cladding laminate on the outdoor fascia, the intensity of the consistent design quality is maintained.

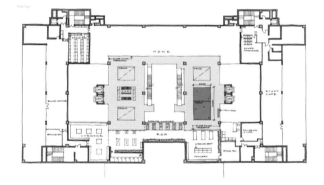

Shoppers Stop, Rajouri Garden

India's retail industry has been enhanced further by a new store format, developed by JHP. The consultancy's Indian client, Arvind Brands, has just opened a discount fashion store, "Mega Mart", in Chennai. The 2,790 square meter store is a new strategy for Arvind and will provide customers with an entry point for brands in a contemporary department store style environment. The store is spread over two floors, and as well as men's, women's and children's casual and smart clothing, it has a marketplace and a café. The project also involved JHP creating a new brand identity, mark and graphic communication suite within the store.

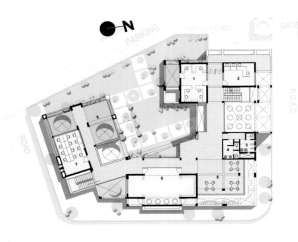

ITM School of Management

The concept is based on the principles of an Indian courtyard where the liveable spaces look into the semi shaded landscaped court and receive soft, diffused sunlight. There is a beautiful symphony of light and shadow and an interplay of textures and surfaces throughout the building, which accommodates a lot of transitional spaces. The context is ever present and the occupants of the Institute are encouraged to be a part of and accept this context on both the micro and macro level through the architecture of the building.

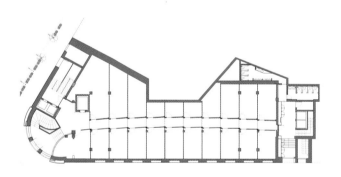

Jewel World

Jewel World is Mumbai's very first jewelry shopping precinct located in the heart of the diamond and gold trading markets – Zaveri Bazaar. After Pahlajani Developers won the bid for the legendary Cotton Exchange Building which is an exemplary example of Art Deco style from Mumbai, they sought to capitalise on the landmark structure's exceptional location, transforming it into a vibrant hub of business. When approached for the design of this to be iconic jewelry destination, Arris Architects were assigned demanding task – not merely to maximizse the retail footprint in a very tight structure but also offer the patrons a visual gratification never experienced before.

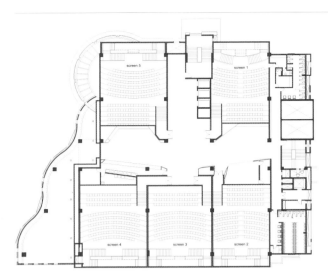

Fun Cinema Mumbai

The concessions for this cinema in Mumbai, the center of India's movie industry, are consciously crafted around the notion of materializing illusions. The attempt is made to amplify the experiences of these illusions by destabilizing the geometric form of a hexagon into a harmonious and functionally stable design which also accommodates the clients' functional requirements. The hexagonal partition acts as the focal point of the design, creating an ambience of a walk through an art exhibit. The location of recessed seating lobbies provides excellent vantage points for spectators, allowing them to appreciate the massive scale of the dynamic partition.

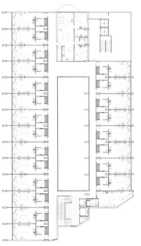
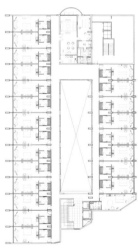

The Park Navi Mumbai

The brief for the public areas was to create a four star hotel with flexibility allowing weekday trade to convert to weekend tourist stays. Therefore, two free-form pods on the ground floor were designed containing the bar, the snug and back office. The orange plastered bar breaks out to address the terrace, while the reception/snug is clad in hand-made plaster jail work addressing the lobby and coffee shop. The bedrooms are characterized by their bamboo floors, teak furniture and brightly colored fabrics.

Cinemax-Mumbai

The designers created an undulating curvilinear ceiling that unified the entire space while connecting the low height areas to the higher height areas at the opposite end in a fluid seamless manner. This ceiling constructed of gypsum is punctuated by varying lengths of indirect light troughs that accentuate the undulating curvatures. The entire flooring of the cinema lobby is of yellow vitrified ceramic tile punctuated by varied lengths of black granite strips.

Fun Cinema Uttar Pradesh

The Fun Cinema in Lucknow is part of the Fun Republic Mall, also designed by Arris Architects. The design approach followed the two main goals of creating a breathtaking atmosphere and optimally utilizing the limited space. A visual vortex came into being with the help of wood surfaces which were broken into facets. Each facet was carefully calculated for maximum space utilization. Complex geometry of surfaces in the hall, along with the material's warmth, result in a noble, comfortable as well as inspiring atmosphere serving as a kind of corridor between the real life of the mall and the fantastic world of the movies.

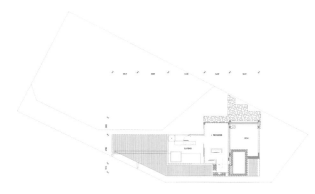

Biasa Boutique

Realized in 2007, in Jakarta, in the Kemang district, the project of the Biasa Showroom is grafted onto a confined and long lot and it is developed on four floors. The first two floors are Boutique while the upper two floors are for the Art Gallery. The main expressive point is the reinforced concrete staircase in the heart of the boutique. It is realized with a series of elements. These elements are profiles with a rectangular section folding up following a G shape. They have been realized on site in reinforced concrete in different heights following the height of the steps. The upper part of the G profile is the step of the staircase, while the lower one becomes the exhibition of the shop.

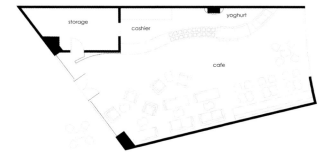

Blu Apple

The main issue for the design was to define a distinctive concept of how to offer frozen yoghurt in the very competitive Indonesian dessert market. The interior design of this café develops out of ice chunks floating in the air, some of which are melting down. White, back-lit slabs are suspended from the ceiling of the space, which is composed of a bar, seating area and storage facility. Colorful murals with phrases decorate the walls. The seating facilities are deliberately very informal with organically shaped chairs as well as sofas to fit in the concept of fluidity. The tables made of glass further accentuate the design idea by referring to ice.

Peres Peace House

Peace is a spiritual condition, an aspiration. The projection of the will into the future is also an expression of hope that our children and future generation will live in a better world. The designer conceived a series of layers, a building that represents TIME and PATIENCE in strata of alternating materials representing places that have suffered heavily. A stone basement raises the building and a meeting place leads via two long staircases to a place of rest, whose size and height, full of light from above, enables visitors to forget the troubles of the world, and fill them with the positive attitude that is necessary to meet and socialize with others.

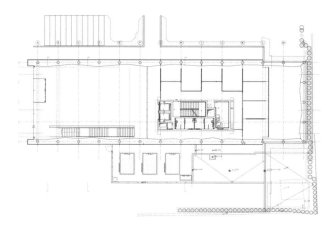

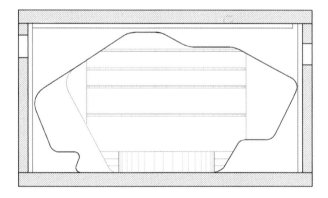

Barber Shop

Hair adheres to the gravity of earth with a dynamics of its own. These concepts were adapted for the interior design to create setting and atmosphere. The work posts and hair styling preparation areas were adjoined in one function: the barber work posts at the start merge into the hair styling preparation area. The process was divided into three stages; each one as a partition between spaces begins as a barber work post. A first partition ends as a hair wash post, the second as a sitting area for clients and the third as a secretary's post. Separated areas were thereby created between the barbers' posts.

Kindergarten in Ramat Hasharon

Situated in a satellite suburb of Tel Aviv, this kindergarten was created from the desire to apply to children's physical surroundings the educational principles that are at the foundation of its activities - respect and equality among children and the opportunity to play and explore new activities in intimate spaces. The design was inspired by Bauhaus concepts: simple and clean forms, long and open views throughout the project and horizontal and minimalist lines. This simplicity allows the children complete imaginative freedom in their environment. Finishing materials such as white plaster, exposed white masonry bricks and large windows complete the serenity of the design.

House O

This project is a weekend house for a couple, located on a rocky coast two hours out of Tokyo. The site is a rocky stretch facing the Pacific Ocean with an approach that slopes down to the water level. The characteristic of its plan, imagined like the branches of a tree, is a continuous one room. All the required spaces, entrance, living and dining area, kitchen, bed room, Japanese style room, study room and bathroom are arranged in this continuous room. Oriented in different directions, one can find various views of the ocean walking throughout the house. The living area, bedroom and bathroom each have a unique relation to the ocean. One could say that the house is akin to a walking trail along a coast.

House in Minamimachi 02

Designing a structure for an especially small plot of land involves unique considerations and challenges. Here, the building was made to slightly exceed its allotted coverage ratio, so each floor fluctuates in shape. The sections that slide out function as lighting design elements, bringing in the outside environment. The shape of each floor is designed according to its intended purpose, but always considering the importance of privacy in this dense urban area. By acknowledging the physical and legal restraints of a small plot, buildings can be created that possess a unique degree of freedom.

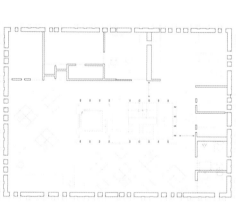

T-Clinic

In this project, the functional constraints of a clinic were set against the creative desires of the architects, who responded with innovative concepts. Instead of keeping places normally used to movement, such as elevator shafts or stairwells, closed, they have been opened up to be used as light wells, collecting light entering from above. Furthermore, much like a traditional Japanese lattice door, the placement of the structurally integral walls and apertures makes the interior difficult to see from the outside, while preserving a clear view of the outside from within, allowing for both functionality and an ideal level of privacy on each floor.

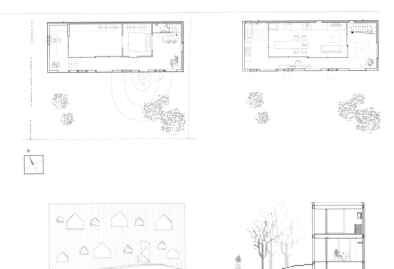

House in Jigozen

Built by the sea in an area prone to natural disasters, this family house presented challenges from the very beginning. A half-outdoor space allows the interior and exterior to flow together - it is at once a terrace, a veranda, an inside room and the outdoors and items normally found inside, such as books, paintings or a bath, can actively participate in this middle-ground. It also acts as a buffer to various natural phenomena, solving the seemingly contrary problems of "protection" and "openness" at the same time. The structure comprises wooden posts placed diagonally; creating a simple framework that does not stifle openness.

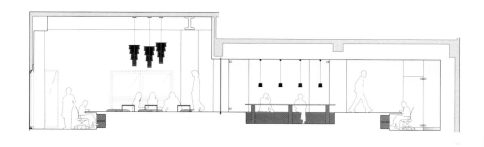

Kayak

Mixing elements from traditional Japanese architecture together with the fluid nature of an innovative web design firm created a 21st century work environment. A raised floor of tatami mats, with cushions and low tables for meetings, and with a horigotatsu (dug out) conference table are very different from the web industry's typical style and offer a comfortable working environment. The tatami floor is surrounded by a continuous wooden desk that seats up to 40 staff members. A meeting and entertaining space on the upper floor makes a more explicitly contemporary interpretation of tatami mats, with a shoes-off raised floor of richly colored sofa-like mats, where staff can sit, brainstorm or unwind.

Itsutsuya

Itsutsuya is a store selling various Japanese craft goods such as lacquerware. It is located at the center of the old commercial area in the castle town. The designers wanted to design the store to play an active role in the lives of the visitors to the town by combining it with the street. The floor planning was based on the following rules conceived: do not place distracting fixtures or furniture in the center area and install different fixtures and furniture in each area. The perspective of the store changes according to the point from which it viewed. The articles are displayed at various heights in the floor according to these principles. The perspective of the store changes according to the point from which it is viewed.

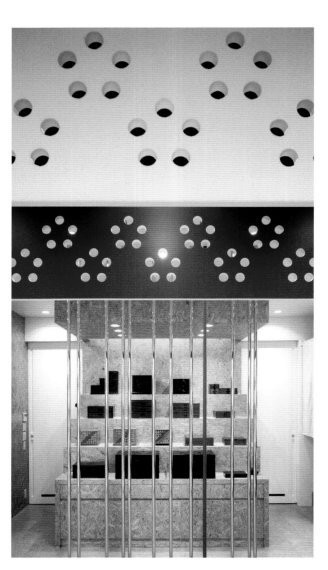

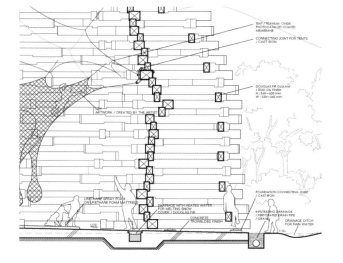

Woods of Net

This permanent pavilion, which was designed as a play area for children, was hand-knitted by the artist, Toshiko Horiuchi Macadam. The design is soft and reminiscent of a forest, creating a space similar to the outdoors, which is also safe for children. It is entirely composed of timber using techniques derived from ancient Japanese wooden temples combined with the most modern structural programs. The members are solely connected by dowel pins and wedges and each member has a different size in order to carry different loads from different directions. The structure has a projected life span of over 300 years.

arp hills

This beauty salon is located in a tranquil residential area of Saitama, the neighboring prefecture of Tokyo. Sliding "Tsuri-Shikiri", a ceiling-hung colored partitions system was designed to create private and semi-private space. Unlike fixed wall panels, this product is flexible enough to be easily relocated at any time. "Shikiri", meaning "dividing space with colors", allows the creation of spaces using colors not as decoration at the end of the design process, but as three-dimensional layers, which themselves work to build the space. The interior combines bright white with dynamic colors in an inviting fusion of atmospheres and emotions.

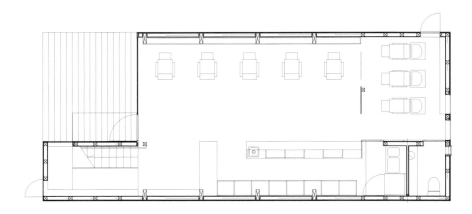

Immanoel

Immanoel is located in Kobe, a small port city in Japan on Osaka Bay in southern Honshu. The total area of this store is only 24 square meters. Though it is small, it contains many of charming goods to attract the female eye. Immanoel is a speciality store for jewelry and accessories. To reinforce the brand image, the emphasis was on chic and charming images. The designers conceived the shop as a jewelry box, with a black wall and tabletop to match the jewellery. The style is simple but the materials well chosen – black stainless steel, black flooring and so on.

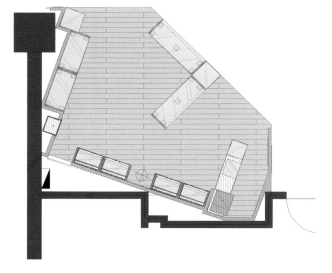

Lotus Beauty Salon

The seamless continuous space is realized by connecting the circular rooms with private space in order to resolve a feeling of closeness and oppression that is the concern of private rooms. The wall height of the rooms except the haircut spaces changes according to the sloped floor, while the function and of the wall tops changes seamlessly between a reception desk, waiting chairs, counters, and display boards. The designer had the joints by using the curving process. Though tangential lines and textures on walls and, floors usually create a sense of distance, removing these elements made the walls less oppressive.

Hotel Screen

Hotel Screen Kyoto is a study project in modernity. Smooth gray stones and large glass windows fit together in a series of overlapping planes, creating an irregular façade full of balconies and terraces. The reception area inside is clean, straight-lined and unadorned. Natural light floods through the area's floor-to-ceiling windows, providing a pleasant contrast to the all-white walls, sofas and tables, which in turn highlight the lobby's few strategically placed elements of color, most notably, an elaborate gold and sapphire chandelier and a lacquered red reception desk. A different artist or designer individually conceived each of Screen's 13 guestrooms and, as such, each has a completely distinctive feel.

House at Shimogamo

In order to meet the requirement of "to be able to see green from every room", the concept of "interface" was used here. The project utilises the typical Japanese apartment style — simple, spacious, and bright. The designers also used lots of bamboo and tatami. The house is multi-functional and accommodates a variety of spaces including a family room, Japanese room, study, guestroom, related sanitary rooms, kitchen and a pergola-clad moon-gazing terrace. The façade of the house is masked by a circular screen of frosted glass. At night, the whole house is illuminated by one large "Andon" or Japanese candle lamp, which also sheds warm light on the neighborhood.

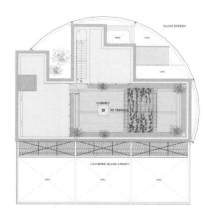

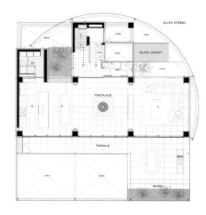

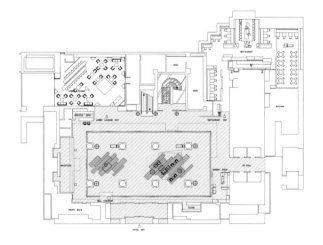

Ana Crowne Plaza Osaka

The project is full of dynamic, contemporary, and luxurious features. The lobby is designed to create a shift or dislocation: when entering the space, an impression of dynamism, elegance and refined modernity is generated by the combinations of special materials and lighting design. The rhythm of thin vertical louvers creates a metallic curtain that wraps the lobby space with a soft and warm light. The large pillars in the center are covered with mirrors, reflecting the metallic louver that seems to disappear within the space and emphasize the height of the lobby. It is a multi-layered space: behind the "metallic curtain", the different functions appear, including the check-in counter and access to the different restaurants and elevators.

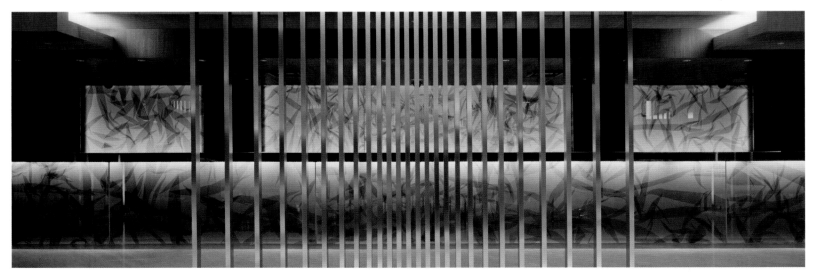

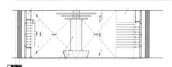

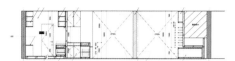

alook

The designer's reference for the design of the shop was the image of the recently-built airport. The process of visiting an optical shop, choosing glases, having an inspection an waiting to receive the finished glases demands a complex operation within the shop. The designer thought that the process is similar to the process at an airport where passengers check in, hand over the baggage, and wait for boarding. The recently built airport provides the facilities for this complex process comfortably and in a way that is easy for people to follow. It therefore seemed to be a useful model for this shop.

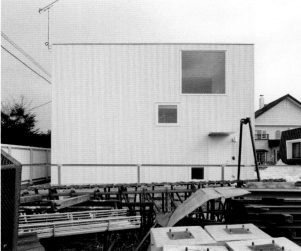

House of through

Located in the east of Hokkaido, this site is bordered by a house to the east and a garage to the north. A buffer zone was set at the north and south sides. The south buffer houses the master bedroom, guest room, entrance and spare room, while the bathroom and study are located in the north buffer. These buffers are punctuated with various openings allowing strong light into the interior, which is reflected by the floor onto the ceiling, filling the space with soft light. A large central pillar gently divides the living space while evoking a sense of strength.

Armani Ginza Tower

The boutiques in the tower were developed to offer the public a comfortable lounge area, outlined by a rug, a clothes-stand and a partition wall created by the interposition of a platinum-colored metal grid between two layers of extra-clear glass, which presents the various merchandise categories. The illuminated walls are lined with brushed glass and the transparent Plexiglas wall display cabinets create a pattern reminiscent of bamboo forest. Retro-illumination, positioned behind the laser-cut linear openings, creates luminous stripes in the wall and on the ceiling. The flooring is in reconstitute marble.

Sunaokuwahara

Essential to any high quality interior, the balace and combination of different materials has proved key to the concept. This project has created not only an engaging contrast of roughness and smoothness, matt and gloss, depth and transparency, permanence and ethereality; but has also formed clean divisions and intersections of coherent light spatial volumes. It is the exploration of the visual and physical boundaries of the environment that suggests a new language of the built domain within a commercial context. This affords visitors a subtly shifting environment as they journey throughout the shop; a series of dynamic views emerge and encourage exploration and anticipation.

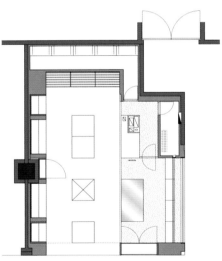

Studio Graphia Marunouchi

Studio Graphia Marunouchi is a general store selling high-quality design goods (stationery, bags, clocks, books and so on). The client is a company dealing with editorial design and stationery production. Close attention was paid to the main creative work of the client being developed in paper mediums. The interior is divided into a white side and a dark gray side. Indirect lighting develops a vague expanse on the left hand side. The down lights on the right hand side emit a narrow beam of light and emphasize shadow. The space on both sides is formed by a polygonal line of steel pipes. Two non-functional objects face each other an create a sense of disharmony.

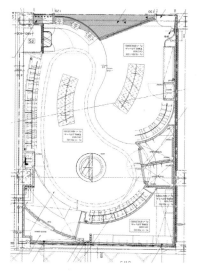

Citrus Notes

Usually, the interior design of "Citrus Notes" expresses nobleness in a relatively square plan with a theme of high quality glamour. However, considering the creative characteristics of Omotesando, this time the designer tried to produce a creative space that stimulates the imagination through using a custom-made rose motif print carpet for the floor, using the height differences to produce different viewpoints, and reassembling the chandelier designed by Angelo Mangiarotti in a glamorous style.

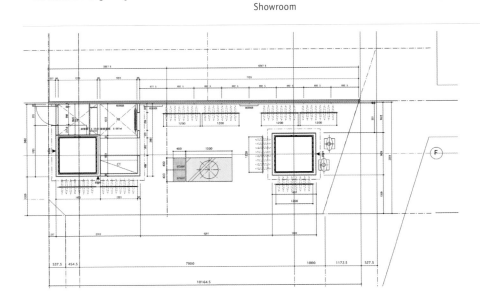

Royal Order

This is the first shop project of Royal Order, which is a mainstream jewelry brand from the American East Coast, breaking into the apparel business. The designers perceived the Royal Design products to be luxurious and contemporary, focusing on high-end consumers. Using materials which have a presence such as a mortar and a black glass, they have couched the design in simplistic European motifs. For the functional capability, the design was simplified and embedded in Zen-like concepts.

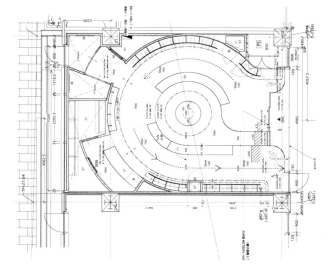

Une Vie Avec Elle

The most attractive point for the designer was to be able to design the shop without a sense of the domestic. The whole design ignores the unique current Japanese trend, and creates the space in line with international trends, namely, it could leave the Japanese trend as an antique and a retro-modern boom to challenge futuristic design. The designer create the fluid organic space that has been missing in recent Japanese design through the spiral-shaped plan and the sloping walkway. As a result, in this fashion mall with its many tenants, the space has become unique and entirely differentiated from the other shops.

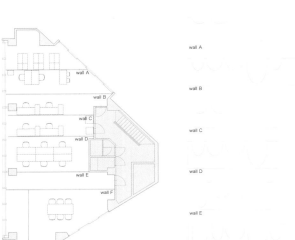

Meguro Office

The office is located near the Meguro river in Tokyo, on the fourth floor of an old office building. The clients wanted the usual spaces and functions — meeting space, management, workspace and storage to be separate, but also to maintain a sense of connection between them. Employees can move between spaces by walking over the parts of the walls that "sag" the most, thus emphasizing the contrast between the uses of the different spaces. Spaces that need more sound-proofing are enclosed with the kind of plastic curtains you might find at a small factory so that people can work without worrying about noise but not feel isolated.

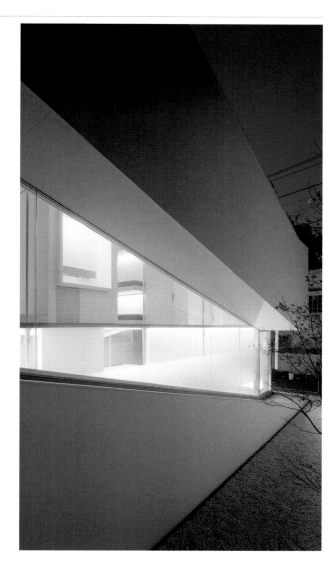

C-1

The basic architectural design, a glass box surrounded by a slope that connects the floors, was designed before the land was found. From the beginning, the basic design included all aspects of the project, starting from the shape of the building to the design of light switches and furniture. Usually an architectural project is developed in sequence; building, interior furniture, products; making it difficult to be totally homogenous. To achieve a weightless architectural space, 25 mm steel slabs were used as the floor. From the slope, the interior is visible from the floor level to ceiling, creating a real three-dimensional interior. C-1 is not a minimalist house but rather on the contrary, it is expressionism.

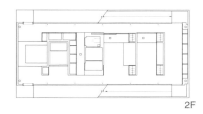

2F

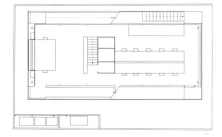

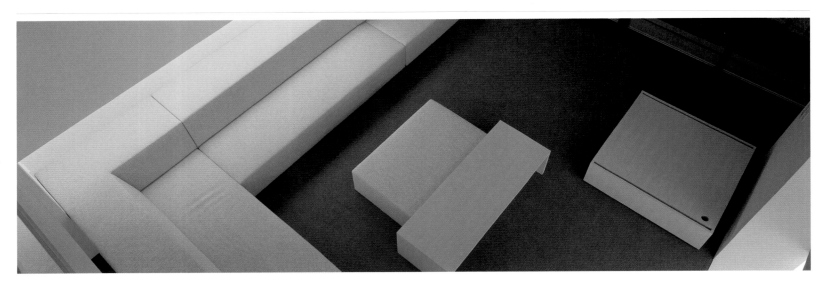

Shinagawa flat

The concept for this apartment is based on the absence of walls and follows the clients' wish to create a space that is as open as possible. Space and function are structured by the use of differing materials. Living room, kitchen and bedroom are characterized by their specific floor treatment, each being selected for visual and functional qualities. The apartment thus awakes the impression that the separating walls have been removed, leaving the various treatments behind. The space's shape is also used to connect function: the form of the kitchen ceiling is visually linked to the dining table. In the upstairs bedroom and bathroom, a similar floor treatment for different room functions was used to create a rectangular space that appears larger than the sum of its functions.

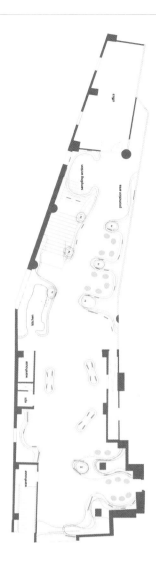

FlatFlat in Harajuku

FlatFlat in Harajuku is a store based on the concept of "the future park" and aims to combine a virtual element with real space accessible to anyone. The designers attempted to create a space where people feel like snuggling up to the organic form that curves based on human body dimensions. On the other hand, the "inorganic principle" consisting of white wall surface fixtures, neon tubes of ceiling illumination and mortar floor creates a virtual element. They used lines which allow neon tubes and the prevention of mortar crack seams to offset the forms of the wall surface fixtures. They stimulate the curiosity of the visitors by synergy with the forms of the fixtures and lead them to the inner part of the narrow space.

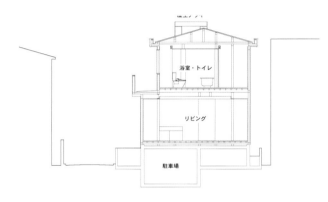

House in Okusawa

An existing house was renovated by covering sections of the exterior and revealing elements of the interior. The project consisted of many small alterations using standard building materials. The brickwork on the façade was painted white and concrete steps were added, while inside beams were exposed and glass partitions installed. These slight modifications introduce change to the neighborhood while avoiding radical innovations. Old touches were given the same importance as the new and were neither denied nor affirmed in a new interpretation of the meaning of renovation.

Nobu

Sunlight, lights from the surrounding buildings, signal lamps and vehicles are reflected and refracted, creating various expressions on the façade. The surroundings are changed and transformed by the duplication of the façade. In addition, an "illusion" is created through the refraction by the mirrors. The designer scratched lines on the stainless steel mirror of a worktable in the shop; when a spotlight projects light onto the worktable, various circular patterns appear at the surface, creating an illusion that the worktable surface consists of two layers.

Magritte's

The site was just 45.61 square meters in area, located in the middle of Tokyo. The width of the front road also restricted the size of the construction machine, so initial conditions presented serious construction challenges. The client was a young married couple aged around 30, and their simple request was the use of concrete for every part of the house including floors, walls, tables and so on. They did not even ask for storage space. To satisfy this request, the architects chose to use a precast prestressed concrete which stresses the preinstalled steel bar, to separate the volume between the ground floor and the basement.

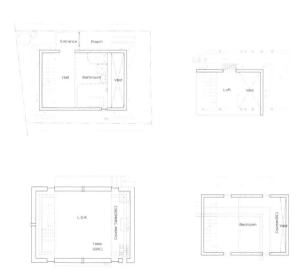

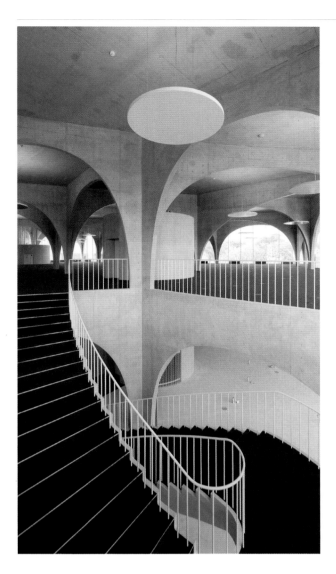

Tama Art University Library

Initially the architects proposed to place the entire library underground. After realizing that this was impossible, the volume was designed above the ground, while still trying to build a subterranean space. The building became a structural system of a series of domes and arches. The arches have been designed to follow gentle curves at different angles. These continuous curves articulate space into blocks of squares and triangles. Due to the strategic placement of the furniture, contradicting characteristics were attributed to the reading area: flow and standstill. The slope of the ground floor follows the natural declivity of the land so that the architecture is well integrated into the surrounding environment, maintaining spatial continuity between inside and outside space.

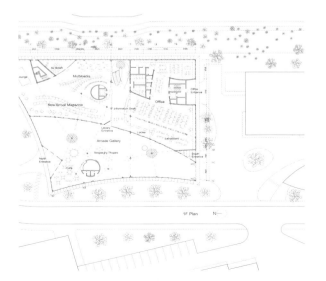

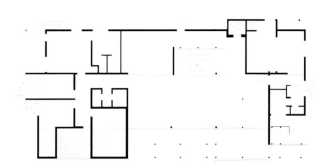

Ginzan Onsen Fujiya

Architecturally, the project consisted of 'a large scale refurbishment' rather than the construction of an entirely new building, which would have abandoned the idea of a 'three-story wooden house'. Instead, the existing structure was preserved by removing the concrete parts that had been added when the hotel was enlarged, and checking every single wooden part to replace the worn pieces with new wood to enhance the building's earthquake-resistance. The existing façade was renovated utilizing wood from the original 100-year old hotel while the interior space was reorganized by the insertion of an atrium. This atrium is surrounded by a delicate screen made of 4 mm-wide slits of bamboo (Sumushiko), while Dalle de Verre, an almost-transparent stained glass, is fit into the opening that faces the outside.

DKNY Flagship Store

Upon entrance, the customer is presented with a ribbon of natural oak planks connecting the entry, split basement and mezzanine levels. This stands in dark contrast to the gray basaltina stone flooring. A mannequin presentation platform flanks the right side of the ground floor, which houses women's wear. To add organic elements for showcasing merchandise throughout the store, hand-shaped powder-coated metal rods with wire-brushed oak bars were installed for hanging clothes, framed by white texturised plaster walls. To contrast these organic elements with a more urban feel inside the store, white polyester lacquer was used to create the cash wrap area and used as a backdrop.

3.1 Phillip Lim-Seoul

The store was constructed in an existing four-story building. The low ceilings of the original structure were accommodated by extending two of the four enclaves vertically to cut out double height spaces. The main entrance to the store is also a type of enclave, cropped and recessed from the façade with a continuous glass storefront. Evocative textures were explored for the façade and interior walls, creating a narrative of atmospheres from one space to another, each offering a new and unexpected encounter with the clothing. Mirror lines the existing perimeter walls, expanding a continuous field of space in which the "cropped" enclaves float.

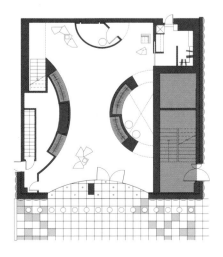

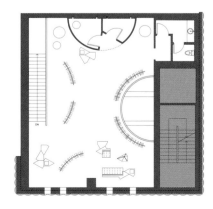

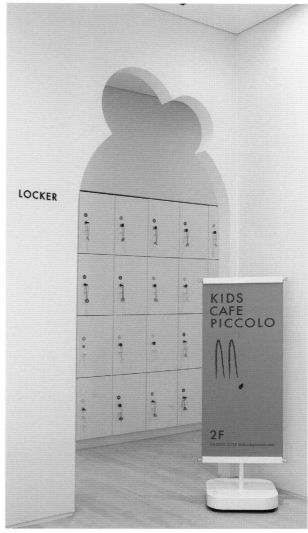

Kids Café Piccolo

The project has been designed for children and their parents to offer a playground, a playroom, a party room, a library and a café. The interior spaces were designed to offer a fairy tale feeling for children with an adult-like atmosphere for their parents to enjoy. The fun should be combined with a learning experience. In the spacious playing area, lengths of soft wood timber floor planks were used at perpendicular angles across one wall to create a series of rectangles and squares, reminiscent of a tree house. In the party room, ceiling roses were used in concentric circles to form a crisp white design on a rich colored wall, whilst a corbel – traditionally seen as a decorative architectural support– is used as a floating shelf without the usual brackets and visible fixings. Below the shelf, corner blocks, which are usually sold as corner pieces to wall panels or door surrounds, are utilized to create a decorative tile effect.

Zouk Club

The design concept is based on a fluid and organic structure, a juxtaposition of two curved lines. The bold expression of the façade is designed as an iconic piece of architecture to create a major statement alluding to the vibrant and energetic environment of the internationally recognized Zouk music style. The overall look of the building façade is clean and simple with white stucco to emphasize the unique and dynamic form. The white stucco walls for the entrance foyer recall mud architecture of the North Africa deserts. Although the finish is rough and textured, the form is bold and visionary. The floor is made of cement screed with mosaic tile inserts to create concentric patterns.

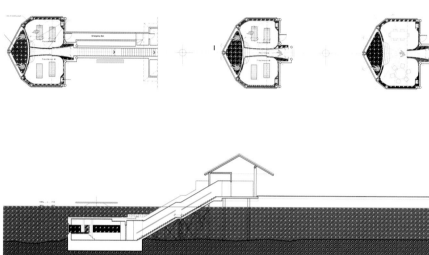

The World's First Underwater Spa

The underwater spa, which forms part of the luxury Huvafen Fushi resort in the Maldives, comprises two double treatment rooms and a separate relaxation area with stunning views under the Indian Ocean. Guests enter the underwater spa along a passageway lit with color-change lights in the ceiling to enhance the overall sensory experience. Once inside, reconfigurable sliding walls allow the space to be opened up to make the most of the spectacular views or closed to create a more intimate space for treatments. The resort itself comprises 43 naturally modern rooms located both on the beach and on stilts over the Indian Ocean.

Six Senses Hideaway Zighy Bay

Positioned as the finest boutique resort in the Middle East, the Six Senses Hideaway Zighy Bay establishes a new benchmark of luxury in the region. Located on the Musandam Peninsula of Oman, the resort is a 90 minutes drive from the gateway of Dubai. The dramatic setting, with mountains on one side and a 1.6 kilometers white sand beach at Zighy Bay, on the other, hosts 82 pool villas – all with butler service. The accommodations of Six Senses Hideaway Zighy Bay are a blend of the surrounding Omani traditional style with modern amenities that provide luxury local cultural themes. The resort has a spa, operated by the award-winning Six Senses Spa, with nine treatment rooms and two Arabian Hammams. Furthermore the resort includes three dining alternatives, including a dinner experience on the top of the mountain with a stunning view over Zighy Bay and the mountains.

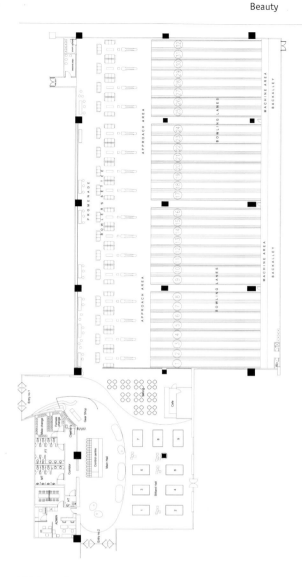

SM MOA Bowling Club

EAT turned a 34-lane bowling center into an entertainment hub which includes a billiard hall, pro shop, café and KTV. The space had to be flexible in order to transform itself into an arena to host major competitions. The bowling center is located in Mall of Asia, Manila's largest shopping mall. The entry to the bowling center is exposed to a semi outdoor space of the mall. At certain times of the year the space is exposed to strong typhoons. Therefore all external elements had to be properly secured for these conditions. The requirements for a 34-lane bowling center meant that designers had a large floor space of approximately 2,000 square meters to design.

Face to Face

This project aims to provide a service office and meeting environment that captures an emerging need for more lifestyle orientated workplaces. The reception counter is de-familiarized as a pantry bar, meeting table cum play table, becoming a magnet for interaction and activity on a daily basis. Next, a full-length graphic wall on an all-black canvas coupled with dramatic lighting and various reflective/matte surfaces provides a dynamic and unconventional setting for an office, but one that is more lifestyle-driven. Furthermore, portrayals of animal and human silhouettes throughout the building provide a quirky and playful sensibility.

Leo Burnett Office

In designing a space for those who bear the legacy of Leo Burnett, the quintessential Ad man, Ministry of Design conceived of three unique environments that separately capture a different aspect of the total creative process but yet connect seamlessly in spirit and tempo. Space to Impress contains a larger than life 'graffiti' style portrait of Leo and a cool white sophisticated counter sculpture. In the Space to Interact, chill-out spaces and formal meeting spaces offer a variety of ways to meet and exchange ideas. Finally, the office is united into a single creative organism via a series of open planned desks in the Space to Create.

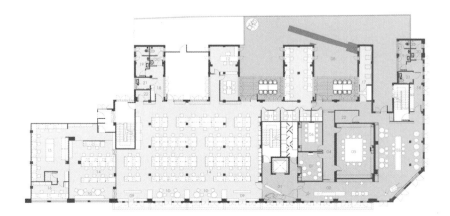

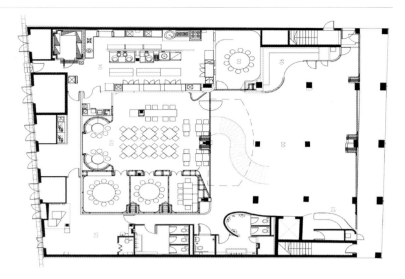

New Majestic Hotel

The New Majestic Hotel comprises four adjoining three-floor commercial buildings, which have been combined and adapted for re-use as an exclusive 30-bedroom boutique hotel. The historical listed façades of the commercial buildings, which date back to 1927, were retained and restored. In a unique design concept, reflecting the inner struggle of a mistress, a curvilinear stairway expressing feminine sensuality was introduced into the hotel as its central feature. The stairway connects the rugged ground floor lobby (where the original ceilings have been retained showing the ravages of time) to the new swimming pool deck on the second floor, symbolizing her passage from initial shame to final relaxation. Terrazzo flooring, a formerly popular but now almost forgotten trade, is used in the front lobby to reinforce the theme of nostalgia.

55 Blair Road

Bringing light into this long plot was the most important consideration. A large air well divides the two sections of the house allowing for maximum light to penetrate the living spaces. Aluminum cladding wraps around the void, reflecting light into the living spaces. The void acts not only as a large light well but also encourages natural ventilation within the house. Continuity of space was a key concept to promote the relationship of internal-external space. The main section of the house is separated by the outdoor pool and frangipani garden.

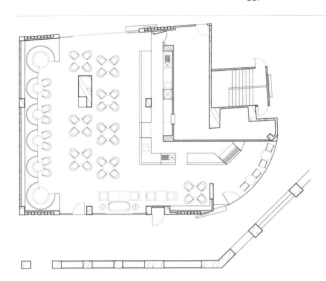

The Coffee Connoisseur

One of the key parameters of the design was to inject a contemporary assimilation of elements into a Victorian influenced café design. Elements on what actually constitutes a look of this type were studied and re-interpreted into different physical forms. There was a purposeful deconstruction of mismatched uses of these elements, turning wallpaper into silk-screened glass motifs, chandeliers into rows of numbered repetitive light sculptures and curtains into spatial divisions that drop from the ceiling. The twists create very interesting nuances of adaptations of culturally strong images into sleeker contemporary counterparts, evoking feelings of grandeur in a setting displaced from its original cultural context and location.

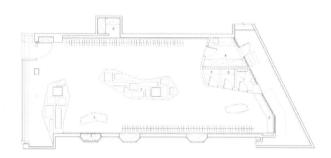

Mesh

A simple but strong visual image of a truly modern shopping window is created through the white colored, exposed metal external wall. From the reflection of the mirrors that wrap the columns, horizontally aligned shelves of metal corrugated boards display luxury accessories, and enliven space. Together with over 300 pieces of laser-cut punched metal webs in the ceiling, the lighting, air-conditioning and hanging displays combine in clarity and simplicity to display the clean, smooth style of digital technology. The streamlined curtains and display cabinets connote a tenderness of space and soften the harshness of the marble flooring and display stands without sacrificing the geometric feeling of modern design. The natural tones of the marble flooring correspond to the rhythm of the ceiling, and a premier display space is thus presented in both delicate and precise design using industrial materials.

Hair Culture Salon

Hair Culture Salon with "black diamond" as the central theme for its interior, a contemporary and re-fined space was created. A multilateral geometrical cut was adopted to depict the quality of the mineral stones. The core space for both the ground and first floor is the mineral modules which are sculpted by black mirror glass. Hiding behind the mineral modules, there are VIP rooms and other functional sec-tions such as the washing area and the staff room. Within the white painted space, the multilateral geo-metrical cut is once again employed on the ceilings, with the addition of brown epoxy floor, reinforcing the image of natural mineral rocks.

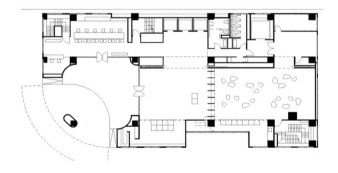

Xue Xue Institute

The aim of the interior design was to promote communication between the different groups as a basis for creative learning and working. The entire complex is structured similarly to an open loft apartment, in which people from different faculties come together and are able to design their environment according to their requirements in a flexible and functional way.

Bernini Fashion Headquarters

The headquarters of successful fashion retail group Bernini contains showrooms for all their main brands as well as reception, meeting areas and general office space. The brands all have show stores within the space representative of the store designs for that brand. The in-between spaces where a pair of leather sofas stands are planned as informal meeting areas, while the entire room can be set up for buyer shows at the start of each season. The reception counter forms part of a "ribbon" that connects all the areas together. Facing this is the design department screened by a full length glass wall printed with graphics based on traditional cutting patterns.

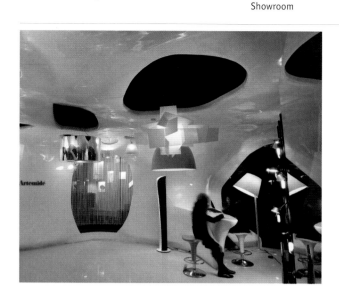

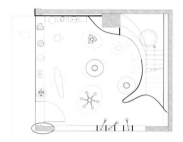

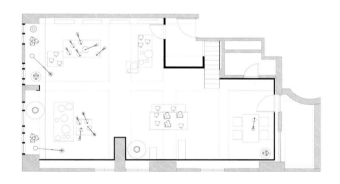

Artemide Flagship Store

Responding to Artemide philosophy, lighting is a source of physical pleasure and mental comfort, CROX International embellishes the first Artemide Flagship Store in Taipei Downtown with the concept of the brightness and the sense of hope by interpretating the scene of sunlight breaks through the could. The ceiling, walls and desk consist of a single, curvilinear form made of fibre-reinforced polymer. This sculptural composition is finished with glossy paint to give a visual illusion of a large store space. Installed with large, glass windows, the interior is finished with glossy paint to give the illusion of a larger space.

SUNONE

A key feature of the design is the pattern of horizontal screening, which preserves the serenity of the surrounding low-rise residential neighborhood as a visual barrier and creates pleasing working environments by serving as a light filter. In contrast to the traditional office space, SUNONE provides a range of work settings including bench desks with task lights for concentrated work, and more informal spaces to encourage group meeting and chats. While the exterior screen reflects the technological character of the company, the interior screen directly reflects the adventurous personality of its owner and staff.

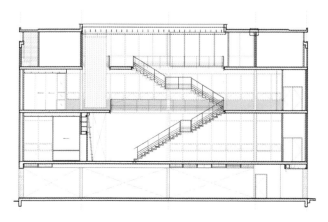

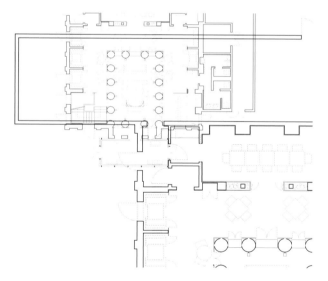

China House Restaurant

Inspired by the vibrant 1930s Shanghai Art Deco, The Oriental, Bangkok's China House restaurant has been re-designed and revived into an avant-garde eatery that serves classic yet contemporary cuisine in a refined atmosphere. The concept of the design rests on a re-thinking of "period" decoration and how one is able to convey the spirit of a time without being overly literal. The end result is a fresh evocation of this cultural period, mixing very few actual Deco furnishings with modern pieces against an interior-architectural setting that aims to balance a new experience of fine dining with a reluctant dosage of nostalgia.

Siam Paragon

"The Pride of Bangkok" is Thailand's first mega shopping complex. It houses many of the world's most prestigious high-end brands and has made an immediate impact on the area by transforming the surrounding district into a region of bustling activity. The biggest challenge for the design team was the creation of a circulation plan and layout. Strategic retail groupings and floor arrangements help minimize pedestrian congestion, supporting a traffic plan that moves shoppers conveniently throughout the center's spaces. Siam Paragon has truly become one of Bangkok's most celebrated destinations, drawing tourists from around the world to its cultural, retail and entertainment selections.

Six Senses Hideaway Koh Yao Noi

Koh Yao Noi is a picturesque island in Thailand's Phang Nga Bay – the unique natural environment setting for the 24-acre Six Senses Hideaway Yao Noi, which exemplifies the Six Senses Hideaway philosophy of redefining experiences from arrival to departure. The natural vegetation and tropical landscaping provide privacy and allow glorious views over Phang Nga Bay. The resort has 54 private pool villas, plus the Hilltop Reserve, and the Retreat; all representing an uncompromised high standard of luxury. The attention to detail and focus on the nature and characteristics of the destination reinforces Six Senses' commitment to the environment. Each villa has its own infinity-edged pool with a sundeck. The dining room features a glass floor with a creek meandering underneath, while the living room presents a wide range of world cuisine, with an emphasis on Thai dishes.

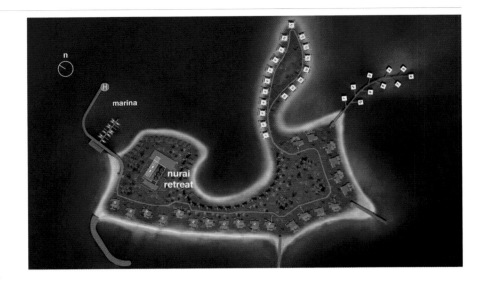

Nurai by Zaya

Derived from the Arabic word "nour" meaning "light", the private island of Nurai is designed to attract the attention of the ultra wealthy. Two strands of water villas extend into the ocean while the project's Beachfront Estates are nestled on the ocean's edge with a rooftop canopy of undulating greenery keeping the houses cool and limiting their architectural presence. The central seven-meter-high atrium is flanked by Musharabiya panels, introducing a dramatic Arabesque touch to what is predominantly a contemporary design. Both the Shoreline and the Seaside Estates house luxurious amenities including infinity swimming pool and gourmet kitchens.

Ritz-Carlton Sharq Village and Spa

The planning was based on a traditional Qatari village ornate courtyard and beautiful furnishings and treasures that found their way here from the seaports create an experience steeped in detail and tradition. Lobby and public spaces flow gently into one another while allowing for intimate seating groupings and moments of interest along circulation corridors. All aspects of detailing were to refer back to authentic Qatari motifs-handrails, stone carvings, and inlaid mosaics create a sense of continuity and refinement that help to reinforce the storyline of the project.

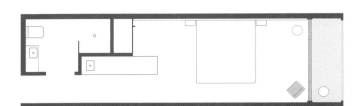

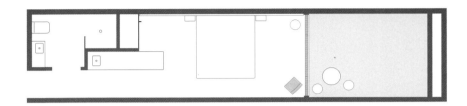

The Limes Hotel

The design approach focused on the hotel in its absolute entirety – considering the intended look and feel, and paying heavy attention to the interiors, furniture, surfaces and finishes, as well as extending the design influence to the Limes' music and drinks list. The Limes façade was tangibly branded with a large-scale Limes logo, which is also found on details throughout the hotel lobby, rooms and rooftop bar and cinema. The bedroom design focused on the efficient use of space, prioritizing use and features. The material selection for the rooms was based on durability, maintenance and appeal. The result is a delicate balance of sophisticated warmth. The rooms feature custom Corian (by Dupont) kitchen benches and toilette vanities, Blackbutt timber bed heads, custom powder coat aluminum door handles, splashback and floating bedside tables, Luna Textiles curtains and bathroom wall tiles by Bisazza.

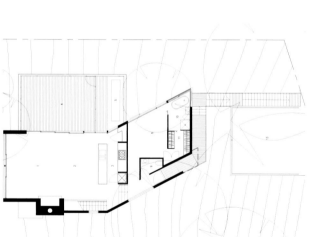

Bundeena House

The houses were designed for a sophisticated style-conscious market, for someone who would live in a luxury contemporary apartment in the city. The top floor maximizes exposure to the northern sun whilst the lower level is directed toward the beach. This design allows for a large north facing deck area in front of the living room which sits above the bedrooms. Thus simple sustainable principles result in a very dramatic form. The upper level is conceived as a timber box for the landscape and the lower level is a white contemporary portal form. The houses have a progressive feel with clean and contemporary lines.

Hotel Realm

This built in flexibility has resulted in a robust formal building structure deliberately conceived to offer flexibility in response to program updates to meet the clients' critical needs. At the detail level, the emphasis on utilization of natural light, ventilation and solar access have largely determined the expression and form of the Hotel Realm. In RAIA Jury's words, "Hotel Realm is commended for considerable control of material and proportion throughout the public and private accommodation spaces, resulting in consistently formal expression of wall planes and openings to the surrounding areas. The level of control is admirable".

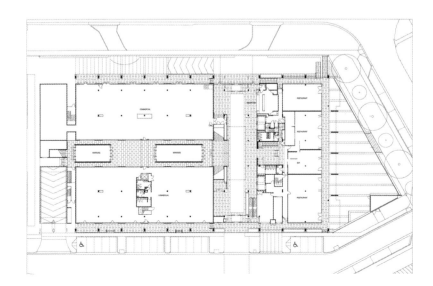

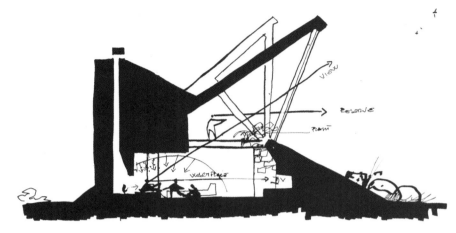

Under the Moonlight House

The project tries to integrate itself in the site through use of materials that have been used before and that are part of local historical background. House's shape resembles typological archetypes used by countrymen and cowboys that lived in the area. Stone, wood and metal are materials used for both structure and construction of the project. The House has been designed in order to comfort seasonal stay, both during summer and winter, and lets visitors appreciate the natural environment surrounding them. This has been done through placement of many glazed frames that grant wider external views. On the second level, two bedrooms are included as well as a master bedroom with bathroom and spa.

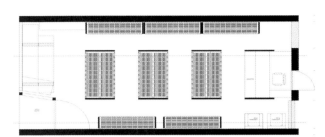

Calibre Collins Street

Calibre Collins Street combines elements of boutique shopping at its best in new ways. Large changing rooms, signature chrome racks, hand-woven seagrass wall panels and custom terrazzo flooring are just a few of the high quality features. With layers of subtle textures, discreet detailing and gracious space planning, homage was payed to the integrity of the Calibre range. The large windows overlooking Collins Street display the artistic and imaginative visuals and clothes for which Calibre are renowned. The store within is somewhat more intimate, providing the shopper with a relaxed and easy environment layered with personal items like the original molded fiberglass chaise designed by Eames.

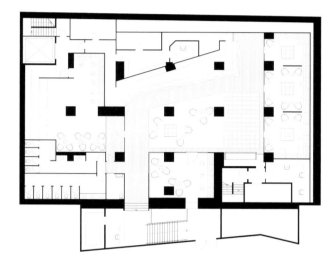

Eve Nightclub and Bar

The inspiration was drawn from the the 1970s and early 80s disco era, when going out was a glamorous event. As the space was located in a basement, the outside world could be ignored, creating an entirely new world. When considering the name of the venue, the designers decided to play on this theme of "The Garden of Eden" and implement it subtly into their concept for the different areas of the club such as the Dragon Bar, the Tiger Room and the central dance floor.

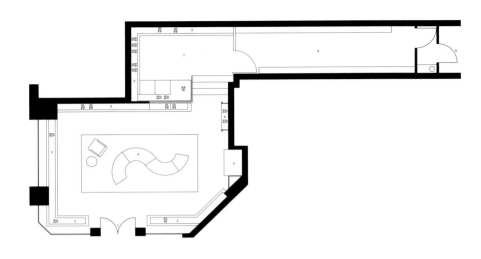

Tino Lanzi

The soft, feminine ladies shoestore was designed to be like a modern summer garden gazebo. The walls are lined in a champagne paint finish and bronze floral wallpaper with little summer wrens and delicate ribbon stripes. The joinery is set in stark contrast using white (antique white USA) polyurethane with sharp lines creating a lattice-like effect. The green carpet creates a grassy floor finish; the oak chevron floor with earthy and organic decorative motifs gives formality. A huge Lily chandelier and sconces seem to grow from the surfaces.

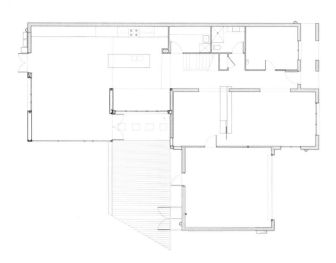

Village Park House

Alterations were made primarily to the rear ground floor plan and roof above the garage. The ground floor, the rear of the house was redesigned to accommodate a new north-facing living area with a new roof and high ceiling. The ceiling height was raised to heighten the sense of space as well as to capture more northern light. The family room has replaced the previous living room at the front of the house. A larger master bedroom has been created above the existing garage which overlooks the courtyard and opens out to a private balcony. As each site brings along its own set of challenges and demands, this project in particular challenged designers economically.

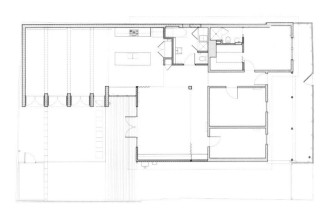

Kelso House

To allow maximum sunlight to penetrate deep into the living areas, three linear roof lights run the full width of the extension, creating an ever-changing light setting as the day progresses. Another roof light is located directly above the shower so that one can experience daylight while showering. Due to overlooking and west facing issues, large unobstructed glazing facing the garden was not feasible. Five vertical fin walls are designed to partially block potential overlooking. The fin walls break up the façade into four openings, allowing doors to be inserted. These are also structural columns supporting the roof and the wide box gutter above.

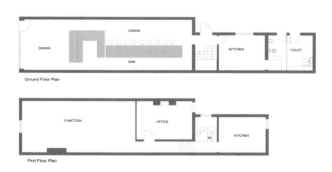

Ground Floor Plan

First Floor Plan

Maedaya Bar

This project demonstrates the possibility of using ordinary recyclable material for hospitality projects without compromising the sophistication of the food and service. Traditionally sake is bottled in wooden casks and secured with ropes. The current commercial method of bottling sake is similar to that of red or white wine. The designers' interest in sake bottling lies in the bounding of the cask using ropes. Thereafter they chose to investigate and translate their interpretation of "bounding" with the use of Manila ropes. The ropes held in tension at specific points form the shape of a house or a hut. A house, whether it be a teahouse or sake house, is a sacred place in traditional Japanese culture.

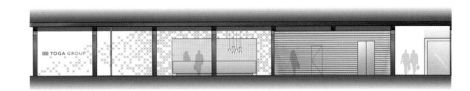

Toga Group Head Office

The project is located within a heritage wool store building that has been adapted to office space. Bates Smart refurbished the base building, removing intrusive additions such as plasterboard ceilings, column claddings and walls, to reveal the original timber ceilings, beams and joists. The lobby was fully refurbished, with all materials and finishes removed to expose the original construction. Concrete floors were exposed and polished and glass was used as balustrades and walls to maintain visibility of the original fabric. The Toga Group's brief called for an environment that encouraged integration, visibility, collaboration and team work.

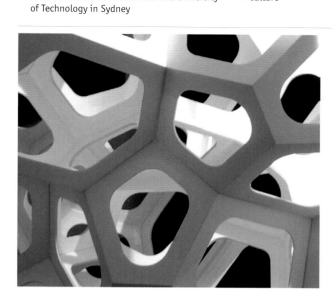

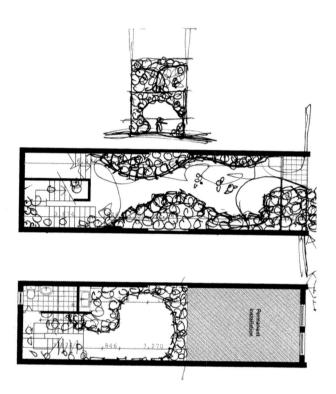

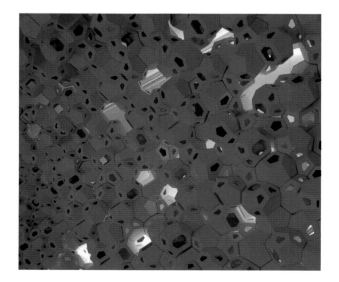

Digital Origami

The danger of digital creations is the virtual worlds they depend on, or rather the lack of constraints in the virtual if compared to the physical world. Most of the time digital creations end as eccentric fly-through computer renderings. With the Digital Origami the designers wanted to realize concepts. They studied and researched current trends in parametric modeling, digital fabrication and material- science and applied this knowledge to create a space-filling installation. The aim was to test the fitness of a particular module, copied from nature, to generate architectural space, with the assumption that the intelligence of the smallest unit dictates the intelligence of the overall system.

Stockland Head Office Sydney

Locating the new head office in this building was seen as an extraordinary opportunity to demonstrate that the building could be 'turned around' to create a contemporary, engaging and sustainable new workplace. A vertical street underpins the new workplace. This street is in the form of a void (8.5 meters x 5.5 meters) that winds its way up the building's eastern side. The void contains stairs that spiral through the eight floors from level 22 to 29, staggered in its vertical location to maximise the views between floors and provide a greater sense of connection. The void and stair not only provide a greater sense of physical connection, but become the symbolic connection of 'one Stockland'.

Fuji Xerox Epicenters

The vision of the center is to offer Fuji Xerox's global customers a complete 'digital print' experience. Visitors are provided with a personalized journey depending upon the reason for their visit and their level of existing knowledge of the Fuji Xerox products and services. A series of "experiential zones" are personalized for each customer, ensuring relevance of brand communication through to sales conversion and customer retention experiences. From arrival the customer's experience is extraordinary. An iconic sphere, projecting welcome messages to the customer, denotes the entry point. Visitors are greeted by a roaming attendee, unrestrained by the confines of a reception desk.

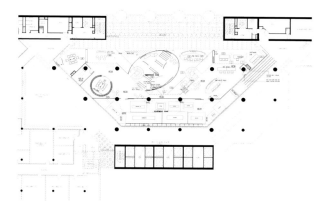

BCS Office

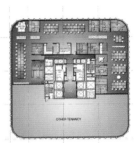

BCS is the brand of household furniture of the Shanghai Ever Rich Furniture Manufacturing Company which is a member of Hong Kong Novel Enterprise Ltd. BCS Concept's design reflects the perfect combination of modern design with European and American classical styles. It is luxurious, yet simple, unique and full of elegance. Combining outstanding design talent, superior craftsmanship, a desire for perfection and years of experience in furniture making, BCS Concepts aims to create furniture that consistently meets the most personalized aspects of the client's demand. BCS Concepts is able to match the pace of European and American furniture companies.

Washington H Soul Pattinson

Washington H Soul Pattinson appointed PCG to manage the refurbishment of their corporate headquarters at 160 Pitt Street Mall, Sydney. In recognition of the building's significant contribution to local heritage, it is listed on the NSW Register of Historical Buildings. The refurbishment and upgrade of the building's existing engineering services enabled the project team to focus on unusual aspects of the building's original architecture. The introduction of a single passenger lift and a new enclosed atrium space at the rear of the building significantly improves the quality of the working environment for Soul Pattinson's staff.

Darlo Bar

The new works to the ground floor of the hotel incorporate a new bar and courtyard which is two stories in height. Deep within the structure of the existing hotel, this space is fully lined with acoustic perforated, lapped aluminium panels. The panels are painted in gold, silver and green colors to accentuate a "garden" room in the heart of the building. The interior of the bar was guided by the "Retro" nature of the ground floor fitout. A collection of old steel wired and framed furniture was collected from auction houses and shops. All were painted white. The concept was simple – the courtyard bar would have the character of a quirky outdoor garden room of the 1960s in Sydney.

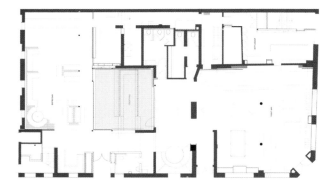

Paddington Inn

The rooms surrounding the courtyard are washed in daylight. The interior planning upholds the various rooms of the old hotel; most notably the small nook – with its "moorish" inspired stepped timber ceiling – and the long bistro/bar/lounge, its end focus being the bar with its bronze mirror reflections. The steel post and beam construction of the courtyard is refined and strong, bracing old structure and supporting new. The courtyard is an outdoor urban room, highly acoustically attenuated so that the patrons can enjoy it both day and night, and the neighborhood is not imposed upon. The stepped section of the courtyard allows for diversity of standing and seating areas.

Cooper Street

All the furniture has been specifically designed for the room. The desks and storage units were created from recycled carcasses from a second hand office warehouse and bespoke steel frames which have then been dressed with form ply. This created seating facilities for eight groups of four to six people, with a central storage unit that could be converted into further desks if required. There is also room for expansion, backing onto the conference room and in the utilities at either end of the main space. The desks have removable sections in the middle creating easy access to all the CAT5, telephone and power cabling, all of which leads back to a large server in the utilities area.

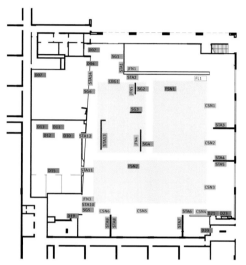

Five Dock Library

Minale Bryce Design strategy wanted to create a memorable, yet state-of-the-art library facility for the new Five Dock Library fitout. From the cosmopolitan café/bookstore to the busy street life of Five Dock village, a feeling of avant garde was devised to complement the library's urban surroundings. Essentially two distinct schemes overlap each other to create a dramatic, vibrant and enticing composition. Brightly sculptured walls make an exciting basis for the library fitout with colors defining various sections of the library. Dividing walls are lined with translucent acrylic and lit from above with bright blue lighting.

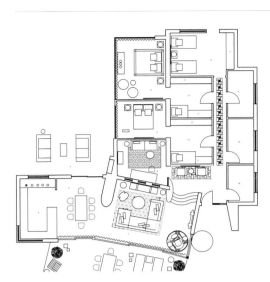

Hardwick Turnbull Beach House

This original 1960s home was already in very good condition but needed updating. The designers re-worked the original 1960s style with mid-century modern iconic furniture of the likes of Eames and Jacobsen. These were mixed with modern furniture from Minotti and new custom-made carpets. The color palette was inspired by the house's surroundings. Being by the ocean the designers chose to use materials that referenced the sand, water, timbers and fauna of the local Palm Beach area. Timbers, blue upholstery and paint finishes, yellow textured fabric and natural stone mimic the outdoors. The room is walled in by the use of bamboo and the floor is paved in natural local sandstone.

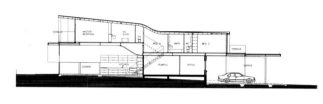

Bondi Wave House

The house is located one street back from the famous Bondi beach. The brief for this house was simple – capture the spirit of Bondi in a home, which is both a beach house and a stylish urban dwelling. As a beach house, it was designed to reflect the natural power of its location, with the intention being that one should feel as though you are in a boutique or café rather than a house. The swish of the roof owes as much to the soft lines of a surfboard as the curl of a wave. The line of the wave is the unifying element, which runs all the way through the house, and forms an entry wing over the garage at the south, while rising to give greater height to the living room at the north end.

CarriageWorks Contemporary Performing Arts Center

The new forms stand free of the rows of original cast iron columns, creating circulation routes in the interstitial spaces with views through the building. The foyer spans the entire width of the building. The linear entry structures to each of the theater spaces are like "ghosts" of the carriages that once moved through the space. The front of house is divided by glass doors from the back of house activities, which are located adjacent to the railway tracks. The new elevated roof echoes the rhythm of the original roof monitors.

Windsor Loft

The design is a reflection on architectural strategies — spatial intervention/differentiation in a fluid continuity; visual/subliminal permeation between private and public domain in contemporary domestic spaces in urban fabric. A cruciform column stands in the middle of the first floor living areas. Traversing floor tiles and recessed ceiling lighting tracks radiate from its four edges, virtually dividing the open plan into entertaining, dining, sitting and circulation areas. With its wall-lined high gloss white joinery and north orientation to the internal courtyard, the kitchen blurs into an inconspicuous whitewash in daylight. At night it becomes an annex to the house.

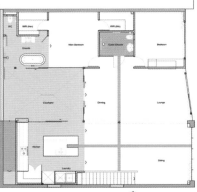

The Credit Valley Hospital

Farrow Partnership Architects designed The Credit Valley Hospital's 30.000 square meters. Cancer Care and Ambulatory Care facility, which includes features such as Complex Continuing Care, Rehabilitation, Maternal Child Care, Laboratory Services, and Emergency Room renovations. These renovations and additions are only phase one for a larger three-phase, $349 million dollar project, designed to serve the future health care needs for the people of Mississauga. The dramatic spaces and warm materials of the new facility promote humanistic healing practices among patients and staff.

Opus Hotel

Opus Hotel Montreal is a unique boutique hotel that blends contemporary style and design with a nod to the historic with a chic Montreal touch. The original avant-garde structure, built in 1914 by Joseph-Arthur Godin, was the first poured concrete building in North America. Created in an Art Nouveau style, the building featured little ornamentation, save for a signature curving staircase. This simplicity of design is reflected in the unmistakably modern concrete addition, created by architect Dan Hanganu of Montreal and interior designer Yabu Pushelberg of New York, both winners of the prestigious "Platinum Circle Award". Inside, Opus Hotel Montreal's intimate one hundred and thirty-six guestrooms combine sleek minimalism with luxurious comfort. Opus Hotel Montreal provides the service and amenities of a luxury hotel in a stylish and intimate environment.

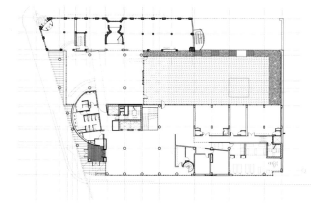

Rain

The first challenge was to solve the planning issues, especially to create an appropriate entrance. The original opening to the leased space was at the corner of the building, quite distant from the building's striking stone-arched main entrance. The designers won Historical Board approval to close the secondary doorway and modify the primary entrance and lobby area. Inside the traditional Victorian oak doors, the designers created a new divided vestibule with a security to the office building and a stunning new passageway leading to Rain itself. To the right, a glossy pebble-finished wall rises above a steel trough of river rocks and bears simple acrylic cut-outs of the restaurant's logo elements.

Offices for Grip Limited

The formal and informal meeting spaces throughout the agency offer various spatial experiences. The double-height atrium visually and functionally links the two main floors. In addition to a stairway related to the bleachers, vertical movement is also provided by a slide and a fire-pole connecting the creative offices. Made of folded hot-rolled steel and stained walnut veneer, the bleachers are used for full office meetings, film presentations and as an alternative workplace, while the meeting area resembles a large hot tub. Clad in stainless steel, the interior is finished with white synthetic grass.

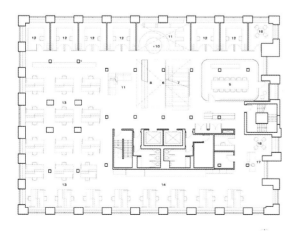

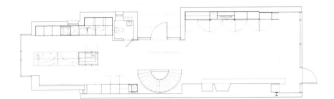

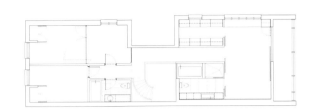

Russell Hill

Built during the 1970s, the house is situated overlooking one of Toronto's downtown ravines. The renovation reopened the ground floor so that it became an open loft-like space from front to back. By installing a new fully glazed wall at the rear garden side of the hose, it was possible to extend the sense of the outdoor space through the interior. Interior finishes were chosen for their neutrality and were stripped back to a more modern style, causing the house to become a neutral shell punctuated by three sculptural elements: a block of stone associated with kitchen elements, a curved stair, and a 20-inch stone bench with a fireplace wall. Each of these elements is associated with windows, skylights, and double height spaces to enhance the spatial experience.

Agnic Eagle Mines Offices

Agnic-Eagle Mines (AEM) is an international company focused on gold, with operations in Canada, Mexico, Finland and the USA. Their LaRonde Mine in Quebec is Canada's largest gold deposit. The design makes subtle references to AEM's core business. At the reception area, the back wall is composed of smooth slabs of horizontally grained travertine that abstractly evoke the geological strata of a mine. Embedded into the wall are random strips of gold coloured bars. A glass display case is also contained within the wall to showcase chunks of the raw mining material. This wall rises up two floors where the slab was cut open to accommodate an open stair that leads to the main boardroom.

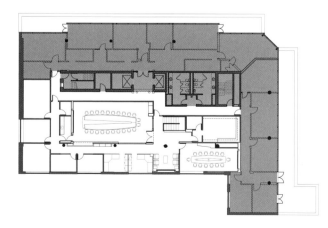

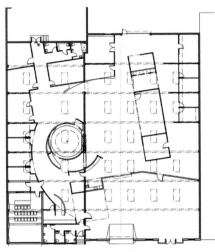

3Ality Digital

This digital film production facility inhabits two bays of an industrial building from the 1940s, separated by a bearing wall that allowed very limited open passage between the spaces. The architects were charged with designing a dynamic work environment with administrative and technical wings that include offices, workshops, editing rooms, equipment cage, screening room and long sight lines for camera staging. They introduced a circular conference room that becomes the vortex of the environment. It straddles the central dividing wall and propels into motion a series of ripples whose trajectories penetrate and diminish the wall separation, while establishing auxiliary spaces for informal gathering.

Bloomingdale's

The three-level store is located in Wisconsin Place Center which is at the border of Washington DC. The main floor is one level above the open plaza. The store continues to demonstrate Bloomingdale's merchandise mix, which emphasizes designer and luxury brands. The design is quite contemporary and continues to pursue variations on the signature "black & white" image of the 59th street flagship in New York City. The new store features a 40-foot circular atrium topped by a skylight. Glass-enclosed escalators traverse the atrium and enhance the sightlines to all the sales floors. There are four three-storied black glass clad columns that punctuate this atrium. Black granite and black mirrors are used generously to accent the space and as architectural icons.

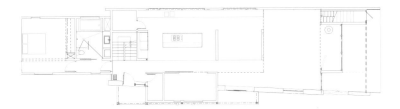
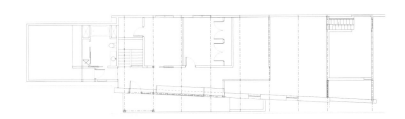

Boxhead

This three-bedroom house has an open plan and a "boxes in boxes" design approach with an economy of scale strategy, in which each smaller box becomes more precious. The plastered insulated concrete block walls and the concrete floor provide thermal mass and a heat sink which works with the super insulation provided by the exposed structural insulated panels. These distinct materials blur the definition of inside and out. A reduction of new materials and waste is also achieved with concrete cut outs and are recycled from a dumpster into floor and wall tile, which were specifically used for the master bathroom.

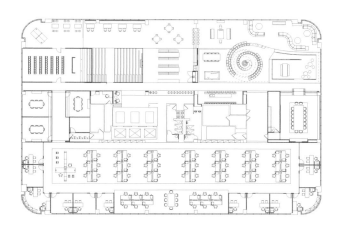

Saatchi + Saatchi

Shubin + Donaldson Architects conceived Saatchi + Saatchi's design to incorporate concepts of "home". This mandate is fulfilled by a grand staircase / meeting space, living and dining areas, and a "backyard" for casual gathering. The centrally located main floor is highlighted by a communal hub to bring staff together to allow for impromptu collaborative moments. The theme of "homing at work" is apparent in a spiral library that imparts the concept of a hearth. The combination of seating and shelving offers employees a central area for reading, as well as a mini amphitheater for small inter-office presentations. The grand staircase serves dual purpose as connector and meeting area.

Taste International

The small but rather incoherent space is wrapped in a sinus corrugated green-flocked steel wall. A plant wall is situated at the deep end of the inner part of the restaurant, a vertical garden with hundreds of plants placed in a multilayered and absorbent felt-surface. Different plants are placed in small pockets and the varieties of species create a living surface in constant change. Diamond shaped mirrors extend different spaces and elements such as the entrance and the plant wall. An additional element of harmony in the restaurant is the mustard colored wooden ceiling with tilted lamellae that diffuses the light from the fluorescent lamps above the ceiling. The black base of the terrazzo floor is customized with green and yellow pieces of glass that matches the walls and the ceiling. Functions such as the toilets and the entrance to the restaurant that extend from the organic green flocked walls are clad in birch wooden panels.

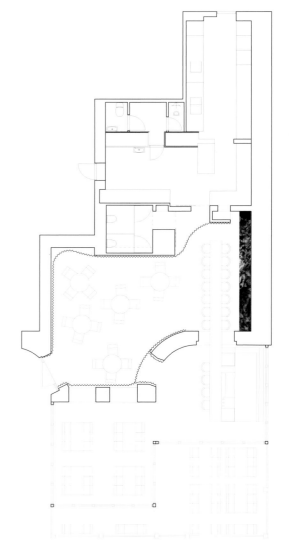

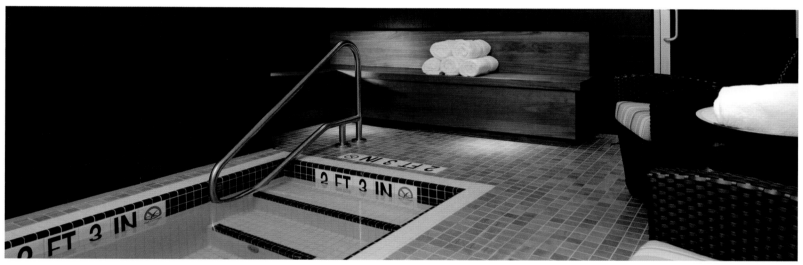

Heavenly Spa by Westin Hilton Head Island Resort

A sense of calmness and renewal is felt immediately upon entering the spa from either the lobby or the porte cochere. A portico of quarter-cut walnut on the walls and ceiling with dropped crystal lights signifies your entry into the spa and leads you to the reception desk of honed black limestone with a white back-painted glass top. A water wall with lacquered glass tiles and stacked white river rock provides a calming backdrop and is the main feature of the reception lobby. The nine treatment rooms are appointed with walnut floors, wenge wood cabinetry, plantation shutters on the windows, and a soft white sheer drapery panel that is lit from above and acts as the light source in the room.

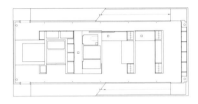

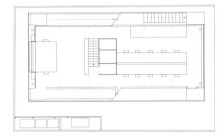

C-I House

Located in the historic Hudson Valley, the four-acre site is situated in southern Columbia County, bordering Duchess County to the south. Overlooking a pond, the house is surrounded by dense vegetation while commanding a vineyard view to the east and a view of the distant Black Dome Mountain to the west. Designed as a weekend retreat, the construction consists of concrete foundation/footings, supporting a wood framed enclosure with spatial layouts based upon standard modular construction dimensions. Opening sliding glass doors give access to a sun-deck, acting as an ethereal transition between the indoors and outdoors.

Alexander Mc Queen

The interior design uses plaster and sheet aluminum to create the illusion of shapes carved from rock, with walls, floors and ceilings that flow into each other. A ceiling below comes up through the floor above to form a balustrade; fixtures behave like stalactites suspended from the ceilings; shelves are cut out of pillars, blurring the boundary between the elements. Iridescent chips of mother-of-pearl sparkle from a terrazzo "carpet" the natural color of wet sand.

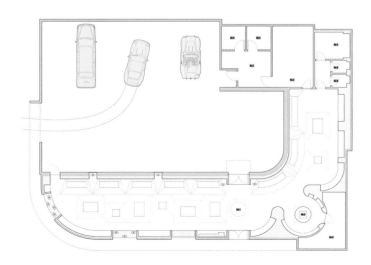

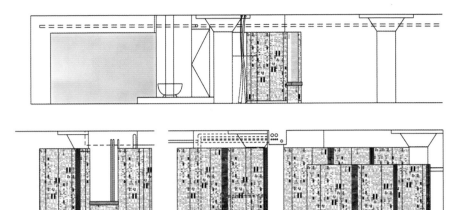

Solomon Loft

Emphasizing the light-filled and expansive space, the designers integrated two units creating an open retreat with only a single element subdividing the expansive loft space. A sinuous double-arced wall divides spatial uses without fully enclosing any part of the unit. The wall defines a screening room on one side while providing visual privacy for the master bath and bedroom on the other. Raised two steps above the floor, the bath area features an open shower comprised of a poured-in-place concrete wall. An antique claw-foot tub sits exposed on the raised platform while the vanity unit and toilet are enveloped in the point of the arcs. The 300 square meters loft is equipped with all the goods of a luxury home.

(Wide) Band Nomadic Café

(Wide) Band is a portable project; it was moved to the A + D Museum in Los Angeles where it functioned as a café by day and as a bar/lounge space at night. The primary material, 3/4" polycarbonate core panels, was chosen for its structural capacity to span large spaces and for its translucency. The walls, floor, and ceiling were shaped by wrapping the panels in a continuous loop. The table bisects the space and becomes a nexus for engagement, promoting the interaction of users with each other as they negotiate. The surface, lit from varying distances, glows in colors ranging from yellow to orange to red and ruby. Even in daylight, the translucent material yields different shades of orange.

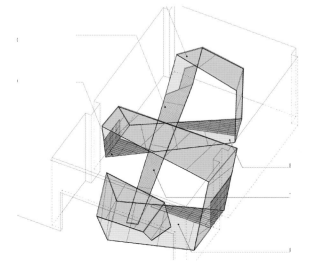

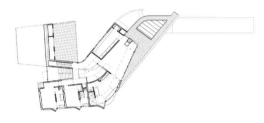

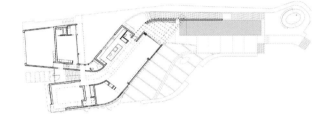

Point Dume Residence

This project explores the nature of fluidity and sequence in the context of space, circulation, and landscape. The site rests atop one of the highest points in Point Dume, Malibu, and offers stunning panoramas, making the organization of views a paramount concern for the project. The home both captures and is captivated by these vistas, creating spaces that flow in to one another and in to the landscape. The smooth, sinuous surfaces that organize the spaces are punctured and intersected in such a way as to break down the barriers that visually and psychologically separate the inside from the outdoors.

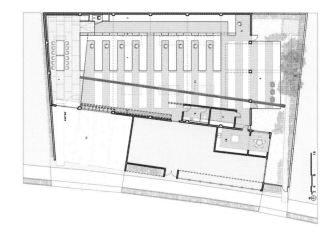

Lehrer Architects LA

The project included succinct interventions, such as blowing out the southern wall, creating 1.22 mm x 2.44 mm work surfaces of white-painted solid core doors, finishing floors with epoxy, installing off-the-shelf storage systems, painting a dramatic red line along the floor to resolve the trapezoidal shape of the space, and creating a strategic landscape design. The office would specifically house architects and they designed a multipurpose working space that simply and clearly honors the rudiments of work: vast work surfaces, lots of natural light, seamless connections to the landscape and fresh air, generous storage, and clearly individuated workstations adding up to a coherent, palpable group.

American Cement Building Loft

With a deliberate contemporary design, huge Silver Travertino marble plaques and walnut oiled wood were used in the great majority of the areas. These materials along with wall color and texture create neutral and warm spaces that welcome a simple and sparse array of furniture and ornamental elements. A diversity of furnishings was used to achieve original material combinations: leather, glass, wood, minerals, metals and colors generated a special harmony within the house. The vertical dividing elements of polychrome gold crystal reflects multiple tonalities depending on light and perspective, enhanced by the use of metal lattice.

Vienna Way

This 372 square meters residence is located on a large lot that divides into thirds. The two main structures exist on the outer edges of the property and maximize the interaction between the indoor-outdoor space as well as the available land. A kitchen spans the two structures and is covered by a green roof. The northern wing contains the private living space with a fireplace. The southern wing contains the formal, public spaces that begin in the front of the property and conclude in an outdoor dining area.

Baroda Ventures

Rios Clementi Hale Studios adapted a surprising, yet delightful, combination of retro and contemporary styles for the renovation of the two-story Baroda Ventures office. The architects applied several themes throughout the design – classic modern furnishings with unexpected fabrics, elaborate ceiling medallions and door escutcheons, glossy surfaces, and repeated patterning at various scales – while incorporating plenty of daylight. An existing quatrefoil window design is a leitmotif throughout, seen in wallpaper and structural details. Timeless elegance was achieved by pairing traditional essentials with the latest in design to create a place of sophisticated opulence.

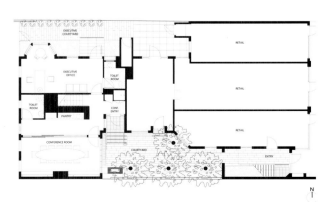

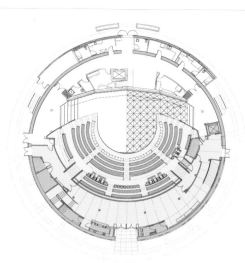

Mark Taper Forum

The architects fully enhanced the interior spaces with modern amenities for patrons and expanded the backstage areas for the actors and production teams. While maintaining the footprint of the original 1967 building, the architects cleverly carved out "found space" within the facility to better serve patrons and crew. From the newly configured entrance into the lobby that showcases an original Tony Duquette mural, to the auditorium with all-new seating, and the expansive lower-level lounge addition that provides patrons with larger restroom facilities, the architects successfully upgraded the space and added accommodations for disabled patrons. The multidisciplinary firm worked closely with the client to design new environmental graphics, including donor recognition walls and plaques, and all interior and exterior wayfinding signage to seamlessly complement the design of the theater.

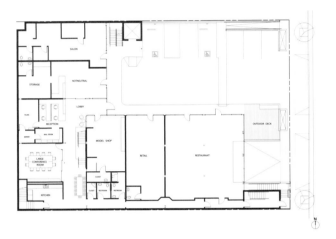

Larchmont Office

Rios Clementi Hale Studios renovated a former mini-mall for its multi-disciplined design staff and its nonhierarchical studio environment with pod work groups of 6 to 19 members. Exterior walls were replaced by window wall systems, and screened porches were created around the second-floor studio space. Exterior panels alternate between mirrored glass and expressive cut aluminum screens. Indoor "parks" are created with artificial turf in unexpected places. A display wall along the staircase exhibits photos, boards, and models of past, current, and future architectural projects of the firm. The "tree house" meeting room features floor-to-ceiling windows overlooking the street trees.

Openhouse

The house is embedded into a narrow and sharply sloping property in the Hollywood Hills. Large steel spans and double cantilevers allow the front, side and rear elevations to slide open and erase all boundaries between indoors and out, opening the architecture to gardens and terraces on two levels. The glazed open spaces are visually counterweighted by sculptural, solid elements rendered in stacked granite and dark stained oak. With the glass walls completely open, the house becomes a platform defined by an abstract roof plane, a palette of natural materials, the gardens and the views.

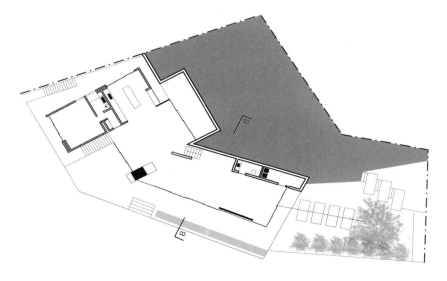

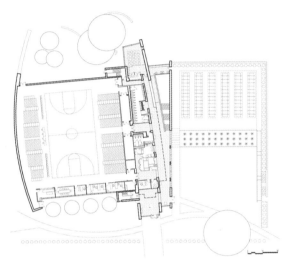

Center for Wellness

The Center for Wellness at the College of New Rochelle is designed as an abstract representation of a paradisiacal garden. The Center merges building and landscape into a physical, intellectual and spiritual experience, through the use of natural materials and light. The natatorium is a grotto carved beneath a contemplation roof garden. Skylights allow daylight to the surface of the pool water below. The gymnasium emerges from the topography like a rock outcropping with its locally quarried granite walls. The lobby concourse is a crevasse cut deeply into the sloping site and connects the gym to the pool.

NYPL Francis Martin Library

The feature elements of the design are bold and graphic, with a palette of oranges, greens, and blues offset by glossy white. The splashes of bright color result in an interior that is animated, expressive, and thoughtful. Reflective Barrisol undulates throughout the room, forming a playful ceiling, which folds away in some areas to increase ceiling height and reveal the existing concrete slab. The increased ceiling height adds lightness and openness to the space. Translucent plastic shelves display books in a clear and visibly inviting manner, while the diagonal arrangement of the shelves behind the reading tables creates a fun, dynamic series of spaces for the children.

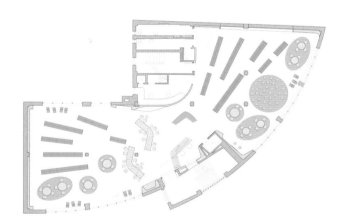

→ bluarch architecture + interiors /
Antonio Di Oronzo

→ Restaurant &
Bar

→ 2008

→ New York (NY)

→ USA

→ Photos: ADO

Greenhouse

This is the first certified eco-friendly nightclub in the country. The design concept was to convey the dynamic richness of nature as a living system. The walls connect to the ceiling via a series of laser-cut ribs creating a shelter within the space. The ribs are lined with series of round panels organized in a self-similar, non-recursive pattern generated through a fractal algorithm. The light points, in total 2,500, are all connected to a computer and describe effects which can come from music beats or video signals. The goal is to offer the experiential opportunity of a "live" landscape. The ceiling is an organic formation of 40-millimeter crystals representing a body of water about to project onto the ground and the sudden character of nature. The crystals are seemingly passively appended, but slightly vibrate with the music and vividly respond to the green lasers and the LED on the walls and ceiling.

Fifth Avenue apartment

This high-end Fifth Avenue apartment includes elements of European design. The client had in mind an apartment where she could recover from her busy life and the city's hectic tempo with her family. On the one hand, the atmospheres to be evoked in each room were defined beforehand, while on the other, the apartment acts as a harmonious whole. The extraordinary works of art by New York painter Rachel Lee Hovnanian contribute to the meditative atmosphere. The most beautiful fabrics are used to add to the serene ambiance, making good use of natural light. Varied materials, ornaments and forms are united using a consistent palette of black and white with a tender violet.

Bliss Spa Soho

During the update of Bliss' original spa and retail premises, the space was reconfigured to create more product display areas and improve client traffic flow. Original signature design elements were maintained as a gesture to the spas' important role in the history and success of the company. An existing circular ceiling mural was preserved and the new fixtures, architectural details and graphic elements were designed in relation to this prominent feature. Freestanding curved fixtures emulate the form of the mural while creating a dynamic spatial flow. A laminated acrylic "feather wall" used in the original design was also re-created and incorporated into the flagship store location.

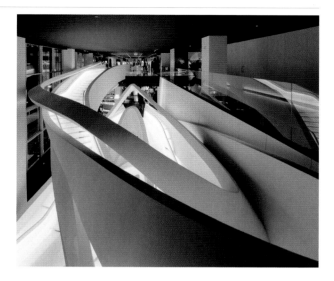

Armani Fifth Avenue

Situated in the center of New York, the project takes up the first three floors of two buildings localized between 5th Avenue and 56th Street. The showroom is developed on four different levels and is conceived of an only space, without clear distinctions, and a singing space connected with the power generated by the whirlwind of the staircase. The nucleus of the project, the staircase, is a structure wrought with the radiator grill of steel, highlighting the look of the sculpture. Every element of the internal design, from the exhibitors, rooms, and armchairs follow the movement concept generated by the staircase.

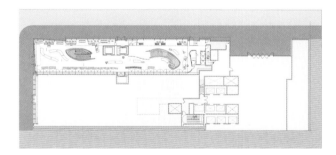

Miyake Madison

This project for the Japanese fashion designer Issey Miyake on Manhattan's Madison Avenue consisted of an interior renovation and a new façade on this historic shopping street. The design breaks the threshold between the sidewalk and the world of Issey Miyake. The flush clear glass façade creates a seamless barrier from which the volume of the shop is extruded. The 241 square meter volume, which terminates in a mirrored wall, extends without end. In effect, the entire shop becomes a giant store window with mannequins dispersed throughout the entire depth of the space. A stretched checker-board pattern of light boxes in the ceiling meanders around these columns adding a figural element to the volume.

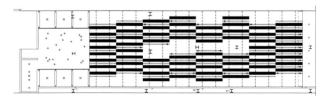

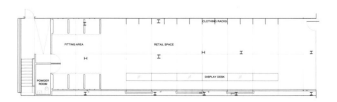

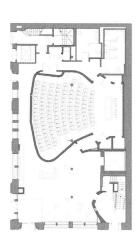
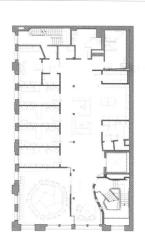

NYU Department of Philosophy

A new stair shaft below a new skylight joins the six-level building vertically with a shifting porosity of light and shadow that change seasonally. Prismatic film was installed on the south-facing stairwell windows which occasionally break the sunlight into a prismatic rainbow. The ground level, utilized by the entire university, contains a new curvilinear wooden auditorium on a cork floor. The upper level floors contain faculty offices and seminar rooms which are done in different shades and textures of black and white, according to the texts in Ludwig Wittgenstein's book "Remarks on Color".

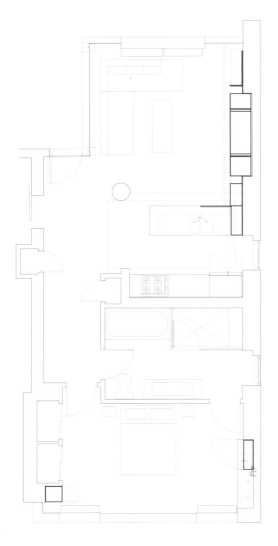

McFarland Residence

The main focus of this project was inspired by a painting the client had received as a gift which has great sentimental value to him. The designer decided to incorporate the abstract artwork composed of vibrant reds and pinks into the built-in cabinetry designed by i-Beam Design. The cabinets accommodate the client's large collection of CDs, DVDs and state of the art entertainment system along with his collection of ceramics and miscellaneous objects. The cabinet doors were painted to incorporate the colors in the painting, and the painting served as a door within the cabinet system. All other cabinetry in the apartment was custom built to the client's needs.

Milne Ojito Residence

The harmonic progressions radiate out from the origin point to generate a variety of spaces including a guest bedroom, a home entertainment center, an office, an open dining area, numerous cabinets and moving exhibition panels to accommodate an evolving art collection. A prime example of this may be seen in the temporary guest bedroom which appears by opening a sofa bed that in turn releases a cantilevered wall which swings out to privatize the bed area while projecting the matrix into space. The only permanent enclosure in the loft contains closets and a new guest bathroom made of acid etched mirror, which gives the impression of expanding space and suspended gravity.

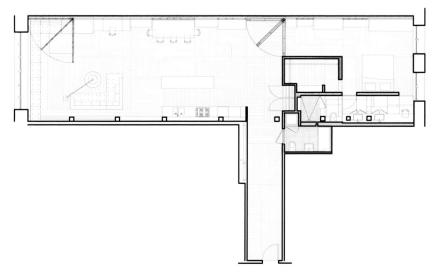

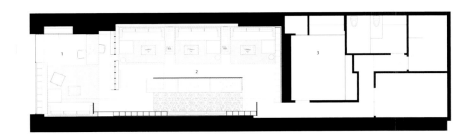

Nike iD Studio

More lounge than showroom, the Nike iD Studio combines and reveals an inherent contradiction between luxury (sedentary, comfortable and elite) and athleticism (active, strenuous and egalitarian). This contradiction is a guiding principle behind the detailing of the space. Flocked wallpaper, seemingly stuffy and Victorian, is made up of sneakers and basketballs. Such visual puns are transposed to three dimensions, as wallpaper peels away from the walls to define seating areas below and a light cove above. No material stays in a single plane: walnut panels hover on one side of the space and then turn 90 degree into the room, taking the viewer's gaze with them. This implied sense of movement is everywhere, lending a sense of restlessness to the space.

Wasch Residence

From the earliest stages of the design of the Wasch Residence a primary goal was to bring natural light into every room of the loft. The high ceilings in the space allowed a continuous band of clerestories to ring the upper level of the main living spaces. The custom steel and glass clerestory panels became an organizing element of the project; they formed a second line of windows within the loft. Many of the clerestories swivel open to allow air to circulate through the rooms. A portion of the living room can be closed off with two large sliding steel and resin doors to form a separate guest room when needed. When there are no guests the large sliding doors disappear into a wall cavity.

Theory NYC

The space brings Theory's offices, showrooms and retail all under one roof. The interiors are completely custom tailored to the clients' specifications. Zeff played with colors, finishes and furnishings, while attempting to differentiate and unify floors at the same time. Rows of desks and workstations are surrounded by executive and private offices. Lounges are furnished with sofas, daybeds, and ottomans — a mix of contemporary, vintage and MARKZEFF. The corporate lobby and the four levels above are connected by a staircase of concrete, glass and polished stainless steel, along with a stainless steel mesh curtain.

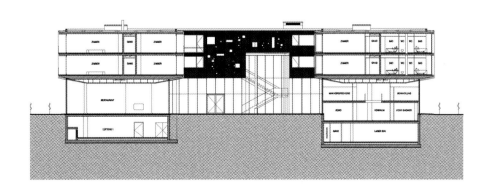

"In Heat, Installation at Henry Urbach Architecture"

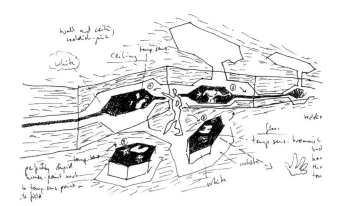

J.Mayer H.'s interior stems from Friedrich Kiesler's design for the 1947 "Blood Flames" exhibition at the Hugo Gallery, New York. His radical new concept proposed merging art, architecture and the viewer into a continuation of painted walls and floors which host and interconnect the artwork. "In Heat" develops this confusion of art, viewer and space an even more radical way by introducing thermosensitive coating as interactive paintings where the viewer, creating a temperature shadow by touching, melts into the overall exhibition design. Everything becomes flattened into an architectural surface, where the depth is temporal rather than spatial.

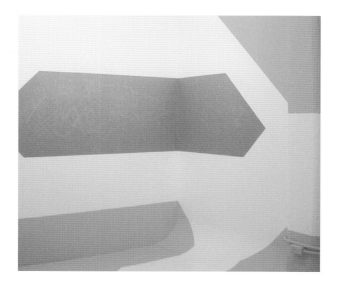

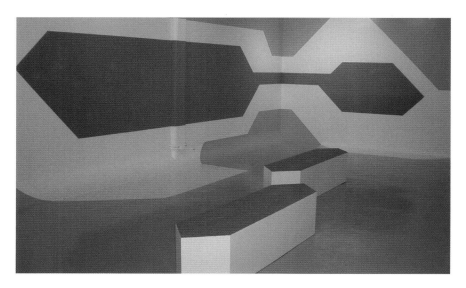

Cristiano Cora Studio

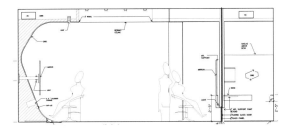

The goal was to create a new essence of salon environment that captures the balance between modern architecture and the needs of the hair dressing industry. The fluid movement of the Cristiano salon truly captures the elements of simple modern design while the functionality of the design enables a smoother process of hair dressing. The aim was to create a space that would be distinctly appealing to women: curved, clean, and stylish, but at the same time comforting and transformational. The simplicity of the design encourages the client's focus to be on the inspiring experience of becoming transformed.

West Village Duplex

The lower floor of the duplex was completely gutted keeping only the original wood floors. The ceilings were raised to the maximum possible adding light and a feeling of spaciousness previously missing. The new stair has a stainless steel stringer, wood treads and an impressive "hardware-less" glass railing. The stair is lit by a new skylight and a series of glass lights above. At the top of the stair the designer created an open study with a built-in desk and bookcases overlooking the upper terrace. The master bathroom was finished with gray stone — a dark consistent gray limestone- and limestone porcelain tile.

Chelsea Gallery

The project was to transform a derelict 325 square meter space into a gallery that could accommodate the growing business and hold art openings in the evenings. Mixed Greens is a gallery that believes that contemporary art should be affordable and a part of everyone's life. Instead of the usual white walls, the architect and designer decided to use white as the core of the space but use different variations of green for the interiors of the space. Thus the inside of the bathroom, the office and even the interiors of the closet are all different shades of green, very appropriate for a gallery named Mixed Greens. The office is grape green, while the art wrapping room is celery.

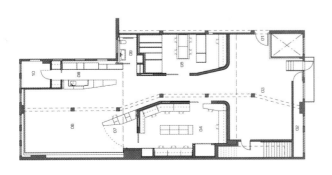

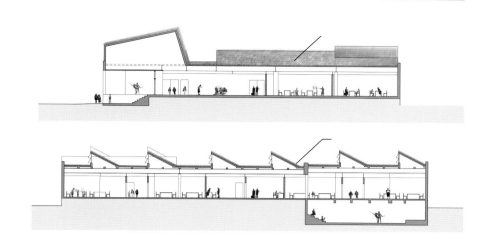

Bronx Charter School for the Arts

Through its adaptive re-use of an old factory, the school plays a role in the transformation of its industrial Hunts Point neighborhood. To achieve a healthy environment that enhances the learning spaces despite budget and site restrictions, a simple innovative approach was needed. Color, space, and natural light create a direct physical connection with the content and aims of the curriculum. The classrooms are conceived of as studio spaces. White and gray surfaces predominate to make the most of the light from the north, with color stripes providing orientation to each of the classroom bays, towards the street and the shared arts spaces along the façade.

NYC Information Center

Graphic banding of floor and walls organizes the interior creating a "mapped", foreshortened space. In order not to compete with the media presentations, lighting glows from integrated "light coves" at floor and ceiling level, as well as from the digital projection mirrors hovering above each Smart Table. The Smart Tables and their digital mirrors simulate the intensity of the city experience. Layers of information, electronic interfaces, brochures, a video wall "Fly NYC" feature, and ticket and metro card vending are carefully incorporated into the design, resituating each individual experience and linking them as a unified system.

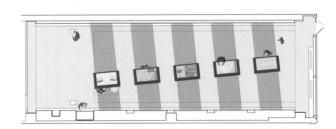

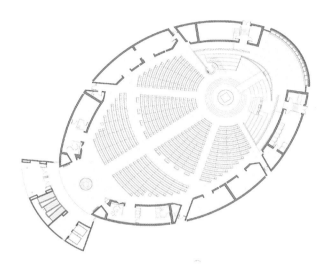

Cathedral of Christ the Light

The project was designed by Craig W. Hartman as a replacement for the cathedral of saint Francis de Sales, which was destroyed by an earthquake in 1989. The cathedral overlooks lake Merritt and has 1,350 seats. Inside there is also a mausoleum, conference center, offices, residences, a book store and a café. Outside, a landscaped plaza links the building with downtown Oakland. Rather than traditional iconography, the cathedral's design focuses on the experience of and space. The base of the building is concrete while wood ribs rise above featuring a glass enclosure and wooden louvers. The cathedral is also designed to withstand a 1000-year earthquake, making sure it will stand the test of time.

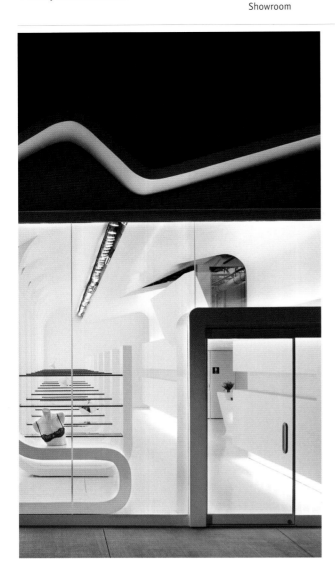

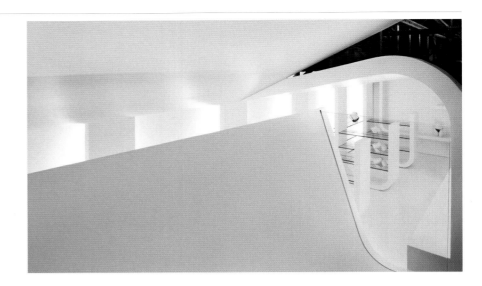

Bizarre Boutique

A women's boutique was the perfect opportunity to challenge the typical retail store conventions where the walls, fixtures, ceilings, and floors are all separate elements. It also provided a chance to test processes of blending these elements to generate space where the store itself becomes the podium to display the merchandise as art objects. The solution was to fabricate a continuous surface to lead you into the space and to define it. This surface bends, folds and is cut to display merchandise and conceal mechanics, creating a visually pure backdrop for a memorable shopping experience. Molded plastic played an important role in the forming of the reception desk and the exterior forms. The display shelves are also a "plastic form" constructed from drywall. Plastic was utilized based on the fact that it provides a sturdy base for the curved forms. Nebraska weather being so unpredictable, it was also used for the exterior due to its weather resistance qualities.

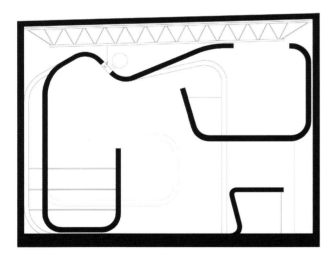

Facebook Headquarters

The new Facebook headquarters facilitates interaction and connection, reflecting the company's mission as a social networking website provider. The former laboratory facility of a high-tech manufacturer brings together more than 700 employees originally scattered throughout ten locations in and around Palo Alto. The design goal for the new facility was to maintain the history and raw aesthetic of the building and create a fun dynamic setting appropriate for the company's youthful staff. Many walls and spaces are left unfinished and employees are encouraged to write on the walls, add artwork, and move furniture as needed, allowing the building to evolve continuously.

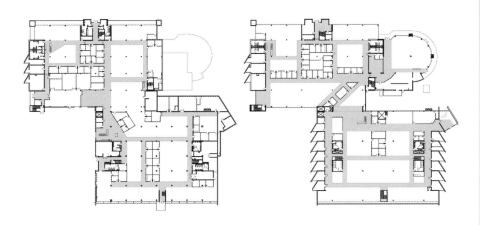

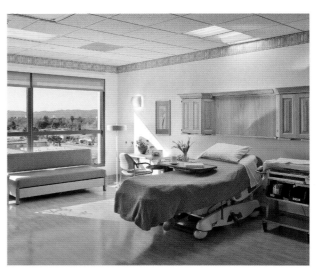

Kaiser Permanent Panorama City Medical Center

The building is organized in a "bundled" vertical design that responds to the urban context of a constrained site. Support and diagnostic & treatment functions are located on the large, lower three floor plates, which are topped with three smaller floors of nursing unit functions. All floors are organized around an east-west oriented "core" of support functions. The clustering of core functions within the building also allows for large, open, flexible 'loft' space on the diagnostic & treatment floors for ever-changing functions such as operating rooms and imaging rooms.

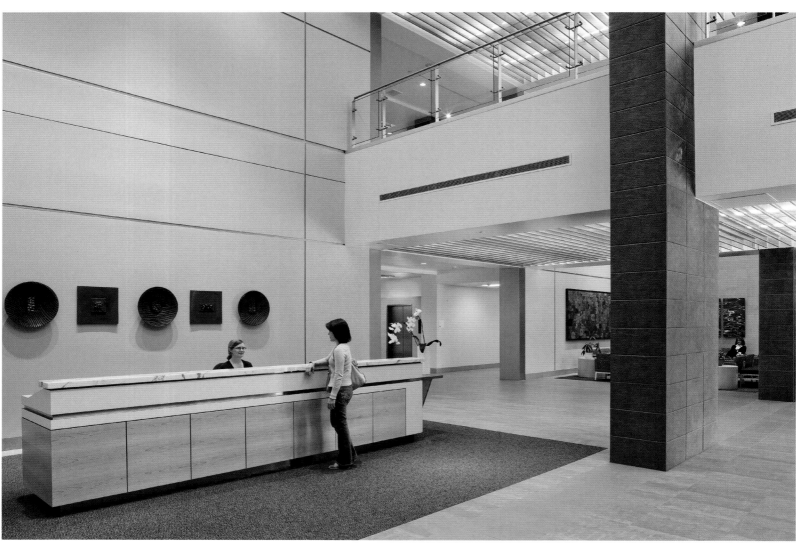

The Disney Store Headquarters

The original wood framed building is composed of three parts. The front portion is a 4.9 meter-high space with large timber trusses. The large rear portion is a double height wooden framed atrium space with a saw-tooth roof, creating dramatic clerestory lighting that spans the width of the space. These two portions are connected by a long interstitial brick walled structure, which inspired the creation of brick-like elements for the interior. These modular elements allude to children's block building games and remind staff of their role in creating products for children. In addition to providing an internal landscaped courtyard and new skylights throughout, the building also connects occupants to the exterior with a new landscaped courtyard at the front. This includes an ivy topiary of "Mickey Mouse ears". Most days the doors to the interior courtyard, which is accessed from the cafeteria, are left open, allowing fresh air and sunlight to permeate the space.

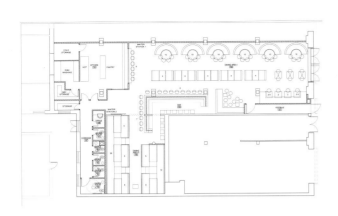

NYLO HOTEL - PLANO

NYLO Hotels is currently the most popular brand of lifestyle hotels. Their hotels are conceived as a diving force behind a high quality, rich social atmosphere, full of art and design and filled with suprises and the fun personality of a civilian-style luxury hotel. The designers avoided commonly used materials such as stone, brick, and wood flooring, going directly to the polished concrete finishes.

Ace Hotel

Ace Hotel Portland is the result of the renovation of an old hotel built in 1912. Many of its original details, such as the deep cast-iron roll-top baths and capacious sinks, have been retained and refurbished. As much of the historical character as possible was retained and combined with clean lines to create a look of warm minimalism. The team at the Ace also turned to local artists, suppliers and craftsmen for a mix of modern and vintage elements to create a distinctive Ace aesthetic which at the same time reflects the hotel's locality. One of the most important aims was that rooms should not look like hotel rooms – instead resembling private homes. Rather than a $15-a-drink cocktail bar, the hotel offers Portland's legendary Stumptown Coffee Roasters, the comfortable communal-seating Clyde Common restaurant, and the retro diner-themed Kenny and Zuke's Delicatessen.

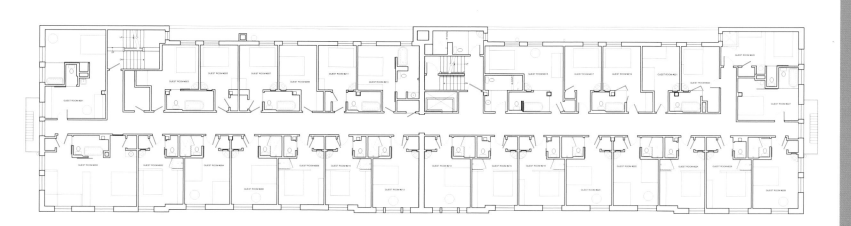

Rhode Island School of Design Library

The approach for the RISD library employed not one, but three distinct architectural tactics: preservation, engineering, and architectural intervention. The library is located in the main hall of the historic Hospital Trust Bank building. It houses an extensive collection of art and design volumes, magazines, and multimedia resources, as well as group study areas, classrooms, and administrative offices. Two new pavilions housing key programmatic components were positioned within the barrel vaulted void of the main hall. The negotiation between the purity of the architecture in the space, and the insertion of new elements defines a strategy of camouflage as a way of threading new elements into the space as inconspicuously as possible.

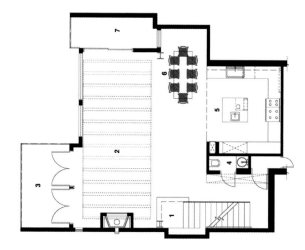

Sausalito Residence

An urbane, elegant home fused with a warm modern ambiance was the main design concept. The interiors are comfortable and playful, open to the expansive view of San Francisco Bay. It has a wide open view to the sea on three sides (north, east, and south). A luxuriant light-fixture opposite the kitchen shows modern style, a green tone embraces the washing room creating a relaxed atmosphere, and the bedrooms have taken good advantage of the sea. The designer's solution was to remove most of the interior walls through the use of structural steel in order to generate a sense of space, create a dramatic stair event, and open the exterior walls to the views.

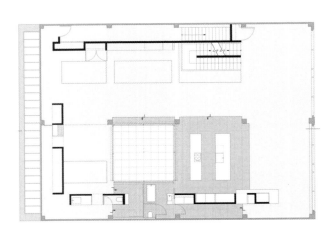

Tehama Grasshopper

A surprising integration of old and new elements, of competing urban forces, brings the remodeled warehouse alive. Three stories of interlocked spaces have distinct personalities and functions: office, main living area, and penthouse. The rigidity of the original concrete structure is broken down in a subtle interplay of light, surfaces, levels, and indoor and outdoor spaces – making the urban living experience as richly textured as the city itself. The second floor is the main living space for the young owners and their child. Its focus is a new courtyard, cut out from the existing floor plate that connects the building to the new penthouse above and to the sky.

Westfield San Francisco Center

The Emporium department store on Market Street was once hailed as the "grandest mercantile building in the world", and its design elements that include a Beaux-Arts grand façade and a signature glass dome were among the most recognizable in the city. In recent decades, the Emporium building stood vacant and fell into disrepair. After an eight-year development and design process, the site, now home to Westfield San Francisco Center, showcases the Emporium's historic elements and integrates an existing retail center located on an adjacent site. The 227 tons dome was raised 18 meters and suspended on a newly built foundation while the rest of the building was constructed around it. The façade restoration engages the surrounding cityscape and has added new energy to the district.

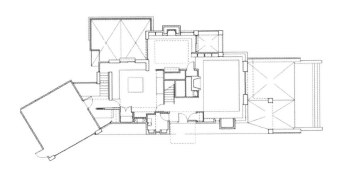

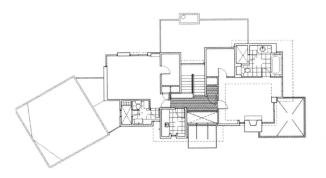

Santa Barbara Riviera Residence

Though not immediately obvious, this house embraces several characteristics of environmentally sustainable design. The basic design strategy is to site the house based on solar orientation, resulting in passive solar gains throughout the year. Photovoltaic power generates household electricity through a 2.8 kilowatt system (when power is not needed, it feeds back into the grid). A passive rooftop solar heating system provides for domestic hot water and a passive solar ground-level hot-water system is used to heat the pool. The natural flow of hot and cool air is fortified by the use of radiant hot-water floor heating and separate central air conditioning in the ceilings.

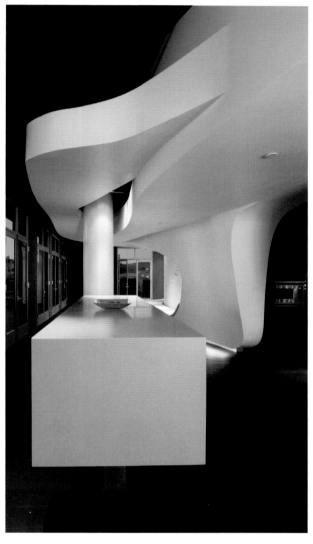

Moving Picture Company

The project explores the notion of light in relation to color in reference to the company's work in the area of color manipulation in film. The developed forms and patterns were produced using studies of light, analyzing and modeling it three-dimensionally. Animation frames were chosen and layered to organize spatial qualities and create movement throughout the office environment. An organic, sinuous spine weaves its way through the suite and an attached soffit grows from the serpentine walls. Light portals pierce the organic forms and are equipped with programmable LED lighting. Patterns derived from the animated studies are emblazoned onto the laser cut walls and circumscribe the interior.

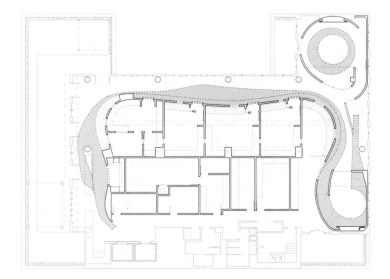

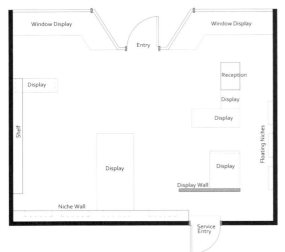

Far4 Store

The space needed to reflect the luxury of the goods and maintain a relationship with the small scale of the ceramic products, with a focus on product itself. The goal was to build a warm, open environment, where shoppers could meander around various displays, closely inspecting each finely crafted piece. To achieve a feel of intimacy in the shop, and to remain true to the building's history and the Northwest's aesthetics, wood was used extensively throughout the space. Wide-plank Dutch oak flooring was used as the material for both the floor and the display areas. Doing so allowed introducing fewer materials into the space, so as not to compete with the ceramics.

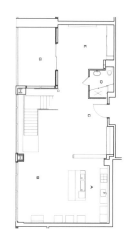

Millennium Tower Loft

The home combines wide open spaces for entertainment with enough privacy for a small family with a child and comfortable spaces for guests to stay. The main floor layout is designed to transform from a single volume entertainment space to distinct kitchen, dining, entry, and guest mini apartment areas with discreet built in closets. The extra deep sofa combines with the ottoman to create a full bed, and the powder room contains a hidden shower tucked away behind angled privacy glass panels. The second level has flexible office space that can be used for different family activities and can, in the future, be transformed into a third bedroom if the need arises.

The Atrium School

The Atrium school looked to Maryann Thompson Architects to design a facility that called for the adaptive reuse of an open warehouse structure on a limited site in a densely populated area. The oblong site presented specific challenges including how best to arrange parking fields, accommodate green space, and orchestrate pedestrian and vehicular traffic through the site. The school's entrance and vehicular access was repositioned to the back of the campus away from the building's prior entrance, which faced a main thoroughfare. Extensive glazing and skylights brightened the previously dark and enclosed warehouse space and also facilitated cross-ventilation. The double loaded corridor was enlivened with special window nooks, which provide moments of rest and discovery and an unfolding spatial experience.

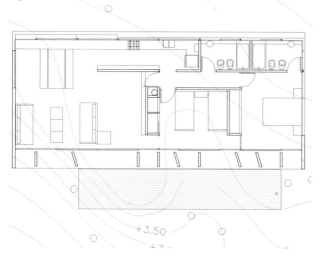

Casa de Hormigón

Mar Azul is a seaside town south of Buenos Aires, characterized for its large dune beach and leafy coniferous forest. The owners chose a field in the forest with a challenging topography, away from the sea and dense zones, in order to construct a cottage without losing the important presence of the landscape. Located on a flat surface in the terrain with a strong diagonal slope, the house was solved like a concrete prism of extended proportions and minimum height. The house does not contain a main entrance, but is rather a flexible construction with entry from anyone of the rooms, assuring natural light throughout.

+3.50

Mercado Design

The Mercado Design project is born from the understanding of the building using a number of concepts: a single flat volume with considerable permeability that is able to provoke the effect of surprise. At first glance, it presents more of a challenge than an explicit revelation. It is not intended to sell material goods, but rather to discuss motivations that lead people to search for bigger values, to desire a better quality of life. The design hopes to aim at something that is not limited to palpable issues, but can rather suggest a wider perception.

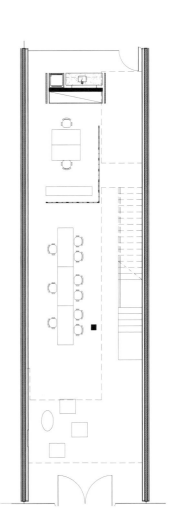

Alphaville

This luxurious apartment is designed to create a harmonious atmosphere. A perfect combination of robust, warm and pure materials like wood, stone, glass and marmoleum and the use of sober colors with colorful accents make it a timeless and stylish residence. If there was a piece of furniture not exactly suitable for this place, the designers would redesign it and had it produced. For example, the gray furniture in the studio, the bed, the bamboo bathroom furniture and the high gloss white cupboards in the living room are redesigned. What is special about this project is that the apartment is designed 'upside down': the design studio is placed on the ground floor, the sleeping rooms on the first floor.

Escape Bar

According to the name of the restaurant, the idea was to provide a kind of refuge in the urban space. To obtain this effect, the architect created an artificial forest of dry trunks separating the lounge and the street, with a mirror in the ceiling. The light of this area, yellowish and very intensive, comes from the floor and bounces off the ceiling with a dramatic impression, as if it comes from a great height. Entering the bar, a pre-programmed indirect RGB fluorescent system suffuses the space in color. The designers chose a palette of colors related to the furniture and the moods that they desired to apply. Soft colors and smooth transitions were used in a way to provoke imperceptible sensations.

Micasa vol.B

The store was built using rustic material and rustic executions. It is both rustic and modern: Micasa Volume B recalls the artisan processes of popular civil construction, and, above all, the modern Brazilian buildings, brutalist projects in a brutalism reinvented south of the equator, attentive to local knowledge. The façades of the store were made in a not-very-common manner using exposed reinforced concrete: the outward appearance of the material, generally done very precisely with new lumber, is used here randomly, chaotically, and some wood was not even removed after curing. The brise-soleil in the offices are made of a net of reinforcing bars used for the concrete.

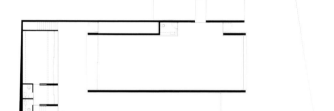

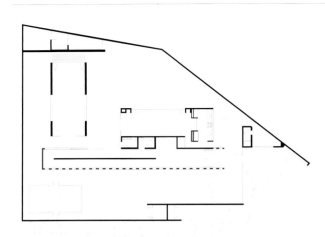

Primetime Nursery School

This project is the first Brazilian nursery developed from a program specially conceived for children aged from zero to three years, based on an exclusive educational concept. The priority was to create of an abstract non-stereotypical space with a ludic character that would meet the functional demands of the numerous procedures involved. The technical team involved offered ideal solutions for the best air and water quality, floor heating and balanced lighting. The landscaping was equally conceived to guarantee the safe interaction among the children. In addition to natural materials, the colors yellow, orange and red were selected to create a stimulating atmosphere.

La Prairie Spa at the Ritz Carlton Grand Cayman

Taking their cue from the purity of a Swiss glacier, the designers have created the luxurious, water-based interiors of the 1,737 square meter Silver Rain a La Prairie Spa. The guests are surrounded by the comforting aura of water in all its states. This unique experience begins the moment the guests open the silver-leafed doors and enter a quietly dazzling space that introduces them to the tranquil experience of the spa beyond. Water rushes beneath the tiled floor and behind screened walls – water that is heard but not yet seen.

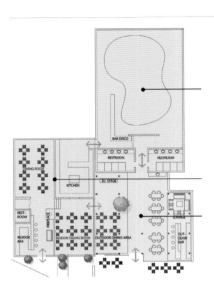

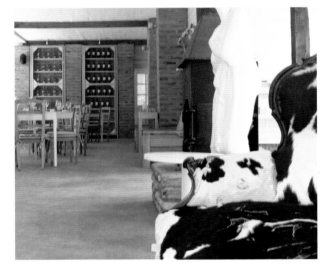

Amandita Bar Restaurant

Located in the town center, this country-style house, which used to be the local club, is situated in an area that has little relation to the coastal spirit of the town. That is why the design of Amandita aims to build up that beach atmosphere that all vacationers are looking for when they escape from the city to go to the coast. The remodeling keeps the original structure of the house, retaining the adobe, brick and native woods. Being a very low-budget project, it favoured a "soft" terrace by building a deck and a wooden roof structure, which, controlling the different light intensities, would support the exterior program.

Engineer's House

The interoir is designed with a transparent structure to bring the user close to nature. The evening glow causes the red wall beside the stairs to dazzle and creates a passionate and welcoming environment. Large glass windows are used in the living room, making it spacious and bright. Thus, the user can save energy and feel the power of nature. A highly unique element was designed for the bedrooms: this volume is connected to other areas via a glass connecting bridge. Through these design elements the designer aimed to create a closer relationship between dwelling and the exterior world.

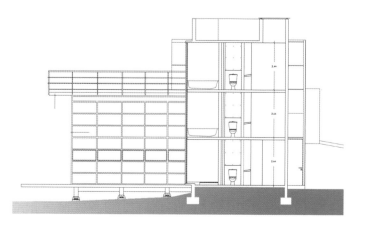

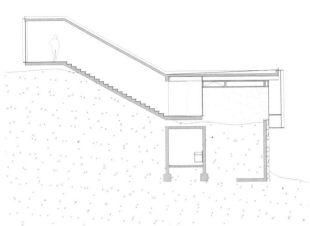

Chalet C7

The project is located at 2,990 meters above sea level in the Andes Mountains. The site is on the south slope of the Inca Lake, just in front of the Portillo Hotel, a few kilometers away of the Argentinean border and Mount Aconcagua. The terrain is a steep rocky slope, facing the immediate view to the lake and the Tres Hermanos Mountains. Over this strong and harsh natural landscape the house disappears from its view uphill, without interfering the view towards the lake. From a protected environment, inside the refuge, the mountain landscape is the main character.

Tierra Atacama Hotel & Spa

For environmental reasons, the whole hotel was built on a platform, leaving the existing historic ground untouched. The surrounding land, neglected for many years, was returned to its agricultural state and planted again with grains, fruit trees, herbs and flowers native to the area. The difficulty of building in a remote location led to a lighter style of building material, reducing the use of various materials such as cement, moldings and water – all scarce in the desert environment. Local labor was used to build walls made of stone and rammed earth, which protect the exteriors and blend with the surroundings. Finally, the setting consists of an extensive and diverse landscape, which is gathered in parts in frames to mark special views, and successive patios which range from very open spaces, passing through intermediate areas with gardens, water and fig trees, to the most private, shady and protected space for each occupant.

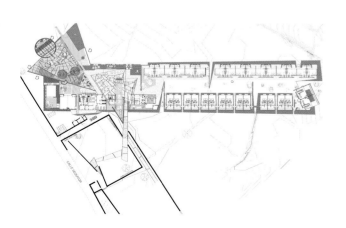

Gonzalo Mardones Viviani Architects Studio

Simplicity and a sense of nature were at the heart of this design. A non-orthogonal L-shaped plan was chosen in order to tense the circulations and the space. The designers worked with one material and one color: all the walls and roofs are white. The floor was furnished with light gray ceramic and the designers separated the spaces with transparent crystals. The furniture is the same color as the walls and roofs and there are no elements that compete with the white scheme.

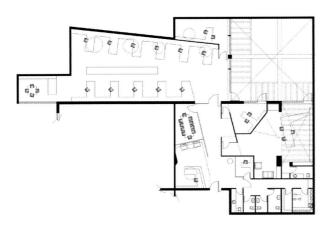

"Ave Fenix" Fire Station

The program includes, in addition to the Fire Station itself, a consultation and training center open to the public; both activities had to be executed separately and the presence of the visitor must never interfere in the work of the firemen. In the case of the main access, the double stair proposed separates the flow of the employers and the visitors and rises from the level of visitor access to a heliport in the roof. This vertical circulation was complemented by the classic tubes where the firemen descend faster. Thus, the proposed solution of the coexistence of the two flows resolves both uses — the station requirements and the public areas.

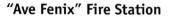

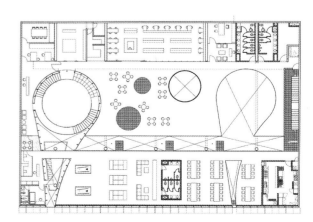

Origami Pavillion

In order to accomplish the objective, the design was based on the art of origami, meaning "folding paper" in Japanese. Composed mainly of geometric shapes including squares, rectangles and triangles, the pavilion creates a very particular form with movements and subtle lines that follow a sense of intuition and not a strict architectonic rationalism. The circulations of the fair were considered in the design proposal; four big openings allow to access to the interior exhibition. The architectural elements filter the light while visitors are surprised by the different movements of the shadows.

Condesa df

This hotel project recycled an apartment building dating from 1928, cataloged by Mexico's National Beaux Arts Institute. The perimeter of the building was preserved up to the first corridor, which was restored to its original state. The inside of the building was demolished to build an opened patio, which is the central space of the project. A dialogue between architectures took place; the circulations leading to the hotel rooms were turned to face this open, public space, where the building connected to the outside. Folding aluminum shades open into the patio, infinitely transforming the space. The shades virtually extend the corridors and offer a play of seeing and not being seen.

Suntro House

This house is located in a residential area of Oaxtepec, a place of exceptional natural beauty. It is contiguous to the north with the hill of Tepozteco and to the south with a highway. The lot is oriented to the northeast with a splendid view of the Tepozteco. The natural light is filtered through the folds of the house in the form of rays that softly flood the spaces. The shape responds to the hard heat of the site, to place every space in the best way inside a curved skin that opens to the immediate context to obtain the best climate and views and allow wind circulation.

Casa Y

A corridor begins in the access zone and continuer above a cupboard before reaching the bedroom, which floats over the empty space crossing the crystal façade, and faces the garden with a view of the sweet gumtree to the west. The bedroom splits itself from the edge generating a strip of light that descends all the way to the living room. All the spaces are connected to the garden but with varying hues of light. The walls and the concrete roofs enhance the feeling of protection. The experience of intimacy is improved by the depth, by the concrete, and by the light.

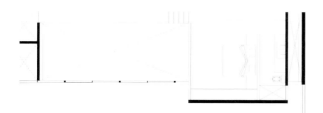

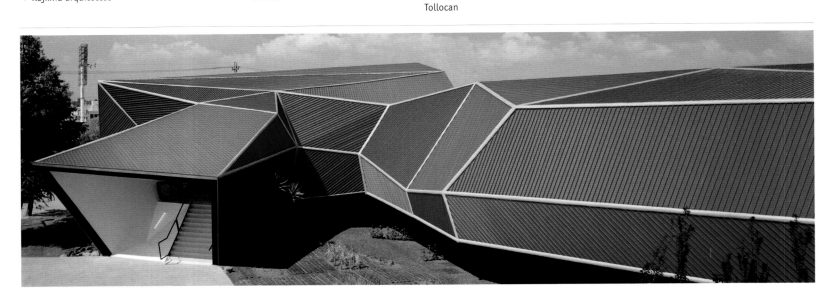

Nestlé Chocolate Factory Museum

Nestlé's chocolate factory in Mexico City was in need of an inner pathway for visitors to witness the production of their favourite chocolates. The idea was to create the first chocolate museum in Mexico and have a 300 meter long façade along the motorway as the new image of the factory was born. The first phase required a 634 meter squared space that could accommodate the main entrance for the visitors to start their voyage into the chocolate factory. As soon as they enter this playful yet striking space, they would be greeted by the reception area, the theater, where they would be prepared for the Nestlé experience, the store or museum shop, and the passage to the tunnel inside the old existing factory.

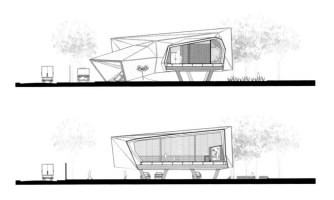

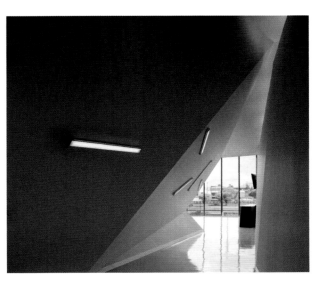

Black House

The covered roof garden is the most important part of the house. The most crowded area in which the family will spend most of the time is also however the most ambiguous place in the house. One- half-house is then one-half-terrace, protected from the exterior conditions when needed by means of four-meter-tall sliding glass panels towards the landscape, and a wall as high as the garage doors towards the street that is detached from the concrete canopy and therefore more of a fence than a wall. The exposed concrete canopy emphasizes views and conforms to an anachronistic local code on context which calls for typical construction elements and materials such as pitched roofs.

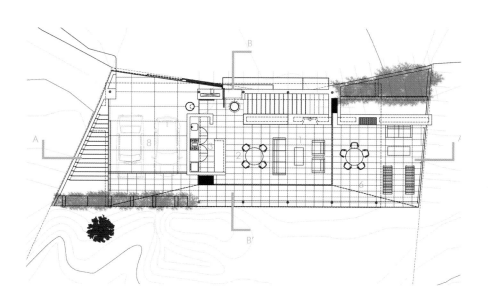

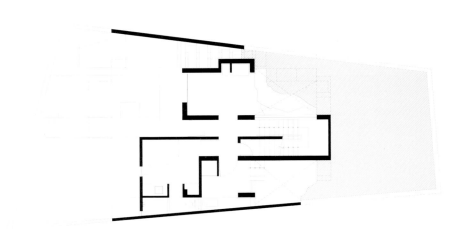

Panfichi Beach House

Located at Honda Beach 130 kilometers south of Lima on the coast of Peru, this beach house is conceived as a floating structure which houses the architectural program while the sloped natural site remains as intact as possible. The connection between architecture and territory is limited to the minimum necessary only to hold the house structurally while it creates outdoor places such as a small pool, a sand garden and a natural rock patio. This "floating box" is separated from both neighbors allowing an ocean view to the rooms located at the back of the site to satisfy one important objective in the design: "to provide an ocean view to all rooms".

House in the Andes

Two concrete volumes with great views to the Andes. The house is set on the top of a sloping field. The program is organized in two parallel and horizontal outdated volumes, based on a simple geometry, where the interior is as important as the exterior. The courtyard entry articulates both volumes under one cover and provides a visual opening of the mountains surrounding the valley. In both volumes transparency is what dominates it. Each room has one side covered entirely in glass, so the landscape forms part of the interior space and expands it.

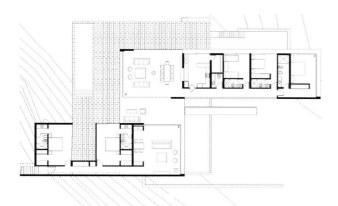

PROJECTS INDEX

ARCHITECTS INDEX